COLTRANE

ON COLTRANE THE JOHN COLTRANE INTERVIEWS

COLTRANE
ON COLTRANE THE JOHN COLTRANE INTERVIEWS

Edited by Chris DeVito

CHICAGO
REVIEW
PRESS

An A Cappella Book

Library of Congress Cataloging-in-Publication Data

Coltrane on Coltrane : the John Coltrane interviews / edited by Chris DeVito. —
1st ed.

    p. cm.

 Includes bibliographical references and index.

 ISBN 978-1-56976-287-5 (hardcover)

 1. Coltrane, John, 1926-1967—Interviews. 2. Jazz musicians—United States—
Interviews. I. DeVito, Chris. II. Coltrane, John, 1926-1967. III. Title.

ML419.C645A5 2010

788.7'165092—dc22

[B]

                               2010011770

Interior design: Jonathan Hahn

Published by A Cappella Books

An imprint of Chicago Review Press, Incorporated

814 North Franklin Street

Chicago, Illinois 60610

ISBN 978-1-56976-287-5

Printed in the United States of America

5 4 3 2 1

To Julia, for everything

CONTENTS

ACKNOWLEDGMENTS

Much of the research for this book was done during my work on a previous project, *The John Coltrane Reference* (New York: Routledge, 2008). I owe a special debt to my coauthors—Yasuhiro "Fuji" Fujioka, Lewis Porter, Wolf Schmaler, and David Wild—as they discovered many of the rare interviews and articles included in this book. Fuji was also instrumental in gaining access to most of the rare photographs printed here, and warm thanks go to Lewis Porter for providing me with the opportunity to serve as editor.

I'm especially grateful to Ms. Antonia Andrews, John Coltrane's stepdaughter, for generously allowing us to publish a selection of John Coltrane's personal writings and correspondence.

Coltrane biographer Dr. C. O. Simpkins and Coltrane researcher David Tegnell were helpful in many ways, not the least of which was allowing publication of Dr. Simpkins's interview with Coltrane's childhood friend, Franklin Brower.

Michel Delorme, Björn Fremer, Tony Gieske, Nat Hentoff, Gene Lees, Steve Provizer, and Valerie Wilmer were all most generous in allowing republication of their work. It was wonderful to hear firsthand accounts of meeting Coltrane from some of these people.

Lars Westin of Berry Produktion AB provided valuable information and assistance, which included access to the photographs of Bengt H. Malmqvist.

Music researcher, author, educator, and librarian-archivist Michael Fitzgerald shared a wealth of information not only on Coltrane but on pretty much everything related to jazz, and the members of the jazz research e-mail list that Mr. Fitzgerald moderates provided information as well. I'd like to thank Larry Appelbaum, Eric Charry, Tad Hershorn, Ashley Kahn, Dan Morgenstern, Samuel

J. Perryman, George Schuller, Chris Sheridan, Bill Shoemaker, Peter Vacher, and Bert Vuijsje for their help.

This book builds and expands on earlier works that have presented Coltrane in his own words. I owe a large debt to Coltrane's biographers: Dr. C. O. Simpkins (*Coltrane: A Biography*, Perth Amboy, NJ: Herndon House Publishers, 1975), J. C. Thomas (*Chasin' the Trane: The Music and Mystique of John Coltrane*, Garden City, NY: Doubleday, 1975), and Lewis Porter (*John Coltrane: His Life and Music*, Ann Arbor: University of Michigan Press, 1998). In particular, parts 1 and 2 of *The John Coltrane Companion: Five Decades of Commentary*, edited by Carl Woideck (New York: Schirmer Books, 1998), served as a springboard. Without the foundation provided by these earlier works, this book would not have been possible.

PREFACE

By all accounts, John Coltrane was a reluctant interviewee. He was also a gracious and conscientious one. His responses were thoughtful and measured; unlike many musicians, he rarely said anything negative or critical about others (though he could be highly self-critical). He freely gave credit to those who had influenced and inspired him. Interviewer after interviewer noted how different Coltrane seemed to be from his music—this quiet, dispassionate man whose music was so intense and energetic, so fiery and volcanic. His occasional dry humor only deepened the apparent divide between the man and the music.

This book includes almost every known Coltrane interview—as well as articles, reminiscences, and liner notes that include quotes by Coltrane—in an attempt to present Coltrane's story in his own words, arranged in chronological order by interview date (as near as it can be determined). Coltrane's stepdaughter, Antonia Andrews, has allowed us to publish some of Coltrane's personal writings and correspondence as well. We also have a firsthand account of Coltrane's youth from his childhood friend Franklin Brower (see appendix A). An interview with Isadore Granoff gives us a good idea of what Coltrane was like as a music student in Philadelphia in the 1940s (see appendix B).

Most of the material collected here dates from 1958 to 1966. Despite a stint performing with Dizzy Gillespie from 1949 to 1951, Coltrane was a virtual unknown when he joined Miles Davis in September 1955—and he wasn't much better known in April 1957 when Davis fired him. Although the Davis group of that time (with the rhythm section of Red Garland, Paul Chambers, and Philly Joe Jones) is now considered to be one of the legendary small groups in jazz, it received little recognition in its own time. Few reviews of the band appeared in newspapers or the jazz press, and most of those that did appear were unfavorable. Philly Joe Jones was too loud; Red Garland was a "cocktail" pianist; Davis was arrogant; Coltrane's tone was "freakish" and he played too many notes. It wasn't until the release of the albums *'Round About Midnight* and *Cookin' with the Miles Davis Quintet* in March and July 1957, respectively, that the group began getting favorable notices. By the time the reviews appeared, however, the band had already broken up.

Being fired by Davis appears to have been the wake-up call that finally led Coltrane to overcome his addictions to alcohol and heroin. Coltrane spent the second half of 1957 playing in Thelonious Monk's quartet, which garnered rave reviews during its extended stay at the Five Spot in New York. By the time Coltrane's album *Blue Train* was released and he rejoined Davis in January 1958, Coltrane had become one of the most talked-about tenor saxophonists in jazz.

Interviews

In all cases where an audio recording of an interview exists, I made a new transcription of the interview directly from the recording. My transcriptions of previously published interviews will therefore differ in some details from the earlier published versions. I transcribed the following interviews:

- Interview with John Coltrane, August Blume
- Interview with John Coltrane, Carl-Erik Lindgren
- Interview with John Coltrane, Ralph J. Gleason
- Interview with John Coltrane, Benoît Quersin
- Interview with John Coltrane, Claes Dahlgren
- Interview with John Coltrane, Benoît Quersin
- Interview with John Coltrane, Michiel de Ruyter
- Interview with John Coltrane, Michel Delorme and Jean Clouzet
- Interview with John Coltrane, Michiel de Ruyter
- Interviews with John Coltrane, Shoichi Yui, Kiyoshi Koyama, Kazuaki Tsujimoto, et al.
- Interview with John Coltrane, Frank Kofsky

I've attempted to transcribe the interviews as accurately as possible, with only minor editing for readability (omitting excessive "um"s and "uh"s, repeated words, and the like). Ellipses in brackets—"[. . .]"—indicate omitted material; ellipses without brackets indicate pauses. Most of the interviews are presented in their entirety (or as much as survives on the audio recordings, some of which are incomplete). The Ralph J. Gleason interview is the main exception; it had to be heavily edited due to constraints enacted by the copyright holder.

Several interviews exist only in print in French publications; the original recordings have been lost. In these cases Coltrane's words were originally translated into French by the interviewers for publication, and they've now been translated back into English by John B. Garvey (with some additional material in the Postif interview translated by Lewis Porter). This, of course, means that we're only reading an approximation of what Coltrane actually said. The following interviews have been translated:

- "John Coltrane: A Modern Faust," J.-C. Dargenpierre
- "John Coltrane: An Interview," François Postif
- Interview with John Coltrane, Jean Clouzet and Michel Delorme
- Interview with John Coltrane, Michel Delorme and Jean Clouzet
- "Coltrane, Star of Antibes: 'I Can't Go Farther'," Michel Delorme and Claude Lenissois

Articles, Reminiscences, and Liner Notes

Writers would occasionally interview Coltrane and then interweave his comments into an article or review. I've attempted to include all articles, reminiscences, and album liner notes that quote Coltrane substantially. (In some cases, only brief quotes by Coltrane were included in a piece; see "Quotable Coltrane" on page 333 for some of the more notable ones.) Ellipses in square brackets indicate omitted material; ellipses without brackets were in the original piece. In most cases I've presented the complete articles, but a few have been edited to eliminate redundant or nonrelevant material. Egregious spelling and punctuation errors have been corrected.

Personal Writings

Antonia Andrews, Coltrane's stepdaughter (for whom Coltrane wrote the tune "Syeeda's Song Flute"), has allowed us to publish a sample of Coltrane's personal writings and correspondence. These works give us a unique glimpse of Coltrane as he corresponded with fans and journalists. On one hand, he humbly responded to fans' requests for autographed photos; on the other, he bluntly expressed his opinions to *Down Beat* editor Don DeMicheal in a June 2, 1962, letter: "You can have this term ['jazz'] along with several others that have been foisted upon us." Egregious spelling and punctuation errors have been corrected, with the exception of Coltrane's poem and the liner notes for *A Love Supreme*.

So this is Trane in his own words.

I have the uneasy feeling that John Coltrane himself would have had serious reservations about this book. As Coltrane told Nat Hentoff in 1967, "I don't know what else can be said in words about what I'm doing. Let the music speak for itself." Of course the music does speak for itself, if we let it. But now, more than four decades after Coltrane's death, "jazz" is a balkanized thing—fractured, fragmented, a patchwork of different and warring schools. Even many of those who appreciate Coltrane's music are limited to a particular Coltrane phase—his sheets of sound (1957–1959), his modal period (1960–1964), or his late period (1965–1967). Here in the twenty-first century, there's no universal theory of jazz, let alone Coltrane's music.

Why not?

As a young alto saxophonist in the mid- to late 1940s, Coltrane grew up "under the spell," as he put it, of Charlie Parker, as did most saxophonists of his generation. Unlike them, at some point Coltrane decided he needed to create something that hadn't been heard before. He needed some new sound, some aspect of music that had nothing to do with anyone—except John Coltrane. "You can only play so much of another man," Coltrane said in 1958. The path Coltrane chose was a difficult one—and certainly, from a commercial standpoint, a risky one. Nevertheless he persisted, and now we have a body of work that stands with the greatest of the twentieth century. It is a collection of music, a life's work, that continues, without any sign of abating, to inspire devotion, adoration, and joy nearly half a century after Coltrane's death.

If someone were to reject this book as irrelevant or unnecessary, arguing that only the music means anything—well, I wouldn't object. Coltrane's music has been an ongoing source of inspiration and motivation in my life, as well as pure enjoyment. But I've also found that John Coltrane is one of the few musicians whose life, thoughts, and words are as inspiring as his music. It's been a privilege for me to be able to collect these interviews and articles into one place and present them here.

—CHRIS DeVITO
Urbana, IL
December 14, 2009

PRELUDE: "A STATEMENT OF MUSICAL PURPOSE"

We should pray for & seek knowledge which would enable us to portray & project the things we love in music, in a way that might, wholly or in some part, be appreciated as having been conceived & composed or performed & presented with dedication & in positive taste.

—J. Coltrane

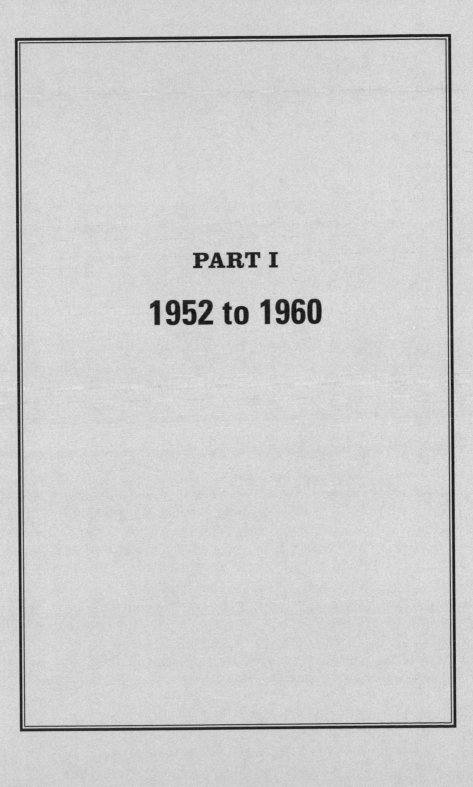

PART I

1952 to 1960

"THE *AFRO* GOES TO A BE-BOP CONCERT"

Rufus Wells

On January 6, 1952, John Coltrane and drummer Specs Wright performed a Sunday afternoon concert in Baltimore, the first in the Adventure in Jazz series. The Coltrane-Wright group played the first set of the concert and the Walt Dickerson group, plus singer Doris Robinson, played the second. The *Baltimore Afro-American* ran two reports on the concert, the second of which is printed here.

Shortly after this concert, both Coltrane and Wright joined Gay Crosse and His Good Humor Six. Coltrane would spend most of 1952 on the road playing rhythm and blues.

DEAR BOSS:

Until this shin-dig last Sunday at the York Hotel Blue Room, my experiences with such concerts had always been harrowing.

In the past, jazz fests had always left me with bruises inflicted by wild jitterbug crowds that seemed to think the music was a signal for mass hysteria.

Sincere Audience

But Boss, I am happy to report that this Adventure in Jazz had about the most refined and sincere audience you'd want to rub shoulders with.

And though I'm no bonafide connoisseur of [this] thing called bop, I'll go on record as saying that if better "sounds" were ever played in this town, I have yet to hear them.

As musicians say when something moves them—it was a goof. Or if you want me to be real "hip," the session killed me.

From the *Baltimore Afro-American*, late city edition, January 12, 1952, pages 1, 2.

If that concert did nothing else, it showed me that foreigners from sophisticated provinces like Manhattan and South Philly are wrong when they claim that we Baltimoreans are square.

Not a Square in Sight

There wasn't a "square" in the joint. Not even a rectangle (an almost square). I understand that patrons had to take a loyalty oath before being allowed to purchase a ticket.

The oath goes something like this: "I solemnly swear that I will dig the sounds, be goofed by the sounds and uphold the sounds against the ravings of infidels like Guy Lombardo and Vaughn Monroe.

"I swear this on the goatee of Dizzy Gillespie and the saxophone of 'Yardbird' Parker."

Well, that's what I heard anyway.

Now for the happenings. The concert began at three-thirty in the afternoon. Some 160 patrons of the cool jazz were crammed into the cozy grotto under the hotel.

"Bones" Mean Girls

I saw some fine "bones" (that's hip talk for nice looking women) and some "down" looking cats (a term signifying sharply-dressed young men) gathered at the tables.

Things were set up cabaret style—the atmosphere in which I think jazz should be presented. You can sit back, relax and concentrate on what's being played up on the stand.

Speaking of the bandstand I had occasion to chat with the musicians before they began to play.

Rehearsed in Men's Room

Johnny Birks,[1] the trumpeter, and John Coltrane, the former Gillespie tenor sax whiz, held an impromptu rehearsal in of all places, the men's room.

Said Birks, "I have eyes for blowing today."

Answered Coltrane, "Yeah."

After that fascinating exchange, they emerged from the rest-room, mounted the stand where pianist Freddy Thaxton, drummer Specs Wright and bassist Ray Drury were poised and waiting.

Coltrane gave them the beat and with a rush and a whir, they teed off on a bouncing ditty called "Seven Come Eleven."

Fans Surprised

I really don't think the fans expected what they heard. They had come a bit skeptical and with critical ears but after the first few bars of the tune, they were delighted and happy as children at the circus. For that matter, so was I.

The tempo increased with each tune and excitement tinged the faces of fans and musicians alike. Birks blew a long other-worldly passage that caused Coltrane to laugh appreciatively.

Everyone's Nerves Upset

Then Specs, the drummer, opened up short flurries of rhythm that had everyone's nerves upset. People applauded him before, during and after his solos.

Coltrane made the fans say "whew." Birks blew and the audience "whewed" some more.

I say again, Boss. It was a goof.

Note

1. Trumpeter Johnny Birks was probably the same John Burks (also Burkes or Burke, as he's listed in various sources) who recorded with baritone saxophonist Leo Parker in 1961. The liner notes for that album, *Let Me Tell You 'Bout It* (Blue Note), state: "JOHN BURKE, the trumpet player, no relation to Dizz, comes from Oceola AK [Osceola, Arkansas], but now makes Baltimore his home. Johnny has played in the bands of Johnny Hodges, Louis Bellson and Eddie 'Cleanhead' Vinson, among others. He plays a clean, controlled horn." Trumpeter Johnny Burkes was listed as playing a Left Bank Jazz Society concert in Baltimore on March 7, 1965 (see http://home.earthlink.net/~eskelin/leftbank.html). There were at least three Adventure in Jazz concerts in Baltimore in early 1952, and Johnny Birks is again listed for the third one, in March 1952. (Coltrane was scheduled to appear at the later concerts, but he'd joined Gay Crosse's rhythm-and-blues group by then. Jimmy Heath took his place.)

INTERVIEW WITH JOHN COLTRANE

August Blume

In early 1955 August Blume helped cofound Baltimore's Interracial Jazz Society, which was formed largely in response to a ruling by Baltimore's Board of Liquor License Commissioners that effectively segregated nightclubs. This ruling was overturned on July 22, 1955 (see "Integration Through Jazz," by George J. Bennett, *Baltimore Afro-American*, September 6, 1955, Afro magazine section, page 7). Coincidentally, this article was published just a few weeks before the new Miles Davis Quintet, with John Coltrane on tenor sax, played a one-week gig at Club Las Vegas in Baltimore. Blume and the other members of the Interracial Jazz Society most likely attended, and Blume may have met Coltrane during this gig.

In June 1958 the Miles Davis Sextet (or the "Miles Davis All Stars," as they were billed) played a week at the Spotlite Lounge in Washington, D.C., and on June 15 Blume invited Coltrane to Sunday dinner at his home in Baltimore. He recorded their after-dinner conversation and, over the following decades, shared the recording freely with anyone who was interested in hearing it. (It should be noted that this was not a formal interview, as Coltrane didn't know he was being recorded until almost the end of the conversation, when he discovers the tape recorder and says, "I was doin' all right till I found this. I didn't think it was on.")

The "interview" starts with the mundane (Blume appears to be explaining the functioning of a reluctant toilet), followed by Blume's remarking on a wide range of reading materials that Coltrane has in front of him (either borrowed from Blume or acquired elsewhere), and moves on to become one of the most comprehensive interviews Coltrane ever did.

Blume: There's something wrong with that, uh, whatchamacallit there, the arm inside that thing it—it makes the tank take a real long time to fill up, you know?

Coltrane: Oh, oh I see.

Blume: You'd better have some reading ahead of you now, huh?

Coltrane: I got something to do here, huh? [*Blume laughs*] Well, this is crazy.

Blume: Have you ever read anything about philosophy?

Coltrane: Well, I—

Blume: What have you read, actually?

Coltrane: I'll tell you what I've read. You know these books that they put out, uh—books—*This Made Simple, That Made Simple*? [*unintelligible*]

Blume: Uh huh.

Coltrane: Well, they got one called *Philosophy Made Simple*. Well I read that. Well that's the only thing I've actually read all the way through. And I bought a few books, little thing, uh, something I picked up called *Language, Truth, Logic*.[1] Stuff like that I just picked up. Some I get into, man, and I don't get any further than the first few pages—you know, and then I start lookin' around, trying to find things.

Blume: What do you think you're looking for—you're interested in philosophy, I mean, what—

Coltrane: I don't know, that's what I—I mean I don't think it's really that I'm looking for as an end, you know? But it seems to be something in it that I kinda like, you know. I guess I'm just sort of seeing what—I'm trying to decide if it would be a good idea to see what other people thought about it, you know. People who think better than I do. See what they think about living, just, you know, life.

Blume: Well, uh . . . Let me ask you this, what do you think about living and life up to this point?

Coltrane: Well, I couldn't give you an answer to that, because I haven't put it together, you know? I don't *think* I have. I couldn't say, you know.

Blume: Do you think there seems to be an overall plan to this thing or do you think that your life is predetermined or that you're your own free agent and you make what you want of your life?

Coltrane: Well . . . it seems like I make, I believe when you say that you make almost what you want, in a way you do, but like *when*. That seems like the part you don't have much to do with.

Blume: Not much control over it.

Coltrane: Yeah, like when is, when, you know   you kind of *set* your course, but when you arrive and things like that, you know. It doesn't always happen as you plan, you know [*laughs; says something unintelligible*]. You can kind of set it.

Blume: Before you got interested in philosophy and, and, uh—

Coltrane: Well I'll tell you.

Blume: —and started to think about philosophy what did you . . .

Coltrane: I can tell you. It started with religion, I guess. [*unintelligible*] And then the first questioning of religion. That brought on everything. You know, when I got to the age where I started to wonder about things.

Blume: What faith were you brought up in, John?

Coltrane: Methodist.

Blume: Methodist? Did you have a very strict religious life or—

Coltrane: Well it was, it wasn't *too* strict, but, it was, it was *there*. My grandfather, *both* of my grandfathers were ministers. My mother, she was very religious. Like, in my early years when I was going to church every Sunday and stuff like that, being under the influence of my grandfather—he was the dominating cat in the family. He was most well versed, active politically. He was more active than my father, who was a tailor; but he [Coltrane's father] never seemed to say too much. He just went about his business, that was *it*, you know. But my grandfather, he was pretty militant, you know. Politically inclined and everything. Religion was his *field*, you know. So that's where—I grew up in that. And, I guess I just accepted it, and I sort of felt certain things. And after I'd say my late teens, I just started breakin' away, you know, among certain things. I was growin' up, so I questioned a lot of what I find in religion. I began to wonder about it. About two or three years later, maybe twenty-two, twenty-three, this Muslim thing came up. I got introduced to that. And that kinda shook me. A lot of my friends, you know, they went Muslim, you see. So I thought about that, anyway, it took me to something I had never thought about—you know, another religion? So that started me to think. But I never did anything about it. [*chuckles*] I just thought about it. I was too busy doing other things, and I forgot it. I think I put it out of my mind for the next several years. I didn't even bother to think about it. And recently, I decided—I mean I started lookin' into, you know, well maybe I can just see what people are *thinkin'*, you know? 'Cause I realized that's what *I'm* trying to do. That's why I sort of turn to things like this, you know. I haven't devoted as much time to it as I want to; I haven't actually learned or covered as much ground of it as I'd like to. I'd like to cover more ground. I'd like to get my own thoughts together, composed the way I feel like it should be, you know. I was like, religion man, I was always—I was disappointed when I found out how *many* religions there were and how—

Blume: You were disappointed?

Coltrane: Yeah.

Blume: In what way?

Coltrane: Not disappointed—I don't know what the hell. When I saw there were so many religions and kind of opposed somewhere to the next and so forth, you know, it screwed up my head. [*laughs*] And, I don't know. I was kinda confused, you know. And I just couldn't believe that, uh, that every—that *one* guy could be right. Because if he's right somebody else got to be wrong, you know?

Blume: If he *is* right.

Coltrane: And vice versa, you know?

Blume: Well, is there a kind of a chance of all the religions that there are, actually being tied in with one another? And by that I mean regardless of what they say, or what they think, that the basic things that are involved in their religion are all actually tied in with the basic things that the next guy believes, and the next guy believes, and so on down the line. And that through history, through time, and through people acting on religion they have tried to say well, what I've got is right and what you've got is wrong because you call yourself this and I call myself that. And that people have actually changed the face of religion, so to speak, but the basic things involved are all pretty much the same?

Coltrane: Sure, I think the basic things will bring them all together, man. If it was just—if there was anybody to *say*, "Well, *get together*."

Blume: In other words then you would like to see something like a universal-type religion where instead of there being all these differences and one guy knocking the next because he belongs to a different faith—

Coltrane: Yeah, there should be. There should be something like that.

Blume: —that there is something basic to all of them and they should all get together.

Coltrane: Yeah, it should be, I think. It should be that way. It's like when you study, you see like what these people say about "good," you know. Philosophers, [*laughs*] when they start talking about "good" and "bad" man, they take those two words and go so far with them. It could be a complicated thing. But it's got to be simple, to really get some good out of it. To really realize something you got to make it simple. And I think religions, they've pretty well, they've got it, they've got it made *if* they can get together because I don't—when they say what they preach is good, I mean, it seems good to me.

Blume: Do you think that when you finish reading a certain number of books and have had time to absorb and think these things over that it will change you in any way or change your outlook on life in any way?

Coltrane: Well, I don't think it'll change me, I think it will help me to understand, you know, like I'll be able to walk a little surer. Just take a little confusion away. I think I'll be the same.

Blume: Do you think very many musicians are more than confused, just like everybody might be, about this religious business? That they might be interested in it, in the same way that you might be interested in it, by trying to gain a little bit more understanding of just what's going on? Do you think a lot of them fall into that category? Have you ever talked to any other musicians about it?

Coltrane: Yeah, well . . . I think the majority of musicians are interested in truth, you know—they, well they've got to be because a thing, a *musical* thing, *is* a truth. If you play and make a statement, a musical statement, and it's a valid statement, that's a truth right there in itself, you know. If you play something phony, well, you know that's phony, [*laughs*] you know, and all musicians are striving to get as near perfection as they can get. That's truth there, you know. So in order to play those kind of things, to play truth, you've got to live with as much truth as you possibly can, you know. And as far as [being] religious; if a guy is religious, then I think he's searching for good, he wants to live a good life. He might call it religious or he might not call himself religious. Maybe he'd say, "I just live a good life." But a religious man would call him, he'd say, "Well that man is a religious man—he lives a good life." So quite a few musicians think about it; I've talked with quite a few of them about it.

Blume: Are there any that stand out in your mind as having views that you feel are closer to the truth than other fellas might have? Are there any musicians that you respect because of their views in this matter?

Coltrane: Well . . . no, I—not offhand, I can't think of any one, any one more than the others. I've talked to quite a few of them. They all seem to be searching, trying to find some way, you know, most musicians I know. And some don't talk about it at all. They seem to be pretty well content, maybe they've found just what they want. . . . I don't know. [*chuckles*]

Blume: It's a long deep subject to try to get into, I know.

Coltrane: Yeah, I get wound up in it, man, you know, and I get confused. Then I have to forget about it for a while.

Blume: Changing the subject a little bit, in your playing and listening experiences in the past few years, who do you feel are the musicians today that you respect most? That's puttin' you really on the spot, I realize, but I'm sure that Monk must fall into a category like this because last night you were, uh, quite positive about the fact that he was a real major contributor and a great writer, and really had something to offer the people. What other musicians fall into this category?

Coltrane: Well . . . I'll name some that I like, you know. I might be leaving out quite a few. [*laughs*]

Blume: That always happens.

Coltrane: Yeah, there might be quite a few I'm leaving out. Horace Silver for one . . . and all the great soloists, you know, like Miles, and Sonny Rollins and guys like that. When I mention a guy like Monk, he's a, to *me*, he's a soloist and he's got, you know, well he *writes* so many things, you know. There are just few like him, really. Charlie Parker was like that. He could play and he could write—quite a few things, you know? Dizzy, he writes quite a bit too.

Blume: What about Benny Golson?

Coltrane: Benny Golson, he's another.

Blume: What about Quincy Jones?

Coltrane: Quincy. Gigi Gryce too. And there's a guy plays, he's in the army right now, he plays tenor, named Wayne Shorter. I think he's going to contribute quite a bit too, 'cause he has this double talent. He can play, you know, and he's got enough stuff to play a whole lot and then sit down and write a lot too.

Blume: What do you think of Johnny Hodges and of Lester Young today?

Coltrane: I like 'em just as well as I did.

Blume: As you used to.

Coltrane: Yeah, just as well as I did in—fifteen years ago.

Blume: Well Rabbit [Johnny Hodges] certainly was, uh, he had to be in the front ranks really of any group of musicians that you'd name—

Coltrane: Sure.

Blume: —because he always played so prettily, man, he was always a beautiful player. I remember reading an interview with Bird [Charlie Parker] in a magazine one time and Bird was very, very enthusiastic about Hodges's playing and said that Hodges was one of his major influences.

Coltrane: Yeah, he was a great—

Blume: He has so much soul.

Coltrane: So much soul, yeah. A whole lotta soul.

Blume: A lot of people say that Lester doesn't play as well today as he used to. I don't know, to me he's always played great.

Coltrane: I think so too.

Blume: He always plays great. He always gets a great sound. He's always got young guys with him too, you notice?

Coltrane: Yeah.

Blume: Well for the last ten years he's always chosen sort of what he felt were the younger talents, like this trumpet player that he had workin' with him for quite a while, Jesse Drakes.

Coltrane: Yeah. He's a very good trumpeter.

Blume: A very very good trumpeter. The trouble is you don't hear enough of him.

Coltrane: That's right. I don't know why. He'll be heard, he's a good trumpeter. He'll find some group somewhere [*unintelligible*].

Blume: When you first started with Monk, before you actually went to work down at the Five Spot, did Monk used to hold rehearsals so that you could learn all the, all the tunes and . . .

Coltrane: Yes.

Blume: How did these things go? I'm kind of curious as to how he more or less, uh, made you familiar with the tunes [and the] changes?

Coltrane: Well, I'd go by his house, you know, by his apartment and I'd get him out of bed maybe, or somethin'—[*laughs*]. And he'd wake up and go to the piano and start playing, you know. He'd play anything, maybe just one of his tunes. He'd start playin' it and he'd look at me I guess, and so when he'd look at me I'd get my horn and start trying to find what he's playing. And he'd continue to play over and over and over and over and I'd get this part, and next time he'd go over it I'd get another part. And he would stop to show me some parts that were pretty difficult, and if I had a lot of trouble, well he'd get his portfolio out and show me the music. He's got music, he's got all of them written, and I'd read it and learn it. He would rather a guy learn without reading, you know, because that way you feel it better. You feel it quicker when you memorize it, when you learn it by heart, by ear, you know. And so when I almost had the tune down, then he would leave, leave me with it. He'd leave me to practice it alone, and he'd go out somewhere, maybe he'd go to the store or go back to bed or something. And I'd just stay there and run over the tune [until] I had it pretty well, and then I'd call him and we'd play it down together. And sometimes we'd just get one tune a day.

Blume: How long did it take you before you actually felt that you were ready to go down to the Five Spot and actually work as a, as a regular unit, you know?

Coltrane: Well—as soon as we got, as soon as he got the job at the Five Spot we went right in, because this goin' over things had started earlier, with this, you know, just—I met him, you know, and I just started hangin' around with him, I went down and I started going down to his house because I like that music. And we'd already recorded one song, "Monk's Mood."

Blume: That was the one you came over from Philly just to do.

Coltrane: Yeah, and I liked it so well I told him that I wanted to learn it, so he invited me around, you know, and that's when I started learning his tunes. We didn't know if we would ever work together. Really enjoyed it, too, I sure enjoyed working with Monk.

Blume: Do you think that was a turning point really in your, in your playing career?

Coltrane: Well . . . I don't know, I don't know whether it was a turning point. About that time I made a decision, you know, myself; that's when I stopped drinking and all that shit. I was able to play better right then, you know.

Blume: Did you used to drink heavily?

Coltrane: Yes. So by the time that he started the group I'd stopped drinking, you know. Found I could—that helped me in all kinds of ways when I stopped drinking; I could play better and think better, everything. And his music, that was . . . a *stimulant*. [*laughs*]

Blume: How did you used to feel when you were working down at the Five Spot and—I know we had seen you a couple of times down there—and in the middle of the tune Monk would get up from the piano and walk around to the side of it and do his little dance [*Coltrane laughs*] and leave you standing there more or less holding the bag?

Coltrane: [*laughs*] I feel kind of lonesome. [*both laugh*] Yeah, I feel—felt a little lonesome up there.

Blume: Well when you're standing up there playing like that [without a piano], how do you hear the changes? Do you think of the changes as you're going along, or does the bass player suggest them to you with what he's playing, or—

Coltrane: Yeah, the bass player, he—I count on him, you know.

Blume: What does he actually do? Like when Wilbur [Ware] would be playing bass, would he play like the dominant note in each chord? I don't know how you phrase this but maybe you can explain it.

Coltrane: Well, at times. But a bass player like Wilbur Ware, he's so inventive, man, you know, like he doesn't always play [*chuckles*] the dominant notes.

Blume: But whatever he plays, does it suggest a note that gives you an idea of which way the changes are going?

Coltrane: Yeah, it may be—and it might not be. Wilbur, he plays the other way sometimes. He plays things that are kind of, you know, they're foreign. If you didn't know the song, you wouldn't be able to find it. [*chuckles*] Because he's superimposing things. He's playing around, and under, and over—building tension, so when he comes back to it you feel everything suck in. But usually I knew the tunes—I knew the changes anyway. So we managed to come out at the end together anyway. [*laughs*]

Blume: Which always helps! [*both laugh*]

Coltrane: Yeah, we managed to finish on time. A lot of fun playing that way though.

Blume: I can imagine.

Coltrane: A lot of fun. 'Cause sometimes he would be playing altered changes and I would be playing altered changes. And he would be playing some other kind of altered changes from the cycle I'd be playing and neither one of us would be playing the changes of the tune until we'd reach a certain spot, and we'd get there together. We're lucky. [*both laugh*] And then Monk comes back in to save everybody. And nobody knows where he is! [*both laugh*] That's what impresses a lot of people anyway. They say, "Man, how do you guys remember all that stuff?" We weren't really remembering much. Just the basic changes and then every-body else just try out anything they wanted to try on it, that's all. And Monk, he's always doing something back there that sounds *so mysterious*. And it's not mys-terious at all, when you know what he's doing. Just like those old things, just like simple truths, you know. Like he just—he might take a chord, a major chord—a *minor* chord—and leave the third out. Yet he says, "This is a minor chord, man," you know? So you don't have a minor third in there, so you don't know *what* it is. You say, "How do you know it's a minor chord?" "That's what it is, a minor chord with the third out." [*both laugh*] And when he plays the thing, man, it will just be in the right place and voiced the right way to have that minor feel. But still it's not a minor because the third is not there. Little things like that, you know.

Blume: Did he pull that on you actually working on the job, or had he done this before, previously, where he'd gotten up and left the piano and left you, so to speak, holding the bag?

Coltrane: Well, he just started that on the job.

Blume: He just started that on the job? How did you feel when he first did it?

Coltrane: Well I was, I was, I started lookin' around for him the first time he did it, but after, [*laughs*] after that I got used to it, you know, and I just tried to hold up till he got back.

Blume: Why do you think he did it?

Coltrane: I don't know. He said he wanted to hear us, he said he wanted to hear the band. [*Blume laughs*] When he did that, he was in the audience himself, and he was listening to the band. Then he'd come back, you know, he got somethin' out of that thing, man.

Blume: I got the biggest kick out of the way he'd do this little shuffle dance on the side.

Coltrane: Yeah, I wanted to see that myself, you know, I couldn't see.

Blume: [*laughs*] Did it ever occur to you to pull your horn away from your mouth and walk over and stand behind him and [*unintelligible*]? [*both laugh*]

Coltrane: Yeah, I should have done that, man. I wanted to see it myself. It was so interesting. Everybody was talking about it. Every once in a while I'd open up one eye and peep at him. He was really enjoying it, he was getting a big kick then.

Blume: Well I'm sure that he must have really enjoyed your playing, I know because—

Coltrane: Well, he said he did, anyway.

Blume: I spoke to him once or twice, I know, and each time he'd say, [*imitating Monk's voice*] "Yeah, he's the man."

Coltrane: I learned a lot with him. I learned little things, you know, I learned to watch the little things. He's just a good musician, man—if you work with a guy who watches the finer points of things, it kind of makes you—helps you to try to watch the finer points sometimes. Little things mean so much in music, like everything else, you know? Like the way you build a house, starting with those little things. You get the little things together and then the whole structure will stand up. If you goof the little things, you don't have . . . [*trails off*]

Blume: Is it the same kind of playing experience playing say with Miles now as it was with Monk?

Coltrane: No, it's a altogether different thing. I don't know, I don't know what it is. It's another great experience, you know.

Blume: [*unintelligible*] . . . a different nature.

Coltrane: Mm hmm. Yes, it's like it is. I can't quite explain the difference either, you know? [*chuckles*]

Blume: Who had you worked with before you worked with Miles when he had Red and Paul and Philly Joe? Who had you been with before that?

Coltrane: Well . . . you want the whole string? [*laughs*]

Blume: [*laughing*] If you feel like sayin' it. [*both laugh*]

Coltrane: Man, let's see . . .

Blume: I know one thing is for sure and certain, you worked with an awful lot of people.

Coltrane: Yeah, I did.

Blume: And it's spread out over a pretty good span of time.

Coltrane: Yeah. Well . . .

Blume: Well like say for example like you said fourteen years ago in forty-four was when you first started playing.

Coltrane: Yeah.

Blume: What did you have your first professional gig with anybody?

Coltrane: Well . . . I usually call my first professional job was a band from Indianapolis led by Joe Webb. This was in '47.[2] Big Maybelle was in this band, you know—Big Maybelle the blues singer. This was, I don't know, this was . . . I don't know what the heck we were, rhythm and blues or *everything* [*laughs*], I don't know *what* that band. Anyway, that's—that band, and then King Kolax—you heard of Kolax, right? Trumpet. And Eddie Vinson, Dizzy, Earl Bostic, Gay Crosse.

Blume: Who?

Coltrane: Gay Crosse.

Blume: I'm not familiar—

Coltrane: He's from Cleveland. He had a little band, he used to be with Louis Jordan one time, his band—he had a little band that was patterned after Louie's band. He sang and played something like Louis. And, um, Daisy Mae and the Hepcats.

Blume: There's another one I'm not familiar with.

Coltrane: [*unintelligible; possibly* "Nothing, really."] Johnny Hodges.

Blume: You did work with Hodges?

Coltrane: Yeah.

Blume: When was that?

Coltrane: Nineteen fifty-three.[3]

Blume: For how long? I had no idea.

Coltrane: Oh, six, seven months, I think.

Blume: Really? Who else was in the band?

Coltrane: Oh, there's Richard Powell on piano, and Lawrence Brown, Emmett Berry. [*Blume says something unintelligible; Coltrane laughs and says something unintelligible.*] And a guy named Jimmie Johnson on drums. And the bass player, I've forgotten his name.

Blume: That surprises me, I had no idea that you'd ever worked with Hodges.

Coltrane: Sure, man.

Blume: I'll bet that was a real gas for you, wasn't it?

Coltrane: I enjoyed it. Yeah, I enjoyed it. Yeah, we had some *true music*, you know. [*laughs*] Lawrence Brown, I like him immensely. He's a great trombonist, you know? Emmett Berry, he impressed me too. And Johnny Hodges. And, uh, Earl Bostic is kinda tremendous, too. I didn't appreciate guys—men like Earl and—after I heard Charlie Parker, you know, but Charlie, he swayed me so much, you know. But after I had come out from *under* it a little bit, after I had *been* under it a little bit, under his spell, then I could listen to other people too. And when I played with these men I find I learn a lot from them. The main thing was trying to, trying to just see how things were, you know, see how—[*unintelligible*]—we have a guy here who plays altogether different, you know, you say, "Well that's so-and-so, I know him anywhere." Then you hear something else you say, "Well that's so-and-so, yeah, I know *him* anywhere." Then you sit down and maybe you can see where, try to see where they both came from, you know, and you find maybe they came out of the same tree somewhere along the line. So I start lookin' at jazz like that, too, you know, collectively, lookin' at the whole thing.

And then after Johnny Hodges . . . it was Miles, that was the next one. I worked with Jimmy Smith for about a couple of weeks before I went with Miles. The organist.

Blume: He's tremendous.

Coltrane: Wow! [*Blume laughs*] I'd wake up in the middle of the night, man, hearin' that organ. [*chuckles*]

Blume: [*laughing*] Give you nightmares.

Coltrane: Yeah, man, those chords screamin' at me.

Blume: You don't work with Bud Powell.

Coltrane: I've played with Bud. I never worked with him. I played about—I think I played one gig with him. Back in 1949 Miles used to get these dance jobs in the Audubon [Ballroom] in New York uptown, way up on Broadway. And I think on one of the jobs he had Sonny Rollins, and Bud, and Art Blakely [Blakey], forgot the bassman, and myself—on this dance job. That's the only time I worked with Bud. He was playing good.

Blume: Whew! . . .

Coltrane: Sonny Rollins, you heard him recently?

Blume: Well, the last time I heard him, let's see, was in November. Last November. And of course the LP that he made, *A Night at the Village Vanguard.*

Coltrane: Mm hmm.

Blume: He had Elvin Jones and, I forget who the bass player was. I know [drummer] Donald Bailey from Baltimore here was on one cut. And I think he had [bassist] Wendell Marshall with him at the concert that I saw him.

Coltrane: Yeah, like some guys you call great, man, and Sonny, he's one. [*unintelligible*] He's just reached that "great" status.

Blume: What do you think of tenor players like, say, Bill Perkins and Richie Kamuca that fall into the so-called—it's a bad word—but the so-called West Coast school?

Coltrane: Well, I haven't heard 'em enough to actually pass comment, you know. I couldn't say. Rickie I know very well, because we came up in Philly together.

And he always could play, you know. But I haven't heard him—I haven't heard him, man, since he was with [Stan] Kenton. I didn't hear him but once then, you know. I didn't hear him like stretch out or anything, he just played a few solos with the band. I'll say that I like his style, you know?

Blume: Mm hmm.

Coltrane: And Perkins, I'm not too familiar with what he's done. I haven't heard any of his LPs or records. What style does he play like, mostly?

Blume: Well, it seems to be out of a Lester. . .

Coltrane: Lester.

Blume: . . . uh, kick. Little bit of, uh, Stan Getz in there. Little bit of Herbie Steward. In that general vein. And it's all derived from Lester [Young].

Coltrane: Yeah.

Blume: He seems to have a little bit more of an individual voice than some of the other guys.

Coltrane: Does he play any bari[tone saxophone]?

Blume: No, I don't think so.

Coltrane: Mm hmm.

Blume: It's a different kind of listening experience than listening to somebody like, uh, like yourself, say—

Coltrane: Sonny.

Blume: Sonny, or any of the really good tenor players on this side of the country.

Coltrane: Well I'm sure they're good, you know.

Blume: They're all very very competent.

Coltrane: Yeah, I'm sure they're good.

Blume: What I wonder about though is that when you listen to something on LP by them—here again I'm in the same position as you, I haven't really had a chance to hear them in person, you know.

Coltrane: Mm hmm.

Blume: I have heard a few LPs, though. And from what I've heard it seems to have been very well thought out, but when it comes to the solos it's like, uh, the whole thing is very well preconceived, so that you don't have the spontaneousness [unintelligible]. It doesn't seem to be a thing of the moment. It happens.

Coltrane: Mm hmm

Blume: It seems to me that whoever the soloist is, he's thought the whole thing out and he knows just what he's going to play before he ever plays it. And he's eliminated any mistakes that he might have made.

Coltrane: Mm hmm.

Blume: Like you remember on the Monk thing that, uh, I forget which tune it was on that LP that you did with [Coleman] Hawkins and them?

Coltrane: Yeah.

Blume: You had forgotten to come in, and Monk was shouting "Coltrane, Coltrane!"

Coltrane: [chuckles] Yeah.

Blume: That's the kind of thing, to my way of thinking, that makes great music. Where you catch mistakes as well as you catch great moments, you know. And even, even Hawkins, Hawkins came in wrong on that thing too.

Coltrane: Yeah, well [*laughing*] I couldn't advise doing that too many times, too often.

Blume: No, but I mean that's just, that's an example.

Coltrane: That's very spontaneous, brother. [*laughs*]

Blume: I guess you were so wrapped up with what he [Monk] was doing.

Coltrane: Yeah, well see at that—when we made that I hadn't played with him too long, I hadn't been playing with him long. And actually he would throw me, you know, quite often he would actually throw me because I hadn't played with him long then and I was unfamiliar with the changes and stuff. But as time went by I got used to him. And he can get awfully tricky, you know. He makes you keep alert, you see—he likes that, you know. He likes to keep, keep the mental process *vibratin'*, you know? [*Blume laughs*] You get to like that thing, you know, after you get to play with him a while. But at first, see, like I was afraid.

[At this point a woman, most likely Blume's wife, interrupts and alerts them to the fact that it's now 6:00 P.M. and they'll have to leave soon so they can get Coltrane to the club by 7:00 P.M. for that evening's performance by the Miles Davis Sextet. They make arrangements to do so. Coltrane, who had been unaware that Blume was recording their conversation, now discovers that the tape recorder is on.]

Coltrane: You know I was doin' all right—this is on?

Blume: Yeah.

Coltrane: I was doin' all right till I found this. [*laughs*] I didn't think it was on.

Blume: What I thought I'd do is take [the recording] down to the clubhouse, you know, and [at] the next meeting play it back for the rest of the club members. I'm sure they'd get a big kick of hearing the thing, and it certainly would illuminate them—

Coltrane: Well—

Blume: —about more aspects of you than they had probably thought about before, you know?

Coltrane: Maybe so. I wish I had something constructive to say, you know, something, something *fine* to say. [*Blume laughs*] I'll just end up like everybody, saying "Keep swinging," or something like that.

Blume: I'll tell ya, another thing I had in my mind, as this thing was going on, and you were talking quite naturally about different things, I got to thinking that I might just—if it's OK with you—I might just sit down and try to go back over this, play this tape over for myself and try to write the thing out and send it in to *Down Beat* and see if they wouldn't print a feature article on you. Because God knows they haven't had one on you, man.

Coltrane: Well . . . well I'd like to have something, you know, to really *say*, like maybe after I search around a little bit, maybe I can find something real concrete to hash over with, you know, about jazz, something like that. And then we can talk it up, maybe. If you'd like to send it in, I mean, you know, just, if you want to—just let me *see* the thing. [*Blume laughs*] Let *me* see it. [*Coltrane laughs*]

Blume: OK, what I'll do, I'll try to write it up and, uh, let me have your address, man, you know?

Coltrane: OK.

Blume: And, uh, let me write it up and I'll mail you [*unintelligible*], if you think it's OK.

[The tape continues to run while Coltrane writes his address. Blume mentions that he'd mailed a Christmas card to Coltrane, care of the Five Spot, and Coltrane says, "I think I got it."]

Notes

1. The book Coltrane refers to is *Language, Truth, and Logic*, written by Alfred Jules Ayer. Coltrane probably had a copy of the U.S. edition, published in 1952 by Dover.

2. Coltrane may have joined Joe Webb earlier, in the fall of 1946, and stayed until early 1947.

3. Coltrane probably joined Hodges in late 1953 and stayed until mid-1954.

CORRESPONDENCE WITH FANS

Crosby K. Coltrane, John Coltrane, and Norman Klein

In 1958 Coltrane's career was on the ascendant; he'd rejoined Miles Davis after a fruitful stint with Thelonious Monk, his classic album *Blue Train* had been released to critical and commercial success, and Coltrane's playing was bursting with powerful new ideas. These letters show Coltrane responding to fans with earnestness, sincerity, and occasionally humor.

On Monday, August 4, 1958, Coltrane responded to a letter from Mr. Crosby K. Coltrane, who also played tenor saxophone. Both letters are typewritten; John Coltrane's is an unsigned carbon copy. Both letters were auctioned by Guernsey's Auction House in February 2005.

Letter from Crosby K. Coltrane

Laramie, Wyoming
April 10—'58

Mr. John Coltrane
c/o Prestige Records
447 West 50th Street
New York 19, N.Y.

I am writing this note in hopes that you will forward it to Mr. John Coltrane.

You see I have the same last name—which is rather odd, so when I read an article in the San Francisco paper by one Ralph J. Gleason I was interested in the name and also the fact that I too have played a Tenor Sax for about 25 years.

Probably has no connection at all, but just as a kick for me and probably him, I'd certainly appreciate it if you would forward this to the above mentioned.

Yours Truly,
Crosby K. Coltrane
1208 Custer
Laramie, Wyoming
AFofM—662

Letter to Crosby K. Coltrane

August 4, 1958

Dear Mr. Coltrane,

I am sorry for the delay in answering your letter, I really have little time to take care of my mail. I know you understand being a fellow musician. Your letter did indeed give me quite a kick. Here in New York I am the only Coltrane listed in the directory. It was the same in Phila. where I lived for a number of years. It is indeed odd to find another Coltrane, especially one playing the same instrument. That adds to the rarity. I appreciate your writing to me. Perhaps we will see each other before it's over.

Yours truly,
John William Coltrane

[Possibly on the same day, Coltrane wrote a letter to a fan named Ernest, respond-ing to his request for a photo. The carbon copy is undated, but it's typed on the same sheet of paper as the first draft of an unrelated letter dated August 4, 1958 (the unrelated portion is xed out at the bottom of the page). This letter was auctioned in February 2005 by Guernsey's.]

Dear Ernest,

Sorry about the delay in answering your letter. What, with travelling, I am always behind in my mail. I am sending you a photo taken at the Palm Gardens concert earlier this year. If you notice, Paul Chambers can be seen between horn and bass. Hope you like it.

Yours Truly,
John Coltrane

Letter to Norman Klein

[In a letter handwritten on lined yellow paper, Norman Klein of Pittsburgh wrote Coltrane asking for an autographed photo.]

Dear John,

    Would you please send me an autographed picture. I would greatly appreciate this.

                    Thank you very much,
                    Norman Klein
                    1203 Malvern Ave.
                    Pittsburgh 17, Pa.

                    August 27, 1958

Dear Norman,

    I'm sorry for the delay in answering your letter. The picture I'm sending you was taken at a record session headed by Art Blakey, with his big band. You can see altoist Billy Graham also. Hope you like it.

                    Yours truly,
                    John Coltrane

CORRESPONDENCE WITH JOURNALIST BOB SNEAD

Bob Snead and John Coltrane

In 1958 Cleveland journalist Bob Snead wrote to Coltrane asking for personal information for an article he was writing; below is his letter. Coltrane's response, which does not survive in full, follows. The article, which includes quotations from the missing part of the letter, eventually appeared in the *Cleveland Call and Post*, an African American newspaper (for the published article, see page 45).

Letter from Bob Snead

Dear John;

I have addressed this letter to you or Mrs. Coltrane to make allowances for the fact that you may or may not be in New York at this time and I would like to open the initial series "Profiles on Today's Modern Jazz Greats" with you. I am hoping that in the event that you are not in town Mrs. Coltrane will be able to supply me with the information I need, for I am sure that she has such personal data as I will need concerning you.

I am in need of such information as where you were born, age, schooling, date of marriage, wife's first name, children, a short sketch of your musical career and any other information you or Mrs. Coltrane can offer to make this series more enlightening to the reader.

I would like to take time out to say that I have worked with bands and musicians for perhaps twenty or more years on newspapers from coast to coast, with artist bureaus such as Mills etc. and in all sincerity I am very much impressed in your playing and in you personally as an example of a clean cut young man. I sincerely believe that in years to come, and not too many, you will by your continued devotion to your music prove that I am not alone in my belief that you as a musician are destined to rank among the greats. Please never lose your sense of values and never forget that the ability you have is a God given grace.

Enclosed you will find some of my reviews of your albums that you may wish to add to your scrap book.

Most sincerely yours,

Bob Snead

In reply address to
9203 Empire Ave
Cleve. 8 Ohio

Letter to Bob Snead

[Coltrane began writing back to Snead on August 4, 1958, but didn't get very far:]

August 4, 1958,

Dear Bob,

I am truly sorry for the delay in answering your letter. I have had much of my important mail misplaced because I am in and out. Things are pretty well ordered now, but I'm afraid the time has hurt me.

Let me first thank you for your very complimentary letter. A very inspiring letter. I thank God for people like you.

Just in case you can still use the information you asked for, I'm sending it. I was born John William Coltrane, September 23rd

[Coltrane resumed work on the letter at the end of August 1958.]

August 31, 1958

Dear Bob,

I am sorry about the delay in answering your letter. I had quite a mix-up [with] my mail due to my wife and me both travelling. We just found your letter along with some other important mail put away with some ads.

Your letter gave me much pleasure. I greatly appreciate your support. It is indeed gratifying to have friends like you. Here is the information you asked for.

I was born in Hamlet, North Carolina, Sept. 23, 1926. My father played the violin and ukelele as a hobby. He was a tailor by trade. My mother had aspirations to become a concert singer. Her Methodist Minister father didn't approve of young girls leaving home until they married so she had to pass it up. She still sings beautifully in the church choir. She also plays the piano.

My family moved to High Point, N.C. where I went to school. After finishing High School, we moved to Philadelphia. It was there that I decided to study music seriously. After a year in the Navy, (1945–46, playing in Navy band,) [I] worked around Phila. until I went with Eddie Vinson in 1947.[1] (I played Tenor here. I started on Clarinet and Alto.) I worked with Eddie about a year, Red Garland and Johnny Coles were in the band at the time. I came back to Phila. and worked around town. Jimmy Heath had a band then that I consider a major influence on the Phila. musicians around that period. I also worked in a group led by Philly Joe Jones. I then went with Dizzy Gillespie (1949) working In his big band until '52. I played alto during my stay with Dizzy.[2] After Dizzy I went with Gay Cross [Crosse] in Cleveland. Short periods with Earl Bostic and Johnny Hodges followed that. Back in Phila., I met Juanita, and married the following year. [*handwritten*] '55

[This appears to be all that survives of Coltrane's letter to Snead.]

Notes
  1. Coltrane joined Vinson in late 1948 and stayed until mid-1949.
  2. Gillespie's big band broke up in mid-1950. Gillespie then formed a small group that included Coltrane on tenor sax. Coltrane left around April 1951.

LETTER TO DICKSON DEBRAH KISAI

John Coltrane

In this fascinating letter Coltrane writes to one Mr. Dickson Debrah Kisai of Ghana, whose letter was published in the *Pittsburgh Courier,* an African American newspaper. Intriguingly, Coltrane asks about job opportunities and the "chances for small business" in Ghana.

September 11, 1958

[*address handwritten*]
To
Dickson Debrah Kisai
P.O. Box 1813
Accra, Ghana

Mr. Dickson Kisai,

I saw your letter in the Pittsburgh Courier. I consider it a great opportunity to correspond with one living in Ghana. Our interest in your country is very high here in America. I am a Musician in the so-called Modern Jazz idiom. I have lived in America all my 30 years. I have travelled the United States to quite an extent, working with different bands. It is my desire to someday see Africa. I'd like to know more about Ghana. What kind of work is in demand? What are the chances for small businesses?

What kind of music do you like? Perhaps we can exchange phonograph records. I am, like you, interested in almost everything. I am starting with music because it is always first with me.

I am hoping to hear from you very soon.

John William Coltrane

"'TRANE ON THE TRACK"[1]

Ira Gitler

This was the first major article about Coltrane to be published. From 1958 to
1962, *Down Beat* ran five feature articles on Coltrane, including a "Blindfold Test"
(all the articles are included in this book). After 1962, however, the magazine
sharply curtailed its coverage of Coltrane and didn't run another major piece on
him until after his death. Coltrane discussed his feelings about *Down Beat* in the
interview with Frank Kofsky (see page 314; for the full article, see page 281).

Asked about being termed an "angry young tenor" in this publication's coverage of the 1958 Newport Jazz festival, John Coltrane said, "If it is interpreted as
angry, it is taken wrong. The only one I'm angry at is myself when I don't make
what I'm trying to play."

The 32-year-old native of Hamlet, N. C., has had his melancholy moments,
but he feels that they belong to a disjointed, frustrating past. The crucial point in
his development came after he joined Dizzy Gillespie's band in 1951.[2]

Prior to that, he had studied music and worked in Philadelphia, assuming
many of the fashionable nuances of the Charlie Parker–directed groups. When
the offer to join the Gillespie band came, Coltrane felt ready.

The feeling turned out to be illusory.

"What I didn't know with Diz was that what I had to do was really express
myself," Coltrane remembered. "I was playing cliches and trying to learn tunes
that were hip, so I could play with the guys who played them.

"Earlier, when I had first heard Bird, I wanted to be identified with him . . . to
be consumed by him. But underneath I really wanted to be myself.

"You can only play so much of another man."

Dejected and dissatisfied with his own efforts, Coltrane left Gillespie and
returned to Philadelphia in search of a musical ideal and the accompanying
integrity. Temporarily, he attempted to find escape in work.

From *Down Beat*, October 16, 1958, pages 16–17.

"I just took gigs," he said. "You didn't have to play anything. The less you played, the better it was."

Plagued by economic difficulties, he searched for a steady job. In 1952, he found one, with a group led by Earl Bostic, whom he admires as a saxophonist even though he disliked the rhythm-and-blues realm the band dwelt in. But this job did not demolish the disillusion and lethargy that had captured him.

"Any time you play your horn, it helps you," he said. "If you get down, you can help yourself even in a rock 'n' roll band. But I didn't help myself."

A more productive step was made in 1953, when Coltrane joined a group headed by Johnny Hodges.

"We played honest music in this band," he recalled. "It was my education to the older generation."

Gradually, Coltrane rationalized the desire to work regularly with the aim of creating forcefully. In 1955, he returned to Philadelphia and, working with a group led by conga drummer Bill Carney, took a stride toward achieving his goal. As he recalled, "We were too musical for certain rooms."

In late 1955, Miles Davis beckoned. Davis had noted Coltrane's playing and wanted him in a new quintet he was forming. He encouraged Coltrane; this encouragement gradually opened adventurous paths for Coltrane. Other musicians and listeners began to pay close attention to him. When Davis disbanded in 1957, Coltrane joined Thelonious Monk's quartet.

Coltrane will not forget the role Davis and Monk played in assisting his development.

"Miles and Monk are my two musicians," he said. "Miles is the No. 1 influence over most of the modern musicians now. There isn't much harmonic ground he hasn't broken. Just listening to the beauty of his playing opens up doors. By the time I run up on something, I find Miles or Monk has done it already.

"Some things I learn directly from them. Miles has shown me possibilities in choosing substitutions within a chord and also new progressions."

Enveloped in the productive atmosphere of both the Davis and Monk groups, Coltrane emerged more an individualist than ever before. In early '58, he rejoined Davis. In the months since he did so, he has become more of an influence on other jazz instrumentalists. His recordings, on Prestige, Blue Note, and with Davis on Columbia, often are matters for passionate debate.

Yet, there is no denying his influence. There are traces of his playing in that of Junior Cook, with Horace Silver's group, and in Benny Golson, previously a Don-Byas-Lucky-Thompson-out-of-Hawkins tenor man.

Coltrane's teammate in the Davis sextet, Cannonball Adderley, recently said, "Coltrane and Sonny Rollins are introducing us to some new music, each in his own way. I think Monk's acceptance, after all this time, is giving musicians courage to keep playing their original ideas, come what may."

When the jazz audience first heard Coltrane, with Davis in 1955 and '56, he was less an individualist. His style derived from those of Dexter Gordon (vintage mid-'40s), Sonny Stitt, Sonny Rollins (the Rollins of that time and slightly before), Stan Getz (certain facets of sound), and an essence of generalized Charlie Parker.

As he learned harmonically from Davis and Monk, and developed his mechanical skills, a new more confident Coltrane emerged. He has used long lines and multinoted figures within these lines, but in 1958 he started playing sections that might be termed "sheets of sound."

When these efforts are successful, they have a cumulative emotional impact, a residual harmonic effect. When they fail, they sound like nothing more than elliptically phrased scales.

This approach, basic to Coltrane's playing today, is not the result of a conscious effort to produce something "new." He has noted that it has developed spontaneously.

"Now it is not a thing of beauty, and the only way it would be justified is if it becomes that," he said. "If I can't work it through, I will drop it."

Although he is satisfied with the progress he's made during the last three years, Coltrane continues to be critical of his own work. Dejection is no longer a major part of this self-criticism. Now, he seeks to improve, knowing he can do so.

"I have more work to do on my tone and articulation," he said. "I must study more general technique and smooth out some harmonic kinks. Sometimes, while playing, I discover two ideas, and instead of working on one, I work on two simultaneously and lose the continuity."

Assured that the vast frustration he felt in the early '50s is gone, Coltrane attempts to behave in terms of a broad code, which he outlined:

"Keep listening. Never become so self-important that you can't listen to other players. Live cleanly . . . Do right . . . You can improve as a player by improving as a person. It's a duty we owe to ourselves."

A married man, with an eight-year-old daughter, Coltrane hopes to meet the responsibilities of his music and his life without bitterness, for "music is the means of expression with strong emotional content. Jazz used to be happy and joyous. I'd like to play happy and joyous."

Notes

1. On the cover and contents page of the issue of *Down Beat* in which this article first appeared, the title is listed as "John Coltrane: A Happy Young Man."
2. Coltrane was with Gillespie from about September 1949 to March 1951.

"JAZZ PROFILE: JOHN COLTRANE —A DEDICATED MUSICIAN"

Bob Snead

The following article, which appeared in the *Cleveland Call and Post*, is based on Coltrane's reply to journalist Bob Snead's request for personal information about his life and career (see page 35). Snead may have met Coltrane in September 1958 when the Miles Davis Sextet appeared at the Modern Jazz Room in Cleveland.

The sounds that flow from John Coltrane's tenor are accomplished as they are by any other sax player in a technical sense by the use of the hands and the mouth. The fact that he has risen above most of his contemporaries is due to a number of reasons. The most important being that he has within him a dedicated desire to be a great musician. Not great in the eyes of the public, but great in his own feelings.

This is not a result of a super ego for John is one of the most humbly shy persons we have ever met. It is however the result of his desire for perfection. It is musicians such as he who are responsible for the public's new acceptance of jazz on a level with other arts. The fact that after more than ten years of professional playing critics and fans all over the world of Jazz are now recognizing him as a gifted tenor voice seems to make little or no impression on him. To be sure he's grateful, but he's more concerned with improving his music.

Coltrane was born some 32 years ago in Hamlet, North Carolina. His father was a tailor by profession, but a violinist at heart. His mother had aspirations of being a concert singer but John's grandfather, a methodist minister, didn't approve. Today she is still singing in the church choir in Philadelphia. With such a background it makes it easier to understand why music is a part of him.

A few years ago John almost gave up music; as he puts it, "I really have much to be thankful for. My father died when I was around twelve. My mother made

From the *Cleveland Call and Post*, December 27, 1958, page 5-C.

many sacrifices to enable me to study music. She never married again. Some years ago I went into a period of depression and almost gave up. I thank God for enabling me to pull out of it. My wife Nita was a great help to me, also. She and daughter, Toni have made my life far happier."

Actually the new Coltrane emerged after a brief period with the Thelonious Monk Combo. Coltrane, who joined Miles in 1955 and remained with him until illness forced Miles to disband, joined Monk shortly after. Of this period he says, "This was a most impressive period for me. Monk is an exceptional musician. The time I spent with him was most stimulating."

Although he has drawn his influences for styles from Dexter Gordon and Sonny Stitt, he has been basically influenced by Monk and Davis especially in his chord structure and musical thinking. Today he is back with Miles exerting a freedom of experimentation that is not hampered but encouraged by Miles.

Coltrane's influence on other saxophonists is being heard today in more and more of his contemporaries. It is almost safe to say that when he has blown his last note he will be recognized as one of the great jazz influences of our time.

"HONEST JOHN: THE BLINDFOLD TEST"

Leonard Feather

Leonard Feather started the Blindfold Test in *Metronome* and then moved it to *Down Beat* (and eventually brought the concept, under a different name, to *JazzTimes*). Coltrane shows a thoughtful and measured listening approach, as well as a wide knowledge of both his contemporaries and the previous generation of jazz musicians.

The Blindfold Test below is the first interview of its kind with John Coltrane. The reason is simple: though he has been a respected name among fellow musicians for a number of years, it is only in the last year or two that he has reached a substantial segment of the jazz-following audience.

It is the general feeling that Coltrane ranks second only to Sonny Rollins as a new and constructive influence on his instrument. Coltrane's solo work is an example of that not uncommon phenomenon, an instrumental style that reflects a personality strikingly different from that of the man who plays it; for his slow, deliberate speaking voice and far-from-intense manner never would lead one to expect from him the cascades of phrases that constitute a typical Coltrane solo.

The records for his Blindfold Test were more or less paired off, the first a stereo item by a big band, the next two combo tracks by hard bop groups, the third pair bearing a reminder of two early tenor giants, and the final two sides products of miscellaneous combos. John was given no information before or during the test about the records played.

From *Down Beat*, February 19, 1959, page 39.

The Records

1. **Woody Herman. "Crazy Rhythm" (Everest Stereo). Paul Quinichette, tenor saxophone; Ralph Burns, arranger.**

Well, I would give it three stars on the merit of the arrangement, which I thought was good. The solos were good, and the band played good. As to who it was, I don't know . . . The tenor sounded like Paul Quinichette, and I liked that because I like the melodic way he plays. The sound of the recording was very good. I'd like to make a guess about that arrangement—it sounded like the kind of writing Hefti does—maybe it was Basie's band.

2. **Art Farmer Quintet. "Mox Nix" (United Artists). Benny Golson, tenor; Farmer, trumpet, composer, arranger; Bill Evans, piano; Addison Farmer, bass; Dave Bailey, drums.**

That's a pretty lively sound. That tenor man could have been Benny Golson, and the trumpeter, I don't know . . . It sounded like Art Farmer a little bit.

I enjoyed the rhythm section—they got a nice feeling, but I don't know who they were. The composition was a minor blues—which is always good. The figures on it were pretty good, too. I would give it three-and-a-half.

3. **Horace Silver Quintet. "Soulville" (Blue Note). Silver, piano, composer; Hank Mobley, tenor; Art Farmer, trumpet.**

Horace . . . Is that "Soulville"? I've heard that—I think I have the record. Horace gave me that piece of music some time ago . . . I asked him to give me some things that I might like to record and that was one of them. I've never got around to recording it yet, though. I like the piece tremendously—the composition is great. It has more in it than just "play the figure and then we all blow." It has a lot of imgination. The solos are all good . . . I think it's Hank Mobley and Art Farmer. I'll give that four-and-a-half stars.

4. **Coleman Hawkins. "Chant" (Riverside). Idrees Sulieman, trumpet; J.J. Johnson, trombone; Hank Jones, piano; Oscar Pettiford, bass.**

Well, the record had a genuine jazz feeling. It sounded like Coleman Hawkins . . . I think it was Clark Terry on trumpet, but I don't know. The 'bone was good, but I don't know who it was. I think the piano was very good . . . I'll venture one guess: Hank Jones. It sounded like Oscar Pettiford and was a very good bass solo. And Bean—he's one of the kind of guys—he played well, but I wanted to hear some more from him . . . I was expecting some more.

When I first started listening to jazz, I heard Lester Young before I heard Bean. When I *did* hear Hawkins, I appreciated him, but I didn't hear him as much as I did Lester . . . Maybe it was because all we were getting then was the Basie band.

I went through Lester Young and on to Charlie Parker, but after that I started listening to others—I listened to Bean and realized what a great influence he was on the people I'd been listening to. Three and a half.

5. Ben Webster–Art Tatum. "Have You Met Miss Jones?" (Verve).

That must be Ben Webster, and the piano, I don't know. I thought it was Art Tatum . . . I don't know anybody else who plays like that, but still I was waiting for that thunderous thing from him, and it didn't come. Maybe he just didn't feel like it then.

The sound of that tenor . . . I wish he'd show *me* how to make a sound like that. I've got to call him up and talk to him! I'll give that four stars . . . I like the atmosphere of the record—the whole thing I got from it. What they do for the song is artistic, and it's a good tune.

6. Toshiko Akiyoshi. "Broadway" (Metrojazz). Bobby Jaspar, tenor; René Thomas, guitar.

You've got me guessing all the way down on this one, but it's a good swinging side and lively. I thought at first the tenor was Zoot, and then I thought, no. If it isn't Zoot, I don't know who it could be. All the solos were good . . . The guitar player was pretty good. I'd give the record three stars on its liveliness and for the solos.

7. Chet Baker. "Fair Weather" (Riverside). Johnny Griffin, tenor; Benny Golson, composer.

That was Johnny Griffin, and I didn't recognize anybody else. The writing sounded something like Benny Golson . . . I like the figure and that melody. The solos were good, but I don't know . . . Sometimes it's hard to interpret changes. I don't know whether it was taken from another song or if it was a song itself.

Maybe the guys could have worked it over a little longer and interpreted it a little truer. What I heard on the line as it was written, I didn't hear after the solos started . . . It was good, though—I would give it three stars, on the strength of the composer mostly, and the solos secondly . . . I didn't recognize the trumpeter.

GIANT STEPS LINER NOTES

Nat Hentoff

Nat Hentoff has covered jazz for well over half a century. Currently, he writes on jazz for the *Wall Street Journal* and *JazzTimes* and is the author of *At the Jazz Band Ball: Sixty Years on the Jazz Scene* (University of California Press, 2010). Hentoff interviewed Coltrane for these liner notes, probably sometime in late 1959. *Giant Steps* was released in early 1960.

Along with Sonny Rollins, John Coltrane has become the most influential and controversial tenor saxophonist in modern jazz. He is becoming, in fact, more controversial and possibly more influential than Rollins. While it's true that to musicians especially, Coltrane's fiercely adventurous harmonic imagination is the most absorbing aspect of his developing style, the more basic point is that for many non-musician listeners, Coltrane at his best has an unusually striking emotional impact. There is such intensity in his playing that the string of adjectives employed by French critic Gérard Brémond in a *Jazz-Hot* article on Coltrane hardly seem at all exaggerated. Brémond called his playing "exuberant, furious, impassioned, thundering."

There is also, however, an extraordinary amount of sensitivity in Coltrane's work. Part of the fury in much of his playing is the fury of the search, the obsession Coltrane has to play all he can hear or would like to hear—often all at once— and yet at the same time make his music, as he puts it, "more presentable." He said recently, "I'm worried that sometimes what I'm doing sounds like just academic exercises, and I'm trying more and more to make it sound prettier." It seems to me he already succeeds often in accomplishing both his aims, as sections of this album demonstrate.

This is the first set composed entirely of Coltrane originals. John has been writing since 1948. [. . .] Miles [Davis] encouraged Coltrane and also stimulated his harmonic thinking. In terms of writing as well, John feels he's learned from Miles to make sure that a song "is in the right tempo to be most effective. He also made me go further into trying different modes in my writing." [. . .]

[Coltrane] has devoted more and more of his time to composing. He is mostly self-taught as a writer, and generally starts his work at the piano. "I sit there and run over chord progressions and sequences, and eventually, I usually get a song—or songs—out of each little musical problem. After I've worked it out on the piano, I then develop the song further on tenor, trying to extend it harmonically." Coltrane tries to explain what drives him to keep stretching the harmonic possibilities of improvisation by saying, "I feel like I can't hear but so much in the ordinary chords we usually have going in the accompaniment. I just have to have more of a blueprint. It may be that sometimes I've been trying to force all those extra progressions into a structure where they don't fit, but this is all something I have to keep working on. I think too that my rhythmic approach has changed unconsciously during all this, and in time, it too should get as flexible as I'm trying to make my harmonic thinking." [. . .]

Of the tunes, Coltrane says of "Giant Steps" that it gets its name from the fact that "the bass line is kind of a loping one. It goes from minor thirds to fourths, kind of a lop-sided pattern in contrast to moving strictly in fourths or in half-steps." Tommy Flanagan's relatively spare solo and the way it uses space as part of its structure is an effective contrast to Coltrane's intensely crowded choruses.

"Cousin Mary" is named for a cousin of Coltrane who is indeed called Mary. The song is an attempt to describe her. "She's a very earthy, folksy, swinging person. The figure is riff-like and although the changes are not conventional blues progressions, I tried to retain the flavor of the blues."

"Syeeda's Song Flute" has a particularly attractive line and is named for Coltrane's 10-year-old daughter. "When I ran across it on the piano," he says, "it reminded me of her because it sounded like a happy, child's song."

The tender "Naima"—an Arabic name—is also the name of John's wife. "The tune is built," Coltrane notes, "on suspended chords over an E-flat pedal tone on the outside. On the inside—the channel—the chords are suspended over a B-flat pedal tone." Here again is demonstrated Coltrane's more than ordinary melodic imagination as a composer and the deeply emotional strength of all his work, writing and playing. There is a "cry"—not at all necessarily a despairing one—in the work of the best of the jazz players. It represents a man's being in thorough contact with his feelings, and being able to let them out, and that "cry" Coltrane certainly has.

"Mr. P.C." is Paul Chambers who provides excellent support and thoughtful solos on the record as a whole and whom Coltrane regards as "one of the greatest bass players in jazz. His playing is beyond what I could say about it. The bass is such an important instrument, and has so much to do with how a group and a soloist can best function that I feel very fortunate to have had him on this date and to have been able to work with him in Miles' band so long." [. . .]

What makes Coltrane one of the most interesting jazz players is that he's not apt to ever stop looking for ways to perfect what he's already developed and also to go beyond what he knows he can do. He is thoroughly involved with plunging as far into himself and the expressive possibilities of his horn as he can. As Zita Carno wrote, "the only thing to expect from John Coltrane is the unexpected." I'd qualify that dictum by adding that one quality that *can* always be expected from Coltrane is intensity. He asks so much of himself that he can thereby bring a great deal to the listener who is also willing to try relatively unexplored territory with him.

NAT HENTOFF

INTERVIEW WITH JOHN COLTRANE

Carl-Erik Lindgren

This interview took place in Stockholm on March 22, 1960, in between shows at the Miles Davis Quintet's concert. Coltrane seems a bit taken aback by the interviewer's "abrupt" opening question but maintains his usual composure throughout.

Carl-Erik Lindgren: Well, it's a pleasure and an honor to have John Coltrane in front of our microphone here, and John, I gotta be abrupt with you, I gotta say it like this: that, uh—your playing has been termed "untenorlike," "unbeautiful," "un-just-about-everything-you-can-think-of." And since the playing mirrors the personality, I guess you have some, some personal thoughts of that kind to say.

John Coltrane: Um . . . well, uh, lemme follow you again. You said my playin' is un-*what?*

Lindgren: I didn't say that; I said that's what the critics said.

Coltrane: See, well, they seem to think that it's an angry sort of a thing, as a rule. Some of them do, I don't know. But the critics here—

Lindgren: Do you feel angry?

Coltrane: No, I don't . . . Um, I was talkin' to a fella today, and I told him that the reason I play so many, so many—it sounds, maybe it sounds angry because I'm—I'm trying so many things at one time, you see, like I, I haven't sorted them out. I have a whole bag of things that I'm trying to work through and get the one essential, you know, and I just—

Lindgren: Would you say, would you say that you're trying to play everything you hear?

Coltrane: Well—

Lindgren: At one time, or something like that?

Coltrane: No, there—there are some set things that I know, some devices that I know, harmonic devices that I know that will take me out of the ordinary path, you see? If I use these. But I haven't played 'em enough, and I'm not familiar with them enough yet to take the one single line through 'em so I play all of 'em, you know, tryin' to acclimate my ear so I can hear.

Lindgren: In the album liners of your latest LP, that was the *Giant Steps* LP, which we have played quite a lot on this show, you claim that you were trying to, to get a—as I understood it—a more beautiful sound.

Coltrane: I hope to.

Lindgren: What do you mean by that?

Coltrane: Well I hope to play a, not necessarily a more beautiful sound—though I would like to—you know, just, say tonewise, I would like to be able to produce a more beautiful sound. But now I'm primarily interested in trying to work what I have, what I know, down into a more *lyrical* line, you know. That's what I mean by beautiful; more lyrical. So it'd be, you know, easily understood.

Lindgren: I'm sure our listeners are, as they are mainly collectors of Coltrane records, I'm sure they would like to hear you express one thought, uh, what you think is listenable among your whole production.

Coltrane: You mean of the albums that I've made?

Lindgren: Yes.

Coltrane: Oh, I, I like *Blue Train,* myself.

Lindgren: I figured you would. [*both laugh*]

Coltrane: There's such a good band on there, you know.

Lindgren: That's a real, that's a really dangerous album.

Coltrane: It was a good recording.

Lindgren: How do you feel about this last quartet recording here, *Giant Steps?*

Coltrane: I think that was my best quartet recording so far. With the exception of maybe *Soultrane,* I'd put them both about the same.

Lindgren: How would you say working with Miles Davis has influenced you stylistically?

Coltrane: Well, it's—it has led me into most of the things that I'm doing now.

Lindgren: He has had a major stranglehold on you in that matter, I mean—he made you play the way you do or you, uh, you got a chance to play like you do—

Coltrane: Well I've been free, I've been so free here, you know, that I, almost anything I want to try is—I'm welcome to do it, you know? [*chuckles*] So that freedom has helped me to experiment.

Lindgren: I heard you were splitting the Miles quintet here and then trying something on your own.

Coltrane: Yes, I am.

Lindgren: How's that? With whom?

Coltrane: I haven't, I have several men in mind but I haven't selected the sidemen yet. I'm gonna try it with a quartet.

Lindgren: What do you feel like working with, a quartet?

Coltrane: Yeah, to begin with, and maybe several weeks after I start I might add a fifth man.

Lindgren: John, which tenor players do you think have influenced you, if any at all?

Coltrane: All of 'em. [*laughs*] I would say all of 'em. But uh—

Lindgren: Do you have a personal favorite, I mean like you put on a record when you're at home and relax and so on?

Coltrane: Well, Sonny Rollins is, I think he's the outstanding tenorman today. That's usually—

Lindgren: That is exactly what Sonny Rollins told me on this show about you—

Coltrane: [*laughing*] That's usually, you know, my *man*, you know.

Lindgren: —so it seems to be a mutual admiration society here.

Coltrane: Yeah, well, he's, he's great. I mean, you know. . . . And of course in the formative days, years ago, it was Dexter Gordon that actually was my major [*unintelligible*]—

Lindgren: Well you do, you do have a strong feeling for tradition, haven't you.

Coltrane: I guess so. I mean I would like to even make it stronger, you know, I'd like to strengthen my roots, so to say, you know? Because I didn't start at the beginning and there's a whole lot back there that's, you know, that all young musicians should hear.

Lindgren: [*unintelligible*]—privately, I mean, when you are listening, you go back there, I mean, just on your own account and listen?

Coltrane: Well I don't have many records in that era now, but I do plan to get 'em. I, I plan to include that in my repertoire, you know, all these old traditional things.

Lindgren: So you got an open mind, huh?

Coltrane: I've been trying, recently, to, uh, to *search myself*, you know, and try to find things that are reminiscent, that sound like those things. But I'm really going to do some work on that soon.

Lindgren: Well John, it seems like you're on with the Miles Davis Quintet here, and—

Coltrane: Oh—

Lindgren: —and thank you very much for taking the time and dropping in on this show.

Coltrane: You're welcome. Thank you very much, I enjoyed it.

"THE JOHN COLTRANE STORY"

As told to Björn Fremer

After attending the Stockholm concert on March 22, 1960, journalist Björn Fremer invited Coltrane to his home. In 2003, Fremer told author and Coltrane researcher Wolf Schmaler that they "talked and talked," so much so that the coffee burned. (Coltrane didn't like the Swedish shrimps Fremer offered because he was used to jumbo shrimps that are easier to find on the plate.) Fremer taped the conversation, but the tape has been lost. Fremer summarized the main points in this article. Coltrane also spoke candidly about his previous addictions to alcohol and narcotics, both of which he quit in 1957, and expressed deep regret that he'd wasted so many years of his life because of them. At Coltrane's request, Fremer omitted this information from the article (phone conversation with the editor, October 26, 2009).

Fremer often met Coltrane in New York, and he saw Coltrane's new group, with McCoy Tynor on piano, at the Jazz Gallery in the spring of 1960. Fremer describes Coltrane as one of the nicest men he ever met in the jazz scene, "like an angel" ("in contrast to Stan Getz, who played like an angel, but . . ."). He often met Coltrane in his home in Queens, which was "very specially decorated," "very spartan." Fremer lost contact with Coltrane around 1964.

I was born in a small town called Hamlet in North Carolina, 1926. I think my family moved from there when I was a few months old—so they moved next to a larger town, High Point, and I spent 17 years there—I went to all the schools, you know, grade school, elementary school and high school.

My father died in 1939, so my mother moved to Philadelphia. I stayed and finished school with my aunt and the rest of the family. Then I also moved to Philly.

From *Jazz News,* May 10, 1961, page 3. Originally published as the liner notes to the Swedish LP issue of *Chambers' Music* (Sonet SLP28), 1960.

My interest in jazz was started in high school. It started through the regular dance we had—from the beginning it was a matter of just dancing to jazz. I liked bands like Louis Jordan's. I enjoyed Louis' music and out of that I started to listen more to the horns. I didn't hear much Duke during that time. We didn't get much of that type of music. It was mostly what you call rock and roll. Before I left school I did hear Count Basie—I heard a few records.

My family liked church music, so there was no jazz in the house. When I was at a party or something like that I heard records of Louis and Duke but I didn't think much of it. I didn't hear much jazz until I was 15.

My father was a tailor. He had several instruments around the house. He played a little on each of them—a violin, a clarinet and a ukelele.

I started with a band in High Point—we didn't have a band in our school. There was a man in the community, Mr. Steele [Warren B. Steele], who knew something about all the instruments. He took a bunch of young men around town and taught them to play as well as he could. I started on alto horn, then went to clarinet and to alto saxophone. This was 1942. I played for a year or so but never thought of making a living as a musician.

I finished school and moved to my mother in Philly. I worked for a year in a signal depot—we had a war, you know. Then I decided to study music again. I took lessons from a private saxophone instructor at Granoff Studios.

I listened to Johnny Hodges, Benny Carter and Tab Smith but the first time I heard Charlie Parker I knew *that* was the thing for me. I went overseas but we still heard Bird's records, copying like mad just to see what he was doing. I spent a year in Honolulu. I was in a band most of the time but we never could organize anything—most of the musicians went home. We came over so the others could be sent back. So there was nothing constructive going on.

When I came back to Philadelphia I went on the road—that was my first road experience. I worked with a guy called Joe Webb and then with King Kolax and travelled all over the U.S. Webb and Kolax were not rock and roll bands—more like jazz bands. They were, [in comparison to baseball, like the minor leagues]. A good place to learn anyway. Kolax had a 17 piece band—just like a big band. When I worked with Kolax I was trying to write and I could write all I wanted. Kolax taught me some and gave me helpful hands [a helping hand].

Fremer and Coltrane sit down for coffee and a chat at the arrival hall of Stockholm-Bromma Airport, November 23, 1961. BENGT H. MALMQVIST/BERRY PRODUKTION AB.

I stayed with Kolax in 1947 and then I went with Eddie Vinson. Red Garland was in that band too. With Vinson I started to play tenor. After him I came back to Philly and worked around town. In 1949 I joined Dizzy's big band on alto and when the big band broke up I stayed with Diz on tenor. I left him in 1951 and went back to Philly.

I wanted to find my own way but I wasn't ready. I had to learn to play straight. There was so much to learn yet. I wasn't trying—not reaching out for too much. Charlie Parker had me strung up. He was way ahead of me and I had trouble just keeping up with him.

I took an offer from Earl Bostic and stayed with him for seven months. The next job was with Johnny Hodges. There was a lot of music going on in that band. I never forget that. It really swung.

All this time musically I was progressing very little in the way I wanted. But I was learning just by being in this great company. But I had not reached the point when I could take active steps by myself. In fact I don't think I reached that point until after I came with Miles.

I left Hodges in 1954, then I played around Philly with an organ trio [Bill Carney's Hi-Tones]. You've heard of Shirley Scott—she was the organist. She swung me out of the place sometimes. Al Heath was on drums and we had a wonderful group. I got a chance to play. I was the only horn so I could stretch out, building up on the horn. That was what I wanted. Being with this group helped me very much.

I had worked with Philly Joe Jones in 1949 and I knew Miles, so when Miles decided to form a quintet I went with him. I always felt I wanted to play with Miles. He really put me to work. All the things that I started trying to do in 1955 when I went with him were some of the things I felt I should have done in '47–'48. So ten years later I finally got back to business. I tried to pile so much up in these past five years, trying hard to bring myself back up—now I like to pile all the things I managed to pick up and spread them out a little. I don't want to play less intensely, but I want to spread it out so I can paint a picture.

I'm preoccupied harmonically now—I want to get through this phase, so I can concentrate on rhythm and melody later. Charlie Parker did all the things I would like to do and more—he really had a genius, see. He could do things and he could do them melodiously so that anybody, the man in the street, could hear—that's what I haven't reached, that's what I'd like to reach.

I'm fascinated by harmonic things and what I want to do is to play these sequences I do now and find a way to put it so that anyone can understand it.

"COLTRANE ON COLTRANE"

John Coltrane in collaboration with Don DeMicheal

During the first two weeks of August 1960, Coltrane and his new group were at the Sutherland Lounge in Chicago. *Down Beat* editor Don DeMicheal's discussions with Coltrane during this gig led to the following article.

The first occasion I had to speak with John Coltrane at length was during his recent engagement at the Sutherland hotel. In our initial conversation I was struck by his lack of pretentiousness or false pride. The honesty with which he answered questions—questions that other musicians would have evaded or talked around—impressed me deeply. We discussed my doing an article about him. But when I saw how really interested he was in setting the record straight, I suggested that we do the piece together.

As it turned out, Coltrane did the vast majority of the work, struggling as most writers do with just the right way of saying something, deciding whether he should include this or that, making sure such and such was clear. The results of his labor is the article appearing on these pages. The words and ideas are John's—I merely suggested, typed, and arranged. —DeMicheal

I've been listening to jazzmen, especially saxophonists, since the time of the early Count Basie records, which featured Lester Young. Pres was my first real influence, but the first horn I got was an alto, not a tenor. I wanted a tenor, but some friends of my mother advised her to buy me an alto because it was a smaller horn and easier for a youngster to handle. This was 1943.

Johnny Hodges became my first main influence on alto, and he still kills me. I stayed with alto through 1947, and by then I'd come under the influence of Charlie Parker. The first time I heard Bird play, it hit me right between the eyes. Before I switched from alto in that year, it had been strictly a Bird thing with me,

From *Down Beat*, September 29, 1960, pages 26–27.

but when I bought a tenor to go with Eddie Vinson's band, a wider area of listening opened up for me.

I found I was able to be more varied in my musical interests. On alto, Bird had been my whole influence, but on tenor I found there was no one man whose ideas were so dominant as Charlie's were on alto. Therefore, I drew from all the men I heard during this period. I have listened to about all the good tenor men, beginning with Lester, and believe me, I've picked up something from them all, including several who have never recorded.

The reason I liked Lester so was that I could feel that line, that simplicity. My phrasing was very much in Lester's vein at this time.

I found out about Coleman Hawkins after I learned of Lester. There were a lot of things that Hawkins was doing that I knew I'd have to learn somewhere along the line. I felt the same way about Ben Webster. There were many things that people like Hawk, Ben, and Tab Smith were doing in the '40s that I didn't understand but that I felt emotionally.

The first time I heard Hawk, I was fascinated by his arpeggios and the way he played. I got a copy of his *Body and Soul* and listened real hard to what he was doing. And even though I dug Pres, as I grew musically, I appreciated Hawk more and more.

As far as musical influences, aside from saxophonists, are concerned, I think I was first awakened to musical exploration by Dizzy Gillespie and Bird. It was through their work that I began to learn about musical structures and the more theoretical aspects of music.

Also, I had met Jimmy Heath, who, besides being a wonderful saxophonist, understood a lot about musical construction. I joined his group in Philadelphia in 1948.[1] We were very much alike in our feeling, phrasing, and a whole lot of ways. Our musical appetites were the same. We used to practice together, and he would write out some of the things we were interested in. We would take things from records and digest them. In this way we learned about the techniques being used by writers and arrangers.

Another friend and I learned together in Philly—Calvin Massey, a trumpeter and composer who now lives in Brooklyn. His musical ideas and mine often run parallel, and we've collaborated quite often. We helped each other advance musically by exchanging knowledge and ideas.

I first met Miles Davis about 1947 and played a few jobs with him and Sonny Rollins at the Audubon Ballroom in Manhattan. During this period he was coming into his own, and I could see him extending the boundaries of jazz even further. I felt I wanted to work with him. But for the time being, we went our separate ways.

I went with Dizzy's big band in 1949. I stayed with Diz through the breakup of the big band and played in the small group he organized later.

Afterwards, I went with Earl Bostic, who I consider a very gifted musician. He showed me a lot of things on my horn. He has fabulous technical facilities on his instrument and knows many a trick.

Then I worked with one of my first loves, Johnny Hodges. I really enjoyed that job. I liked every tune in the book. Nothing was superficial. It all had meaning, and it all swung. And the confidence with which Rabbit plays! I wish I could play with the confidence that he does.

But besides enjoying my stay with Johnny musically, I also enjoyed it because I was getting firsthand information about things that happened way before my time. I'm very interested in the past, and even though there's a lot I don't know about it, I intend to go back and find out. I'm back to Sidney Bechet already.

Take Art Tatum, for instance. When I was coming up, the musicians I ran around with were listening to Bud Powell, and I didn't listen too much to Tatum. That is, until one night I happened to run into him in Cleveland. There were Art and Slam Stewart and Oscar Peterson and Ray Brown at a private session in some lady's attic. They played from 2:30 in the morning to 8:30—just whatever they felt like playing. I've never heard so much music.

In 1955, I joined Miles on a regular basis and worked with him till the middle of 1957. I went with Thelonious Monk for the remainder of that year.

Working with Monk brought me close to a musical architect of the highest order. I felt I learned from him in every way—through the senses, theoretically, technically. I would talk to Monk about musical problems, and he would sit at the piano and show me the answers just by playing them. I could watch him play and find out the things I wanted to know. Also, I could see a lot of things that I didn't know about at all.

Monk was one of the first to show me how to make two or three notes at one time on tenor. (John Glenn, a tenor man in Philly, also showed me how to do this. He can play a triad and move notes inside it—like passing tones!) It's done by false fingering and adjusting your lip. If everything goes right, you can get triads. Monk just looked at my horn and "felt" the mechanics of what had to be done to get this effect.

I think Monk is one of the true greats of all time. He's a real musical thinker—there's not many like him. I feel myself fortunate to have had the opportunity to work with him. If a guy needs a little spark, a boost, he can just be around Monk, and Monk will give it to him.

After leaving Monk, I went back to another great musical artist, Miles.

On returning, this time to stay until I formed my own group a few months ago, I found Miles in the midst of another stage of his musical development. There was one time in his past that he devoted to multichorded structures. He was interested in chords for their own sake. But now it seemed that he was moving in the opposite direction to the use of fewer and fewer chord changes in songs. He used tunes with free-flowing lines and chordal direction. This approach allowed the soloist the choice of playing chordally (vertically) or melodically (horizontally).

In fact, due to the direct and free-flowing lines in his music, I found it easy to apply the harmonic ideas that I had. I could stack up chords—say, on a C7, I sometimes superimposed an E♭7, up to an F#7, down to an F. That way I could play three chords on one. But on the other hand, if I wanted to, I could play melodically. Miles' music gave me plenty of freedom. It's a beautiful approach.

About this time, I was trying for a sweeping sound. I started experimenting because I was striving for more individual development. I even tried long, rapid lines that Ira Gitler termed "sheets of sound" at the time. But actually, I was beginning to apply the three-on-one chord approach, and at that time the tendency was to play the entire scale of each chord. Therefore, they were usually played fast and sometimes sounded like glisses.

I found there were a certain number of chord progressions to play in a given time, and sometimes what I played didn't work out in eighth notes, 16th notes, or triplets. I had to put the notes in uneven groups like fives and sevens in order to get them all in.

I thought in groups of notes, not of one note at a time. I tried to place these groups on the accents and emphasize the strong beats—maybe on 2 here and on 4 over at the end. I would set up the line and drop groups of notes—a long line with accents dropped as I moved along. Sometimes what I was doing clashed harmonically with the piano—especially if the pianist wasn't familiar with what I was doing—so a lot of times I just strolled with bass and drums.

I haven't completely abandoned this approach, but it wasn't broad enough. I'm trying to play these progressions in a more flexible manner now.

Last February, I bought a soprano saxophone. I like the sound of it, but I'm not playing with the body, the bigness of tone, that I want yet. I haven't had too much trouble playing it in tune, but I've had a lot of trouble getting a good quality of tone in the upper register. It comes out sort of puny sometimes. I've had to adopt a slightly different approach than the one I use for tenor, but it helps me get away—lets me take another look at improvisation. It's like having another hand.

I'm using it with my present group: McCoy Tyner, piano; Steve Davis, bass; and Pete LaRoca,[2] drums. The quarter is coming along nicely. We know basically what we're trying for, and we leave room for individual development. Individual contributions are put in night by night.

One of my aims is to build as good a repertoire as I can for a band. What size, I couldn't say, but it'll probably be a quartet or quintet. I want to get the material first. Right now, I'm on a material search.

From a technical viewpoint, I have certain things I'd like to present in my solos. To do this, I have to get the right material. It has to swing, and it has to be varied. (I'm inclined not to be too varied.) I want it to cover as many forms of music as I can put into a jazz context and play on my instruments. I like Eastern music; Yusef Lateef has been using this in his playing for some time. And Ornette Coleman sometimes plays music with a Spanish content as well as other exotic-flavored music. In these approaches there's something I can draw on and use in the way I like to play.

I've been writing some things for the quartet—if you call lines and sketches writing. I'd like to write more after I learn more—after I find out what kind of material I can present best, what kind will carry my musical techniques best. Then I'll know better what kind of writing is best for me.

I've been devoting quite a bit of my time to harmonic studies on my own, in libraries and places like that. I've found you've got to look back at the old things and see them in a new light. I'm not finished with these studies because I haven't assimilated everything into my playing. I want to progress, but I don't want to go so far out that I can't see what others are doing.

I want to broaden my outlook in order to come out with a fuller means of expression. I want to be more flexible where rhythm is concerned. I feel I have to study rhythm some more. I haven't experimented too much with time; most of my experimenting has been in a harmonic form. I put time and rhythms to one side, in the past.

But I've got to keep experimenting. I feel that I'm just beginning. I have part of what I'm looking for in my grasp but not all.

I'm very happy devoting all my time to music, and I'm glad to be one of the many who are striving for fuller development as musicians. Considering the great heritage in music that we have, the work of giants of the past, the present, and the promise of those who are to come, I feel that we have every reason to face the future optimistically.[3]

Notes

1. Coltrane performed in Jimmy Heath's big band as early as 1947.
2. By the time the article was published LaRoca had been replaced by Billy Higgins, who would soon be replaced by Elvin Jones.
3. C. O. Simpkins's book, *Coltrane: A Biography*, includes some material from an early draft of this article that didn't make it into the final version:

- "A cold audience will make you fear that you're not pleasing them. It can kind of put a damper on your spirits. You learn that you've got to override this. If you give up and let them dampen your spirits, you can't play. You might as well give up. You've got to bear down and give them all you've got" (page 114).

- "When I first heard the phrase ['angry young tenor'], I didn't know what the writers were talking about. My playing isn't angry. It's strictly a musical venture with me" (page 117).

- "Jazz is made by the men who make it. [Ornette] Coleman is definitely one direction—there it is and there he is. Others will follow in it" (page 118).

- "Announcements help. There may not be much need for Miles to do it, since everybody who comes to hear him knows the tunes from his records anyway, and in his case it's probably right not to make announcements. But for a group like mine that does tunes that haven't been recorded, it's probably necessary to make announcements. I haven't done so recently, but in the future I will" (page 118). (From audience tapes and radio broadcasts we know that Coltrane did occasionally make announcements, particularly around this time (1960–1961), but this was the exception rather than the rule. Coltrane was clearly uncomfortable speaking to the audience; his announcements tended to be awkward and almost painfully earnest.)

PART II

1961 to 1962

"COLTRANE—MAN AND MUSIC"

Gene Lees

Gene Lees probably met Coltrane in March 1961 when Coltrane did a two-week gig at the Sutherland Lounge in Chicago. This obscure article, which was originally published in the now-long-defunct British magazine *Jazz News*, gives us a particularly interesting view of Coltrane.

Since the days when George Bernard Shaw was writing music criticism, the profession has degenerated, in all too many cases, into a kind of amateur psychoanalysis or aesthetic palmistry.

For all that this sort of writing sometimes has the fascination of back-fence gossip, it is usually useless as an aid to understanding art. Even Freud recognized that there are mysteries about the creative process that his quasi-science could not explain.

Yet, although I'm opposed in principal to personality discussions in music, there is an exceptional case, one in which some understanding of the personality of the man would, I think, help the listener better to understand the music. I refer to John Coltrane.

No man in my experience is less like the impression he at first creates than Coltrane.

There is something forbidding about him, the first time you see him. He stands there, horn held stiffly in front of him, feet apart and firmly planted, eyes shut. Nothing moves but his fingers. Tall and heavily-muscled, he looks like a man of granite, a rigid, frigid monolith. Further, he seems arrogant, and as that hard tone pours from his saxophone in cascades of notes, you may feel that this is a man you would not want to know. No doubt he is temperamental, touchy. No doubt he has a short fuse. No doubt he is, in fact, or in sympathy with, a part of that anti-white Negro element in jazz that is known, with grim humor, as the Mau-Mau.

From *Jazz News*, September 27, 1961, pages 5–6.

My first impression of Coltrane was that he was dangerous. What's more, I walked out on one of his solos with the Miles Davis group, convinced he was a musical fraud. It was one of the most profound errors of judgment I have ever made, and left me with a permanent reluctance to come to conclusions quickly on matters of music.

For, as I came to know Coltrane (somebody or other had insisted that I should make friends with him, that knowing him was an enriching experience), I began to see that this is one of the gentlest, one of the kindest, one of the most modest, one of the most sincere men I'm ever likely to meet, aside from being a phenomenal musician.

Then why does he seem forbidding? It's simple, really: Coltrane is almost painfully shy.

John has a facial expression that all his friends know—sort of a puzzled frown coupled with a deferential smile. It makes me think of a deer, surprised in a forest. One of his friends said, "I think he's blushing, but he's so dark you can't tell."

Coltrane's modesty is illustrated by the manner of his leaving Philadelphia a few years ago. Already well-known among musicians, he was reluctant to try his luck in New York. Tenor saxophonist Wayne Shorter, one of his friends, says John just didn't believe he was good enough.

Now among the many gifts nature has provided John Coltrane, one of the most valuable is an understanding wife who believes in him. Shorter thinks she is the ideal of womanliness. John's wife urged him to make the big career move, to try— to take a chance. This, of course, is contrary to the pattern of so many musicians' wives, who want them to give up their careers and take some sort of "steady" work to provide the family with security. John still wouldn't go to New York.

One day he came home and found that his wife was gone. So was their furniture. All she had left behind was a note, saying that if he wanted her, he would find her in New York.

That's how John Coltrane went to New York and national prominence.

As for his kindness:

One night John and I were discussing a gifted musician who was working for him. The musician had had narcotic troubles. Now he was making a sincere and valiant fight to lick it and had been "clean" for six months.

"It's so hard for anyone," John said, "and it's even harder for a musician, because there's so little to look forward to. It's such an uncertain business. If only somebody could give him a little encouragement, you know, give him a lift." He paused for a moment, thinking, then said gently, "I think I'll give him a raise."

Remember that the man showing this insight and sympathy doesn't smoke, drink, or swear. He rejected all these habits a few years ago. (He does have one habit, though: he's hopelessly hooked on rum candies, which he carries in a small box in his coat pocket.)

One night John was coming to my home for dinner. We met in downtown Chicago, and then drove north along the shore of Lake Michigan. In his shy way, he communicated that he was grateful for a dinner invitation: this was his off-night at the club where he was working, and, since his wife was not with him, he had nothing to do.

We started talking about music. I told him that there had been a time when I had very much disliked his playing, but I had come to enjoy it—and not in some obscure intellectual way but emotionally. I said I didn't know whether his playing had changed or I was simply understanding it better. Perhaps, I said, it was a combination of both, though it did seem to me that his period of experimentation was over and he now knew what he wanted to do. His music felt more cohesive and directed than it had during his days with Miles. Did he himself think his playing had changed?

"I guess it must have," he said with that smile-frown. "You're the second person who's told me that this month."

"Who was the other?"

"My wife."

Coltrane was inevitably quite shy when I introduced him to my wife. But my wife is French and responds quickly to people like John, people who do not push her. She is also a superb cook, and so John became at ease comparatively quickly. He was at first hesitant to eat much. But when I pointed out that, as usual, my wife had cooked too much and it would only be wasted if it weren't eaten, he began eating with verve. My God, can John put away good food! It warmed the cockles of my heart.

Afterwards, I played him Bartok's Concerto for Orchestra through a stereo headset. He'd never heard stereo on a headset, nor had he heard the concerto. He sat silent and engrossed for half an hour.

Later, he made an apologetic little remark about not being too schooled in classical music, unlike Miles and many others, and said he was just now getting into it. It was obvious that he did not feel himself to be an educated man.

Needless to say, he is, in his own area, an intensely educated man. No more dedicated musician exists. When he is out of town, instead of chasing girls or warming bar stools as other musicians are prone to do, he spends his off hours in his hotel room, practicing. He practices incessantly. This is how he mastered soprano saxophone—an instrument that holds increasing appeal for him—in less than a year. Now, he said, he had decided to learn to play harp too. Why harp, of all instruments? "I like it," he said simply.

Is Coltrane an angry man, as those who know him only through his playing have often concluded? Not at all. "I guess they say that because I play with a hard tone," he said.

Actually, if you listen past the tone, Coltrane is an intensely lyrical player. I believe that John expresses himself best and most fully on soprano, not tenor. And the performance that comes closest to mirroring the man I know is the exquisitely done "My Favorite Things" on the Atlantic album of the same name. Here you will hear something of the gentle man—and that is what any natural gentleman is—with the hesitant smile.

In re-reading what I have written, I see that I have failed, thereby demonstrating my own thesis of the futility of explaining personality in the attempt to clarify music. What little I have been able to tell about Coltrane provides only a crude sketch of the man. After all, Coltrane isn't a "character," he isn't a spectacular oddball; he's a quiet, kind, and reliable man. This makes him difficult to portray.

Yet, if I have disencumbered even a few readers of the notion that he is a forbidding and esoteric musician, then I have perhaps made the atmosphere a little warmer, a little more sympathetic, for him and his music.

For myself, when I see him on a bandstand, those powerful biceps and the big chest making his suit seem not quite large enough, and those dark shirts he wears making him look like a working man ill-at-ease in his Sunday best, I know now what to listen for: the gentleman in the heart of the hardness.

INTERVIEW WITH JOHN COLTRANE

Ralph J. Gleason

Among his many other activities, Ralph J. Gleason covered jazz and popular music for the *San Francisco Chronicle* for nearly a quarter century. On May 2, 1961, he interviewed John Coltrane, who was then in the middle of a two-week engagement at the Jazz Workshop, a San Francisco nightclub. Following are excerpts from the interview; the full interview will be published in *Ralph J. Gleason's Conversations*, a book of interview transcripts scheduled for publication in 2010, and *Ralph J. Gleason's Conversations in Jazz*, a radio series of the audio interviews to air in 2010. See www.jazzcasual.com for more information.

John Coltrane: I have yet to write a song that had a melody. [*laughter*] [. . .] "Syeeda's Song Flute" was one of the few, that had a melody. And—well, "Naima" had a melody. That was a ballad, though. But these other things that I write, I've just been goin' to the piano, gettin' chords, and then I'll take a melody, after a while, somewhere out of the chords, you know? [. . .] I think I've done enough of that. [*laughs*] And in the future I'm gonna really try to sit and think of these things, of the song. I've gotta take in more, you know? Musically and maybe some other ways too. And then maybe I'll be able to write, build melodies, think from melodies and write melodies. Then I might be able to do some arranging for another horn too. That's why I haven't had another horn, because I haven't [written] any melodies. [. . .]

I ran across a little, a funny thing. We went into the Apollo. We went in there and the guy said "Man, you're playin' too long, see. You gotta play twenty minutes." So now sometimes we get up and play a song and I'll play a solo that's maybe thirty minutes. Or at least twenty minutes. We can look forward to a song being no less than twenty minutes long. And so I say "How the hell are we gonna do this," you know? [*laughter*] And man, we ended up, after around the third time we did it, we ended up playin' three songs in twenty minutes. And I played all the highlights of the solos that I'd been playin' in hours in that length of time, you know? So [*laughs*] I had to think about that, you know, I said "Now what have I been doin' all this time. What the heck have I been doin'." [. . .]

[But] I could really go on just playin' just like I am now. I mean I enjoy it, playin' that long. It does *me* a lot of good to just play until I don't feel like playin' anymore. Though I found out I don't say that much more, you know? [*laughs*] [. . .]

Ralph J. Gleason: What other plans do you have, things that you want to explore?

John Coltrane: Well . . .

Ralph J. Gleason: 'Cause you're an explorer, this is obvious, right?

John Coltrane: I don't know. [*laughs*] I don't know, man. I'd like to . . . at the moment, I really don't know.

Ralph J. Gleason: Well that doesn't mean now, does it, that you're satisfied.

John Coltrane: No, it doesn't mean that, it just means I don't know. [*laughs*] I don't know what I'd like to do. I know I don't want to *stop*. [. . .] I'll tell you one thing, I have done so much work from *within*, now what I've gotta do is go out and look around me some. And *then* I'll be able to say well, I want to do so much on this or so much on that. But actually I've been within myself, you know, I've been—like I told you foolin' around at the piano, and just trying to look at musical structure and trying to find a way that I feel about it. Certain things. And trying to work on *that*, you know? And I don't know, I've just—I've run into a blind alley on this thing, you know, and I don't see what else—like I get a bunch of [chord] changes, and I changed "Body and Soul," or I changed this song or—well there's just so far you can go with that. I don't think I want to continue to do that because [. . .] I don't think it's gonna get me into as many things and as broad a field that I need to get into, you know?

Ralph J. Gleason: Are you still practicing a great deal?

John Coltrane: Not too much, not much now that the quartet is taking quite a bit of my time. And recording, too, because I mean I feel—I *know* I gotta make three records a year, and I'm always walkin' around tryin' to keep my ear open for another "Favorite Things" or something. [*laughter*] So I can't go to the closet, you know, I can't get in the woodshed like I used to. I'm commercial, man. I used to go in the woodshed, you know, and just stay in there all day and practice and that was all there was to it, I didn't have to worry about it, you know, makin' a good record, because that wasn't important. I don't know, maybe I should just go on back in the woodshed and forget it, you know?

Coltrane at Ralph J. Gleason's home, May 2, 1961.
PHOTOGRAPH BY JIM MARSHALL.

"COUNTDOWN AT ABART'S: NEW KING OF JAZZ TAKING FLIGHT HERE"

Tony Gieske

This blow-by-blow account of what it was like to experience John Coltrane's music in person is a prelude to the interview that follows.

ONCE EVERY four or five years a new jazz king is crowned, and it's an event that—unlike "My Fair Lady" or the World Series—sneaks past everybody. In jazz, it's only afterwards that you realize you were there when history was being made.

So it is with John Coltrane's new quintet. The few that hear it while it is in Washington will have an ineffaceable memory. After nearly 20 years, Coltrane has got it all together and he's burning.

Yesterday morning at 12:02 a.m. I walked into Abart's Internationale, a night club at 1928 9th St. NW., ordered a drink and sat down. At 12:05 a.m. Coltrane, a big, glum, dedicated fellow of 34 who has been mingling with jazz royalty—Dizzy Gillespie, Miles Davis—for a number of years, began playing a brisk blues called "Shifting Down," by Kenny Dorham.

Coltrane played this blues without letup until 12:55 a.m. During that period, he demonstrated:

- That he has mastered everything that has been done with the tenor saxophone in the past 25 years.
- That there will be few jazz musicians who will not be indebted to him in, conservatively, the next five years.
- That, for the present, Coltrane wears the crown.

From the *Washington Post*, June 17, 1961, page A13.

COLTRANE STATED his theme baldly enough, and for a few choruses it almost seemed that it didn't really interest him. He was circling, mellow, ruminative. Then a door came open and it was like being hit with a straight stream from a 2½ inch fire hose, with the notes spraying every which way.

Yet I had heard that when he was playing with trumpeter Davis. The same avalanche, the same maintenance of a constant climax; it was enough to show mastery.

Now came the adventure and the experimentation. For a few choruses, Coltrane stated his phrases at a hair-raising bias from what would have been the ordinary well-tempered pitch.

A single chorus was next devoted to the timbres and rhythmic variations that could be extracted from a single pitch. Drummer Elvin Jones, absorbed in every note, spotted a triplet pattern by Coltrane and proceeded, without losing the intense meter, to play three triplets on a single beat—on the bass drum, with his foot.

Coltrane relaxed into a Davis-like lyricism for a few choruses. There were some compelling pedal-point patterns in the rhythm section. Then Coltrane launched into a long passage during which he managed to blow two and sometimes three notes simultaneously. He was playing chordal sequences on the saxophone.

THE AUDIENCE sat transfixed. It was now 12:35 a.m. Coltrane kept playing, shaking his instrument as though to see if there were any notes left. There were. The pressure mounted.

Coltrane left the key. Bassist Reggie Workman followed right along with him. At this point, my notes read, I felt like I was being nailed to the wall.

12:42 a.m. Jones, a wiry little fellow, begins to tire, not slowing down, but shoving a little too hard.

12:43. Coltrane stops dead. Pianist McCoy Tyner solos. Workman solos. Coltrane repeats the opening theme statement. It is all over. Flat pause. Then applause. It is 12:55 a.m. And all us jazz types pay tribute to our new leader.

"ACCENT ON JAZZ: THE KING WEARS A COCKEYED CROWN"

Tony Gieske

The John Coltrane Quintet—with McCoy Tyner on piano, Elvin Jones on drums, and both Reggie Workman and Art Davis on bass—appeared June 13–18, 1961, at Abart's Internationale in Washington, D.C. *Washington Post* columnist Tony Gieske had previously tried to get an interview with Miles Davis while Coltrane was still in Davis's band. "I spoke to Miles," Gieske recalls, "as he left the stand after a set. 'Why don't you interview him?' he said, pointing to the diffident young player. 'He needs it more than I do.' Being a trumpet player, I was not all that interested in Coltrane, a mere tenor man, [but] I was to be enlightened eventually."

Gieske interviewed Coltrane in his hotel room during the gig. "Coltrane sat on the single bed in a tiny room on the second floor somewhere near the venue. He was holding a dull and dusty old soprano saxophone across his lap, fingering the stiff old keys. Right away, I felt we'd be talking as one musician to another. That's the way these guys are, from Dizzy on down. 'This didn't come from the attic,' he said, looking at me in a friendly way. 'They must have kept this on the roof!'" (Tony Gieske, e-mail message to the editor, July 30, 2009.) For more of Tony Gieske's writing, as well as his photos, see www.tonyspage.com.

WHEN I WROTE UP John Coltrane last Saturday in a near-hysterical article and called him the new King, etc., I knew full well I was playing into the hands of the Aesthetic Fascists, but I felt it was worth it to get people out to see him while he was really on.

An Aesthetic Fascist is a person who bows down before musical führers, such as Beethoven or Charlie Parker, no matter how empty and worthless the product.

From the *Washington Post*, June 25, 1961, page G4.

The Aesthetic Fascist, for instance, will write letters in to NBC thanking them for putting on "Fidelio," a transcendently corny opera. He will write because he has been told that Beethoven is a "genius" and that opera is a "higher form" and that it is good to bring "Culture" to the "Masses."

The Aesthetic Fascist will sometimes even pretend that he enjoyed "Fidelio," having been led, by writers capable of much more high-toned ecstasy than I, to believe there is something in it. More often, he will sit complacently through this dismal void, wondering contentedly what it is that's supposed to be good. He never asks if it's really there.

Now I didn't tell any lies in my article. If you're in that frame of reference—kings and heroes and such, Coltrane is it right now on tenor saxophone. But by broadcasting it around, one attracts a lot of Aesthetic Fascists, who, so to speak, get in without paying their dues, thereby rousing the indignation of the regular, hardworking members of the club. (In jazz, the Aesthetic Fascist is called a "hippy.")

Coltrane is only metaphorically a king, then, and when I talked to him for a couple of hours at the Woodner, this was brought home to me by the fact that he spent the first 5 or 10 minutes trimming his toe-nails, which I thought was a little chilly, king or not.

EVEN THOUGH he had just got up and dressed, King Coltrane had already got out his saxophone, a French Selmer, and was fooling with the reed. Stacked neatly on a table were copies of *The Negro Digest,* "The Universe and Dr. Einstein," "Guide to the Planets" and "Astronomy Made Simple."

"What about this Turkish thing?" I began.

"What Turkish thing?"

"This thing with the endlessly circulating chords, just one or two chords, or maybe just a key, where you repeat, like a vamp over and over. Like Ahmad Jamal used to do. How did that get started? It seems to be the big thing right now."

"Oh, that. Yeah. Miles (Davis) used to do that, too. He made some whole pieces like that. We use that a lot. But that's only one of the threads."

"What are some of the others?"

"Well, Ornette (Coleman) has this 'spread' rhythm. They don't play four. It's implied, and this bass player, what's his name—"

"Charlie Haden."

Coltrane talking to Chico Hamilton backstage at the Newport Jazz Festival on July 3, 1961. PHOTOGRAPH BY RAYMOND ROSS. COURTESY OF YASUHIRO "FUJI" FUJIOKA COLLECTION.

"Yeah. Well, he does slashes and things that are not right on the beat."

"What do you hear in Ornette's stuff? Do you hear keys, pitches . . . what?"

"Well, I hear keys, all right. Sometimes just one key, and sometimes he gets into another key. But I don't know. Every time I talk to him, he's into something different. He's moving very fast. I don't think he uses chords. At least not the way I would use a chord."

"What is all this talk about the way you use chords to make these 'sheets of sound?' I don't hear any sheets. I hear a lot of notes going by very fast."

"Sheets of sound. Well, that was when I got tired of certain modulations. Like when you want to get back to C, and you've got to go D and then G and then C. I was fooling around with the piano, and I figured out some other ways to do it. But you had to go to a lot of places very fast, and that was why it seemed like sheets of sound. Sometimes I couldn't even hear the notes myself until they played the record.

"I thought I would try to figure out how to do that with just a few notes, horizontally, but I haven't had time yet with my new band."

KING COLTRANE, who had put on his shoes and was now pacing the room, went into the bathroom to brush his teeth. I thought I might as well say good-bye and let him figure out how to get back to C, horizontally.

"FINALLY MADE"

Newsweek

This article, written by an uncredited *Newsweek* writer, focuses on Coltrane's adoption of the soprano saxophone—and the popularity of his version of "My Favorite Things"—as the key to his success.

John Coltrane put down his tenor saxophone and acknowledged the applause of the assorted beatniks, pseudo beatniks, and uptown jazz lovers who came to his opening last week at New York's Village Gate. Then the husky, 34-year-old musician picked up a smaller, golden horn, thrust its mouthpiece between his lips, and began flooding the cheerless cellar with the lilting, heart-stopping sounds which they had all come to hear.

At first, playing the theme from Rodgers and Hammerstein's fragile waltz "My Favorite Things," Coltrane produced the sinuous wail of a snake charmer—eerie, tremulous, faintly melodic. Then the tone shifted, the timbre became more strident, the rhythm more insistent. His eyebrows knit in an agony of concentration, his fingers moving in a studied frenzy, Coltrane hammered away relentlessly, sweeping the audience along with him. Slowly the tension mounted until in a final convulsion of sound, Coltrane found his release and slipped back to the graceful cadences of the opening theme. The audience, which had been stunned into momentary silence, suddenly exploded in successive waves of applause.

Tortured: It was a typical demonstration of why many eminent jazzmen consider Coltrane—who last week won three awards in *Down Beat*'s International Jazz Critics Poll—one of the finest musicians alive. After sixteen years of bouncing from one combo to another, sixteen years of searching for a coherent style, Coltrane, who organized his own group last year, has finally managed to discipline "the restless, tortured convolutions of his early work." New Yorkers last week heard an assured, purposeful, highly imaginative jazz voice.

From *Newsweek*, July 24, 1961, page 64.

Much of Coltrane's shimmering freshness is due to his finesse with the soprano saxophone, an instrument all but ignored by most other modern jazzmen. Not since the late Sidney Bechet was in his musical prime has anyone employed the clarinet-shaped soprano sax with such skill and imagination. Ironically, Coltrane, who made his reputation on the tenor saxophone, discovered the higher-pitched soprano quite by accident.

Relief: "Three of us were driving back from a date in Washington late in 1959," the shy, North Carolina–born Coltrane recalled last week, between shows at the Village Gate. "Two of us were in the front seat and the other guy, a sax-player, in the back. He was being very quiet. At Baltimore, we made a rest stop, then got back in the car and 30 miles later realized that the guy in the back wasn't there. We hoped that he had money with him, and drove on. I took his suitcase and horn to my apartment in New York. I opened the case and found a soprano sax. I started fooling around with it and was fascinated. That's how I discovered the instrument." (The saxophone's rightful owner reclaimed the instrument soon after. He has since left the music business to become a newspaperman.)

"It's hard to say whether I prefer the soprano or tenor," says Coltrane. "I find myself playing the soprano more and more, though. You can play lighter things with it, things that have a more subtle pulse. After the heaviness of the tenor, it's a relief to shift to the soprano."

Coltrane, who has been criticized for being "too far out," is a horn innovator who insists that there are still "quite a few avenues open for jazz and they're all going to be explored. I know that I'm going to try everything."

AFRICA/BRASS LINER NOTES

Dom Cerulli

Dom Cerulli interviewed both Coltrane and Eric Dolphy for these liner notes, probably in early summer 1961 (*Africa/Brass* was recorded May–June 1961 and released in September).

John Coltrane is a quiet, powerfully-built young man who plays tenor saxophone quite unlike anyone in all of jazz. His style has been described as "sheets of sound" or as "flurries of melody." But, despite the accuracy, or lack of accuracy, of such descriptions, it is a fact that Coltrane's style is wholly original and of growing influence among new tenor players. [. . .]

Most recently, as this album will attest, Coltrane has become absorbed by the rhythms of Africa. During the editing sessions for this album he noted, "There has been an influence of African rhythms in American jazz. It seems there are some things jazz can borrow harmonically, but I've been knocking myself out seeking something rhythmic. But nothing swings like 4/4. These implied rhythms give variety." [. . .]

For this record, Coltrane composed two of the three selections, then discussed the orchestration thoroughly with Eric Dolphy, a reed player of enormous talent. Pianist McCoy Tyner[1] of Coltrane's group was the third member of the discussion group.

"Actually," Dolphy recalled, "all I did was orchestrate. Basically John and McCoy worked out the whole thing. And it all came from John; he knew exactly what he wanted. And that was, essentially, the feeling of his group."

"Africa" has an unusual form. Its melody had to be stated in the background because Coltrane is not tied down by chords. "I had a sound that I wanted to hear," Coltrane remarked of this composition. "And what resulted was about it. I wanted the band to have a drone. We used two basses. The main line carries all the way through the tune. One bass plays almost all the way through. The other has rhythmic lines around it. Reggie and Art have worked together, and they know how to give and take." This work began with Coltrane's quartet. He listened to many African records for rhythmic inspiration. One had a bass line like a chant, and the group used it, working it into different tunes. In Los Angeles, John hit on using African rhythms instead of 4/4, and the work began to take shape. Tyner began to work chords into the structure, and, in John's own words, "it's been growing ever since."

The instrumentation—trumpet, four French horns, alto sax, baritone sax, two euphoniums, two basses, piano, drums, and tuba—is among the most unusual in jazz. But, Dolphy explained, "John thought of this sound. He wanted brass, he wanted baritone horns, he wanted that mellow sound and power."

Coltrane heard the playbacks and nodded. "It's the first time I've done any tune with that kind of rhythmic background. I've done things in 3/4 and 4/4. On the whole, I'm quite pleased with 'Africa.'"

"Greensleeves" is an updating of the old, revered folk song. It's included in this set because Coltrane, in recent months, has been studying folk music. "It's one of the most beautiful folk melodies I've heard," he said. "It's written in 6/8, and we do it just about as written. There's a section for improvisation with a vamp to blow on."

The quartet has been playing this theme recently, and the arrangement is based on Tyner's chords. Dolphy notated it. "For me," Coltrane said, "'Greensleeves' is most enjoyable to play. Most of the time we get a nice pulse and groove. It was a challenge to add the band to it. I wanted to keep the feeling of the quartet. That's why we took the same voicings and the same rhythm McCoy comps in."

"Blues Minor" is a piece the quartet has been playing of late. It was assembled at the recording session. "It's a head," Dolphy said. "McCoy gave me the notes. I wrote out the parts, and the band did it in one take." It swings loosely with the ease and drive of a head arrangement.

All in all, this album is representative of the state of musical mind of John Coltrane, 34, on his way to something new and exciting, but pausing along the way to sum up the fresh and provocative work he has accomplished this far.

DOM CERULLI

Note

1. Tyner was misidentified as "McCoy Turner" in the original liner notes.

"THEATRE NOTES: JAZZ MASTERS AT LUNCH"

Paul Adams

In early August 1961 both Coltrane and Cannonball Adderley were appearing in Detroit with their respective groups, Coltrane at the Minor Key and Adderley at Baker's Keyboard Lounge. Journalist Paul Adams, writing for the *Michigan Chronicle* (an African American newspaper), had lunch with them.

The world of jazz is in free-wheeling, improvisational orbit. The experimentalists are attempting every new concoction of notes in an effort to plunge jazz into volumes never heard by the human ear.

John Coltrane, tenor sax, is one of the most respected researchers in the movement, as is Julian "Cannonball" Adderley, his friend and colleague.

The two jazz masters met last week at Mr. Kelly's Enterprizes on Chene at a luncheon prepared exclusively for them by song stylist Frances Burnett. Local, well-seasoned piano man Johnny Griffith made it a quartet and was attentive throughout. [. . .]

Theatre Notes had long tried to arrange such a meeting of the above personalities. My efforts were well rewarded. Here was an opportunity to get the facts and formulas directly from the horse's mouth, as it were.

Who had exerted the prominent influence upon "Cannonball's" artistry?

CANNONBALL: "The most profound early influence was Cleanhead Vinson. He blew a strong, explosive sax unlike the sweet melodic altos of the time. But in 1942 I heard a guy that was saying everything there was to say with his horn. It was 1945 before I knew it was Charlie Parker."

To Cannonball, Charlie Parker's style was contagious; he modified it. Frances Burnett, a very progressive singer today, is a convert. Who converted her?

From the *Michigan Chronicle*, August 12, 1961, section 2, page 4.

FRANCES: "When I met and worked with Dizzy I began to learn and appreciate jazz. Now I do everything I can with a song, including 'God Bless America.' Yes, jazz is definitely an excellent art form, purely American and a great source of pride."

John Coltrane, quiet and unimposing, has a mind that races ahead like wild fire. It burns into every nook and cranny looking for new ideas. Who influenced him?

COLTRANE: "Cannonball influences me. Of course, there were Lester Young, Coleman Hawkins and the Bird. But when you total it up I think I feel something from everyone."

The most fascinating discussion to emerge from the luncheon was the concept of the simultaneous note execution. What is it?

COLTRANE: "Well, it's simply playing two notes at the same time on your instrument. It has great possibilities but at present it is admittedly a gimmick though when developed it could have a definite musical value."

In summation the question was asked: Where will jazz go from here?

CANNONBALL: "There is that intangible something in musicians that makes them follow a certain lead—like Coltrane. Maybe in the future some 12-year-old in Africa will come up with something far-reaching and inspiring and all the musicians will follow him. But jazz is free and cannot be dictated to, so no telling."

And that's a point well taken.

INTERVIEW WITH JOHN COLTRANE

Benoît Quersin

The exact date and location of this interview are unknown; however, based on information given in the interview, it must have been held during the summer or fall of 1961 in the United States, after Eric Dolphy had joined Coltrane's working group around July but before the November 1961 tour of Europe.

Benoît Quersin: I've been listening to your music since nineteen forty—fifty-seven, or something, and I—

John Coltrane: Oh, yeah?

Quersin: —love it, you know. I've been very fond of it since then. You've been—well there's—there has been an evolution in your music. Like, you've been exploring new ways of playing jazz. Well, it's kind of hard for me, you know what I mean? I mean, the conception of jazz music, following new patterns, or something.

Coltrane: So, you think it's changing?

Quersin: It *has* been changing.

Coltrane: Yeah.

Quersin: Well, it changed a lot in the last few years. It has been improving. Also, new patterns.

Coltrane: Yeah. Yeah, there have been some new things introduced. And it's good for jazz that they have been introduced, you know, because [they] breathe new life into the whole field. And, I think young men now, they have quite a bit to listen to, and all the men that they listen to, they can take things from what they're doing, and add into their own conceptions, and go their own way and maybe produce something themselves, you know, which might help promote this extension in the music.

Quersin: "Extension" in what way?

Coltrane: Well, in rhythmic and melodic and possibly harmonic directions.

Quersin: So, you're trying to get out of the standard harmonic structures and all that? Well, that's where you started from.

Coltrane: Yeah. I tried to get out of it, because I worked—I went at it in a harmonic, trying to work through harmonic structures because that was—I was—that was my strongest point. I mean I was better equipped to work that way than I was rhythmically or melodically. And that has been about the extent of my work. In what I've done, I've tried to add things to my playing harmonically which I hadn't been playing over the years, you know. And I started in nineteen fifty-seven to do this for myself. Well, almost all of the guys who are out here now are doing so many things that are help—helping to expand the music, it's going, like I said, in other directions. It's going in rhythmic directions and also melodic and harmonic, too.

Quersin: Well, the music—

Coltrane: It's getting a little larger. There's more—there's more that a guy will attempt to play now than he would in—whatever—1955, you know? And things that guys are doing now that's—in '55, they would say, "Well, man, I don't know. It's a little too daring," maybe, you know? But now it doesn't seem that anything can be too daring for a musician nowadays in jazz.

Quersin: So, well, there was an extension in the language—trying to extend the language the—I mean the vocabulary.

Coltrane: How's that?

Quersin: Extend the vocabulary, and—

Coltrane: Oh, yeah.

Quersin: —broaden.

Coltrane: Yeah.

Quersin: Well, the freedom, but organized, organized freedom, as far as you are concerned.

Coltrane: Well, I don't—maybe it is, I don't know. I have to—I'm kind of— actually, I'm groping, I'm trying to find my way, you know. I can only try to work out of what I've been in. Work my way forward, so I just try to set one stone upon another as I go.

Quersin: Maybe, uh, *Giant Steps* album was the first step, or the first definite step toward original music of yours.

Coltrane: Well, that album—that album represented a few things that I'd been thinking of for about five or six months before it was made. The things that I was—the harmonic structures that I was working on there, I hadn't fully developed them and I didn't understand them. Actually, *Giant Steps* was, in quite a few respects, I don't know, an experiment, you know? And the things—some things I could have used in there—in *Giant Steps*—that I made a whole song out of, I could have probably taken—taken them and applied to something else and they might have taken up a few bars and that have been it. But at that time, I was obsessed with the thing and it was all I had in my mind, because it was my first step into playing some extended chord structures, you know, as I was trying to do, and that was those songs that were on there. Some of them had these particular structures in 'em, you know? That was the first one—record that I made with them in there. And since then I've done it, but it hasn't been so obvious because I've learned to use it as a part of something and not as a whole.

Quersin: And then, the next step was—because it sounds—the music I hear in *Giant Steps* seems to—well, it's a wide exploration in harmony, because the harmonic structures are kind of uncommon, really new. But now, in your latest, in the latest things I heard, like *Favorite Things* album and *Africa/Brass* and *Olé*, it's something else.

Coltrane: Well, I'm trying to learn, I'm trying to broaden myself melodically and rhythmically, too, you know? These things that are coming along now are the culmination of—whatever—the things that I'm thinking of in these aspects, rhythmic or melodic. I haven't forgotten about harmony altogether, but I'm not as interested in it as I was two years ago.

Quersin: Harmonic structures, you say.

Coltrane: Hm?

Quersin: Harmonic structures.

Coltrane: Harmony structures?

Quersin: No, the latest album. Yeah, what you just said, [*unintelligible*] two years ago. What's that?

Coltrane: Well, I was more interested two years ago in harmony than I am now, that's what I'm saying. Then it was solely—I was only interested in harmony. Now, I'm trying to learn about melody and rhythm.

Quersin: And so, get more freedom melodically with simpler—one seems to—you seem to play—I don't know if I'm right, but you seem to play a kind of mode, a kind of scale, modified scale.

Coltrane: Yeah, well, I've gone into that now. I've followed Miles's lead in that, I think. He was doing that, that kind of work, when I was with him. And, at that time, I was working on the chords, but he was in the modal thing then. So, since I've had my own group, it has become necessary to use this modal concept because it does free the rhythm section in it. They don't have to keep their strict chordal structure. And the soloist can play any structure he wants to. But the rhythm section is basically unhindered or uncluttered, you know. So, most of the things we're doing now are in modes for parts, in sections, then there are sections when there are no harmonies at all, underlying, that is.

Quersin: How do you like George Russell's music?

Coltrane: He has some good music. He has what is—it's the type of music that seems to be coming into the fore nowadays. I've heard a few records of his, one that Eric Dolphy was on, that I heard, that I—several things on there I like very well. And he understands quite a few of the problems, you know, that musicians are running across today and he's probably gonna do a great deal to contribute to solving of such things.

Quersin: And, what's the reason for adding Eric to the—to your quintet? To your band?

Coltrane: Well, he just came in and started playing! [*both laugh*] Yeah, he just came in and started playing. He played, I forgot where the job was, he brought his horn down and sat in. And, it was on a weekend, so he just played the whole weekend. And the next job we worked, he came down, I think it was in Philadelphia, he said, "Man, I don't have nothing to do." He was bored, just sittin' around New York, so he said, "I'll just come on over." And, after a while I just said, "You're in the band." [*both laugh*] And, that's fine, I really—we've always—I was always calling him on the phone and he was calling me, and we'd discuss things, you know, musically, so we might as well be together. Maybe we can help each other some. I know he helps me a lot.

Quersin: Yeah, he worked on the album *Africa/Brass* with you, didn't he?

Coltrane: Yeah, he was—he did quite a bit of work on that album. Quite a bit.

Quersin: How do you like Ornette Coleman?

Coltrane: I love him. [*laughs*] Yeah, I love him. I'm following his lead. He's done a lot to open my eyes to what can be done, you know.

Quersin: Very subjective.

Coltrane: Huh?

Quersin: Very subjective, he is—

Coltrane: Ornette?

Quersin: Ornette. Very intelligent, fresh and sincere, but—

Coltrane: He's beautiful.

Quersin: He's a beautiful cat. And I think he thinks a lot about his music, but isn't it kind of an intellectual approach to music? And it's good, you know, I feel it's good.

Coltrane: Yeah, well, I feel indebted to him, myself. Because, actually, when he came along, I was so far in this thing I didn't know where I was going to go next, you know. I don't know whether I would have thought about just abandoning the chord system or not. I probably wouldn't have thought of that at all. And he came along doing it, and I heard it, I said, "Well, you know, that—that must be the answer," you know? And I'm of the opinion that it is, now. That's the way I feel now. The way we do, we play, we do—right, since I have a piano, I still have to consider it, and that accounts for the modes that we play, but after all, you can't—we only—we only got a few, and after a while, that's going to get a little monotonous to do it on every song, so it might—there probably will be some songs in the future that we're going to play, just as Ornette does, with no accompaniment from the piano at all. Except on maybe the melody, but as far as on the solo, no accompaniment.

Quersin: Yeah, just to set the climate and then go.

Coltrane: Hm?

Quersin: Just set the climate and then go.

Coltrane: Yeah.

Quersin: Yeah, it's really close to some aspects of the modern music, the so-called classical modern music.

Coltrane: Hm?

Quersin: So, it's more or less close to the modern classical music, you know, that kind of freedom.

Coltrane: You mean the movement now in jazz?

Quersin: Mm hmm. But jazz was something more.

Coltrane: Well, it still retains its—that thing, whatever it is, that it has. And, that's what keeps it going, that—that feeling. Whatever it is, it's hard to define.

Quersin: I heard that you're going to Europe soon.

Coltrane: Yeah.

Quersin: France? You know where?

Coltrane: No, I don't—I don't know where, yet. I know, well, France is there, London is there. And, what else, I'm not sure.

Quersin: Because, I sure hope you come to Brussels, you know, I'll be there.

Coltrane: Ah? [*both laugh*] All right.

Quersin: Well, if they don't hire you, I will.

Coltrane: Well, thank you.

Quersin: I'll try to—

Coltrane: Thank you.

Quersin: —anyway. OK, thank you.

Coltrane: Thank you.

"LIVE" AT THE VILLAGE VANGUARD LINER NOTES

Nat Hentoff

Nat Hentoff interviewed Coltrane for these liner notes sometime in late 1961. *"Live" at the Village Vanguard* was recorded in early November 1961 and released around February 1962.

The Man

This newest addition to the collected works of the insatiably exploratory John Coltrane was recorded on November 2 and 3, 1961, at the Village Vanguard in New York. With Coltrane were Eric Dolphy, bass clarinet; McCoy Tyner, piano; Reggie Workman,[1] bass; and Elvin Jones, drums.

Coltrane had told Bob Thiele, Impulse's recording director, that he would like to try recording "live" because of the added freedom of an on-the-job performance by contrast with the formal aura of a recording studio. "I like," Coltrane said after the taping, "the feeling of a club, especially one with an intimate atmosphere like the Vanguard. It's important to have that real contact with an audience because that's what we're trying to do—communicate."

The Music

"Spiritual" is by Coltrane and is based on an actual spiritual he had run across and that had remained in his mind. "I like the way it worked out," he said. "I feel we brought out the mood inherent in the tune. It's a piece we'd been working with for some time because I wanted to make sure before we recorded it that we would be able to get the original emotional essence of the spiritual."

After the somber opening in which Coltrane on soprano saxophone states the brooding theme, he expands reflectively on that keening line, illustrating the passionate lyricism that is at the core of whatever he plays. Worth noting is the further command of the soprano that Coltrane now has. Using both soprano and

105

tenor has presented difficulties because the soprano requires a tighter embouchure, but as this track demonstrates, Coltrane has made the instrument as natural an extension of himself as the tenor. His tone is full and firm and capable of varying textures to add more details to particular moods. Coltrane is followed by Eric Dolphy in one of his characteristic speech-like solos on the bass clarinet. In his case too, his sound has become warmer and he has increased technical flexibility.

McCoy Tyner's solo demonstrates what Coltrane admiringly refers to as his "fine sense of form and the fresh sound he gets on piano by the way he voices his chords." Another point that Coltrane makes about Tyner is less evident in this predominantly gentle number, but it does become quite clear in Coltrane's more churning pieces. "McCoy," says Coltrane, "has a beautiful lyric concept that is essential to complement the rest of us." To which observation might be added the impression that McCoy's particular kind of lyricism is calmer than Coltrane's often becomes, so that the balance is between kinds of lyricism, not opposites. Coltrane adds: "I've known him a long time and I've always felt I wanted to play with him. Our ideas meet and blend. Working with McCoy is like putting on a nice-fitting glove." After Tyner, Coltrane ends the piece by invoking a yearning intensity that is considerably more convincing than much of the factitious gospel-like "soul jazz" that has been pervasive in the last couple of years.

"Softly as in a Morning Sunrise" was included, Coltrane notes, "because I like to get a sensible variety in an album. It seems to me to round out the two originals, and I especially like the swinging by Jones in this particular take." Coltrane is again on soprano. Tyner opens with a brightly relaxed, crystalline solo which leads into an intriguing Coltrane series of thematic variations in which he doesn't spare himself technically while proving how malleable even the stubborn soprano saxophone can be.

"Chasin' the Trane" is a blues. "Usually, I like to get familiar with a new piece before I record it, but you never have to worry about the blues, unless the line is very complicated. In this case, however, the melody not only wasn't written but it wasn't even conceived before we played it. We set the tempo, and in we went." In view of the length of this and a number of Coltrane's other performances, I asked him if my own theory was valid that he was trying to create and sustain a kind of hypnotic mood so that the listener in time becomes oblivious to distractions and becomes drawn into the music with his usual emotional defenses down. "That may be a secondary thing," he answered, "but I haven't reached the stage yet where I'm trying consciously to produce effects of that kind. I'm still primarily looking into certain sounds, certain scales. The result can be long or short. I never know. It's always one thing leading into another. It keeps evolving, and sometimes it's longer than I actually thought it was while I was playing it. When things are constantly happening, the piece just doesn't feel that long."

This extended blues and the two previous numbers led to further Coltrane observations about his musicians. "For a long time," he said, "Eric Dolphy and I had been talking about all kinds of possibilities with regard to improvising, scale work, and techniques. Those discussions helped both of us to keep probing, and finally I decided that the band was here, after all, and it made sense for Eric to come on in and work. Having him here all the time is a constant stimulus to me. As for Elvin Jones, I especially like his ability to mix and juggle rhythms. He's also always aware of everything else that's happening. I guess you could say he has the ability to be in three places at the same time. Reggie Workman has a rich imagination and he has a good sense of going it alone. That's important in this band. Most times, the other musicians set their own parts. Reggie, for example, is very adept at creating his own bass line. In this band, nobody can lean on anyone else. Each of us has to have a firm sense of where he's going."

Coltrane is on tenor in "Chasin' the Trane" and plunges in from the top. The solo is particularly fascinating for the astonishing variety of textures Coltrane draws from the full range of his horn and the unflagging intensity of his inventions. Listening to Coltrane in this unyielding performance is so absorbing because it allows the outsider to be present at an uncompromising act of spontaneous creation. Usually, even in jazz, some polishing has been done beforehand to avoid at least some of the dangers of unbridled improvisation; but here the whole piece comes newly and unpredictably alive before us. It is possible, therefore, to experience vicariously that rare contemporary phenomenon—a man going-for-broke. And in public no less. If you can open yourself emotionally to so relentless a self-exploration, you can gain considerable insight into the marrow of the jazz experience and into Coltrane's own indomitably resourceful musicianship throughout this whirlpool of a blues.

Coltrane continues to work ahead. A couple of months after this date was completed, he was saying, "I've got to write more music for the group. I've really got to work and study more approaches to writing. I've already been looking into those approaches to music—as in India—in which particular sounds and scales are intended to produce specific emotional meanings. I've got to keep probing. There's so much more to do." And it is precisely this total commitment to the infinite possibilities of music that was so drivingly and sometimes furiously alive in Coltrane's playing on those two nights at the Village Vanguard.

NAT HENTOFF

Note

1. The bassist on "Chasin' the Trane" is actually Jimmy Garrison.

"I'D LIKE TO RETURN TO BRITAIN— AND I'D LIKE TO PLAY YOUR CLUBS"

John Coltrane tells Bob Dawbarn

From November 11 to early December 1961, the John Coltrane Quintet featuring Eric Dolphy toured Europe with Dizzy Gillespie for the Jazz at the Philharmonic tour series. On Friday, November 17, 1961, Bob Dawbarn interviewed Coltrane in his London hotel room. It was the final day of a week-long UK tour that stirred up quite a bit of controversy in the British music press. Unfortunately no concert recordings were made, although a number of recordings exist from the following tour of Europe, including a German TV program that featured the quintet. It was the only time Coltrane performed in the UK.

JOHN COLTRANE is undoubtedly the most controversial jazz musician to make a concert tour of Britain.

On my way to see him at his London hotel last Friday I reflected that, if his music was any guide, he was probably an aggressively dedicated character crusading for a new approach to jazz.

I was quite wrong. This quiet American turned out to be a man of great personal charm and remarkable honesty.

Far from showing the expected contempt for those who failed to understand his musical attitudes, his chief desire seemed to be to communicate with his audiences.

Here are some of the questions I put to Coltrane, and his frank, if sometimes complex, answers.

Puzzling

I found your Quintet's music completely bewildering. Can you explain what it is you are trying to do? Surely you and Eric Dolphy are not following the normal chord sequences?

From *Melody Maker*, November 25, 1961, page 8.

Coltrane: I can't speak for Eric—I don't know exactly what his theory is. I am playing on the regular changes, though sometimes I extend them.

I do follow the progressions. The sequences I build have a definite relationship to the chords. Can you give me a particular example of something that puzzled you?

Take your two soprano solos on "My Favorite Things." The first I found reasonably easy to understand. The second I couldn't follow at all.

Coltrane: That tune has a melody in the major key and a short vamp in the minor. In the first solo I played straight through. You could follow the melody in it.

The second was more ad lib. It was in the same form except that the vamp parts were stretched out.

Different

It seemed to me that the three members of the rhythm sections were playing completely different things—often in different time signatures.

Coltrane: They are free to play anything they feel. Tyner plays some things on piano. I don't know what they are, but they are based on the chords.

The bass works from nothing but the basic E natural and plays it in as many different rhythmic ways as possible. The drummer is playing basically in 3/4 time.

Your playing seemed so different from anything we have heard on your records here.

Coltrane: So many people have told me that, it must be true. I've got to listen to those records again. I guess I've changed in the last year. I'm in the process of changing things around and finding areas that haven't been exploited.

Problems?

Does the soprano present special problems?

Coltrane: It certainly does. You need to play it with such a tight embouchure that I've been frightened of losing my tenor embouchure.

I have my suspicions that that is beginning to happen. I'm not getting the tenor tone I'd like at the moment.

The soprano seems to take over and I may have to choose between them.

Do you plan to keep this Quintet together?

Coltrane: I'm not sure, but it will probably revert to a Quartet. Eric just came in and played with us one night. He wasn't doing anything else so we invited him along.

Most of our things were conceived for a Quartet, and the group sounds more like a quartet plus one than a quintet.

Have you enjoyed the British tour?

Coltrane: We're very inexperienced at playing concerts. We're used to playing at great length in clubs and find it hard to cut things to fit a concert. I don't get a chance to stretch out. With Dolphy added it makes things even harder.

Some people sound as good on concerts as in clubs. Dizzy is one. He really knows how to put it over. I haven't the ability yet. I'm just becoming aware of the problems involved.

Since we went out of London I've been trying to play things the audience are more familiar with. It seems we might get it right too late—at the end of the tour.

I see a guitar on your bed. I didn't know you played it.

Coltrane: I just bought it for company. I got lonesome and had read everything I had. I can't play it, but every instrument has its own personality. Maybe I'll stumble across something I wouldn't get on piano.

Any other comment on the tour?

Coltrane: I would really like to come back, particularly if I could work in a club. I really want to communicate with the audiences.

"CONVERSATION WITH COLTRANE"

Valerie Wilmer

This interview from the UK tour, done in Coltrane's London hotel room, offers alternate perspectives on some of the continuing themes running through Coltrane's interviews: the perceived difference in sound between his recordings and his live band, the soprano sax, the harp, the use of two bassists, Miles Davis's and Ornette Coleman's influence on Coltrane, and freeing the rhythm section from chordal structures.

"Melodically and harmonically their improvisation struck my ear as gobbledegook," wrote John Tynan in the November 23rd [1961] *Down Beat*. He was speaking of the recent musical experiments of John Coltrane and Eric Dolphy, experiments which confounded even ardent Coltrane supporters when he toured England last year.

The in-person sound of Coltrane was so different from his recorded work that most people wondered whether their auditory processes were in order. It seems they were, for Coltrane himself confirmed that his music had radically altered over the last twelve months or so.

Meeting the man himself, it is hard to believe that such a quiet, calm and serious individual could be responsible for the frantic "sheets of sound" which emanate from his tenor saxophone, or that such a sensitive person could think of some of his uglier wailings on soprano as beautiful.

"The sound you get on any instrument depends on the conception of sound you hear in your mind," he told me. "It also depends on your physical properties, such as the shape and structure of the inside of your mouth and throat. I only tried to find the sound that I hear in my mind, a sound any artist hears and hopes to be able to produce. I suppose I did strive to get it with using different reeds and things as any artist does, but now I've settled on a reed at least, and I use a hard one."

From *Jazz Journal*, January 1962, pages 1–2.

I mentioned that everyone had remarked on how different he sounded in the flesh as opposed to on records. "I've discussed this fault with the engineers because the playbacks haven't sounded right," he said. "They get too close to the horn with the mikes and don't give the sound time to travel as they should. Consequently, they don't get enough of the real timbre and they miss the *whole* body of the sound. They get the inside of it but not the outside as well.

"I've heard one or two albums with this fault and I've tried to clear it up, even suggested that I play away from the mike as I'd do in a club, which makes a much more pleasing sound. And of course the loudness also varies according to the reed you have. If you have a good one you don't change it—my good ones usually last about two weeks."

Whatever one thought of the actual *sound* of John's soprano, it was good to know that a leading modernist had taken up the instrument seemingly doomed to oblivion with the passing of Sidney Bechet. He has, in fact, been playing it for about three years, and as so often happens, took it up quite accidentally. "A friend of mine had one and as I hadn't seen one too often before, I looked at it, tried it, and liked the sound. I thought I'd like to use it a little but I'd only just formed my own group and didn't think I'd actually use it in public.

"I don't consider my work on it a success, because I'm at the same place on it as I am on the tenor. Of course the tenor has more body to it, but the soprano lends itself to more lyrical playing. There are times when I feel the need for one and sometimes I feel the need for the other. I try to use either one according to what the tune feels like."

It is also interesting to note that he has recently started playing the harp because "I like the sound. It's one of the most beautiful things and just for the fact that it's different, that's what I like about it. I got interested in it around 1958 when I was interested in playing arpeggios instead of just straight lines, and so naturally I looked at the harp. It's just pure sound, it's not even like a piano where you've got to hit the keys to make the hammers hit the strings. A harpist friend of mine showed me some fingering but I don't have time to sit down and make much out of it. Right now I don't see any chance of making jazz out of it."

Another of John Coltrane's innovations was his recent use of two basses— well, not quite an innovation because Duke had the idea twenty years ago—but his regular bassist Reggie Workman has been playing the rhythm parts, while the group was augmented with the excellent Art Davis. It was through the latter that the idea came about:

"I'd heard some Indian records and liked the effect of the water-drum," said 'Trane, "and I thought another bass would add that certain rhythmic sound. We were playing a lot of stuff with a sort of suspended rhythm, with one bass playing a series of notes around one point, and it seemed that another bass could fill in the spaces in the straight 4/4 line.

"Art and I had been working quite a bit together before the band started and I was interested in bass lines and sequences and he could help me. I actually wanted Art to join me as a regular bassist, but he was all tied up with Dizzy and so I had to get in Steve Davis and when he left Art still couldn't make it, so I got Reggie.

"Once I was in town and I said to Art to come on down because I liked him so much and I figured that he and Reggie could exchange sets. But instead of that they started playing some together and I got something from it. Reggie played as usual and Art countered it and it was very good. I only wish I could have brought Art over with me."

One night, according to Eric Dolphy, "Wilbur Ware came in and up on the stand so they had three basses going. John and I got off the stand and listened and Art Davis was really playing some kind of bass. Mingus has some 'know-how' of bass that he won't tell anyone," said Eric. "But Art sure does have some 'know-how' of bass like Mingus. John made a date with two basses, one called *Africa* on the Impulse label, and another called *Olé* on Atlantic, and Art plays fantastic."

There certainly seems no chance of Coltrane's group becoming stagnant, a thing which he fears more than any other, with the constant change of person-nel combinations. "We had Wes Montgomery out on the Coast," he said, "and I wanted very much to have him here in England. He's really something else because he made everything sound that much fuller."

As for Eric Dolphy, whose playing disappointed so many people when heard in person, John said: "He just came in and sat in with us for about three nights and everybody enjoyed it, because his presence added some fire to the band. He and I have known each other a long time, and I guess you'd say we were students of the jazz scene," he smiled. "We'd exchange ideas and so we just decided to go ahead and see if we could do something within this group. Eric is really gifted and I feel he's going to produce something inspired, but although we've been talking about music for years, I don't know where he's going, and *I* don't know

Coltrane and Leo Wright (left) in England, probably November 17, 1961.
PHOTOGRAPH BY BILL WAGG. COURTESY OF MITSUO JOHFU.

where *I'm* going. He's interested in trying to progress, however, and so am I, so we have quite a bit in common."

Apart from the epic performance of "My Favorite Things" which lasted for half-an-hour at all the London concerts, the majority of Coltrane's material is original. Of his writing he said: "I think playing and writing go hand in hand. I don't feel that at this stage of the game I can actually sit down and say I'm going to write a piece that will do this or that for the people—a thing which some artists can do—but I'm trying to tune myself so I can look to myself and to nature and to other sounds in music and interpret things that I feel there and present them to people. Eventually I hope to reach a stage where I have a vast warehouse of study and knowledge to be able to produce any certain thing.

"Duke Ellington is one person who can do this—that's really *heavy* musicianship and I haven't reached that stage yet. I've been predominately a soloist all my natural life, and now I'm a soloist with my own band, and this has led me into this other thing: what am I going to play and why?

"My material is mainly my own, and I find some of my best work comes from the most challenging material. Sometimes we write things to be easy, sometimes to be hard, it depends on what we want to do.

"A year ago we had quite a few standards which made up a third of the book, but now a number of people, certainly Ornette [Coleman] and Eric, have been responsible for other influences.

"At the time I left Miles I was trying to add a lot of sequences to my solo work, putting chords to the things I was playing, and using things I could play a little more music on.

"It was before I formed my own group that I had the rhythm section playing these sequences forward, and I made *Giant Steps* with some other guys and carried the idea on into my band. But it was hard to make some things swing with the rhythm section playing these chords, and Miles advised me to abandon the idea of the rhythm section playing these sequences, and to do it only myself. But around this time I heard Ornette who had abandoned chords completely and that helped me to think clearly about what I wanted to do.

"It was Miles who made me want to be a much better musician. He gave me some of the most listenable moments I've had in music, and he also gave me an appreciation for simplicity. He influenced me quite a bit in music in every way. I used to want to play tenor the way he played trumpet when I used to listen to his records. But when I joined him I realized I could never play like that, and I think that's what made me go the opposite way.

"Recently I've been doing songs with the rhythm section having more freedom and not being bound to chordal structures, but still giving the soloist just as much freedom. Sometimes we start with one chord and drop it later, and improvise on the bass line or the piano, and this I find much easier to do on original material. I haven't done it on a 'standard' yet, but maybe I will soon. But unless I find a simple one, there are no more breakthroughs on those standards for me.

"There are some great songs that have been played in this music and only need a new approach to revive them. Faced with this fact, I couldn't revise my musical approach drastically, and so I said well, maybe I'm really doing something with this harmonic approach and should stick with it for a while.

"There are going to be songs with one chord and songs with no chords, which in my case means freedom to see if I can develop more in a melodic fashion through these unlimited harmonies."

Although he himself is not certain of the exact directions in which his music is going, this highly intelligent musician is striving for a music that will doubtless be entirely different to any we have heard before. He has been called the only important jazzman since Bird, and I asked him what he thought of his own contribution to jazz.

"Basically I am trying not to stagnate. I go this way and I go that way and I don't know where I'm going next. But if I should get stagnant, I'd lose my interest.

"There are so many things to be considered in making music. The whole question of life itself; *my* life in which there are many things on which I don't think I've reached a final conclusion; there are matters I don't think I've covered completely, and all these things have to be covered before you make your music sound any way. You have to grow to know.

"When I was younger, I didn't think this would happen, but now I know that I've still got a long way to go. Maybe when I'm sixty I'll be satisfied with what I'm doing, but I don't know . . . I'm sure that later on my ideas will carry more conviction.

"I know that I want to produce beautiful music, music that does things to people that they need. Music that will uplift, and make them happy—those are the qualities I'd like to produce.

"Some people say 'your music sounds angry,' or 'tortured,' or 'spiritual,' or 'overpowering' or something; you get all kinds of things, you know. Some say they feel elated, and so you never know where it's going to go. All a musician can do is to get closer to the sources of nature, and so feel that he is in communion with the natural laws. Then he can feel that he is interpreting them to the best of his ability, and can try to convey that to others.

"As to the music itself and its future, it won't lessen any in its ability to move people, I feel certain of that. It will be just as great or greater.

"But as to how it's going to do that, I don't know. It's left to the men who're going to do it—they would know!"

"JOHN COLTRANE TALKS TO JAZZ NEWS"

Kitty Grime

Coltrane was interviewed by Kitty Grime, assistant editor of *Jazz News*, in his London hotel room during the UK tour. (The interview took place just after Valerie Wilmer finished her interview.) Coltrane's responses were edited into essay form for this unsigned article.

WHEN I first joined Miles in 1955 I had a lot to learn. I felt I was lacking in general musicianship. I had all kinds of technical problems, for example, I didn't have the right mouthpiece, and I hadn't the necessary harmonic understanding. I am quite ashamed of those early records I made with Miles. Why he picked me, I don't know. Maybe he saw something in my playing that he hoped would grow. I had this desire, which I think we all have, to be as original as I could, and as honest as I could be. But there were so many musical conclusions I hadn't arrived at, that I felt inadequate. All this was naturally frustrating in those days, and it probably came through in the music.

I've been told my playing is "angry." Well, you know musicians have many moods, angry, happy, sad—and since those early days perhaps more sides of my musical nature have been revealed on records. I don't really know what a listener feels when he hears music. The musician may feel one way and the listener may get something else from the music.

Some musicians have to speak their anger in their playing. The beauty of jazz is that you're free to do just what you feel. But while their playing might express anger, I wouldn't know whether they're angry as people or not. If a man can play well, I get an elation from his music, even if he's playing angry and hard. An aggressive frame of mind can create pretty stern music. But this may well be a very rewarding experience for the listener. You can get a feeling of expectancy

From *Jazz News*, December 27, 1961, page 13.

and fulfillment in a solo, and an artist of ability may lead you down paths in music where many things can happen. I'd hate to think of an audience missing out on music, because they think it's nothing but anger.

Change is inevitable in our music—things change. A big break with the dancing tradition of jazz came in the forties with Diz and Bird. You got broken rhythms, complicated harmonic devices. There is so much beauty still in this music.

Then almost ten years later, Miles, who'd been with them at the beginning, swung over to the other side again. You can dance to most of Miles' most popular things—like "Green Dolphin Street." Now, in the music of people like Cecil Taylor and Ornette [Coleman] you have a swing back to broken rhythms again. It's a fact that everything in life is action and reaction. Things evolve, not necessarily consciously. But there are certain elements that are inherent in jazz, and you must be watching for them. If those elements are there, you'll get it.

Mingus says "the beat must go" and I admit I don't love the beat, in the strict sense. At this phase I feel I need the beat somewhere, but I don't really care about the straight 4/4 at all—though this is just a personal feeling. In a rhythm section I like propulsion and a feeling of buoyancy, which fits under and around the horn, and has a lift to it. A sense of the pulse, rather than the beat, can take you out of a stodgy approach. And, of course, you can swing on other time signatures than 4/4. But what happens depends on the musicians I have playing with me.

Choice of material is entirely individual. I've played some jazz forms so long and so much that I feel the need for other forms, and perhaps for no form. When I started the group, I used to plan routines like mad, now I don't have to plan so much, as I learn and get freer. Sometimes we start from nothing, no "in" plan, no intro or solo routines. I know how it's going to end—but sometimes not what might happen in between! I try to accept songs as they are, with a different approach for everything. I make suggestions to the group, as to what I feel, and we use this as a starting point.

I like extended jazz works, and written compositions, if they're well done. I'm studying and learning about longer constructions. If I become strong enough I might try something on those lines. I don't study the music of any particular period, but harmony and form from a natural standpoint. I try to look at it all. I want to understand music, so that I can do things in an objective way. So far, I've only written from the piano, with melodies that come out of the chords. I'd like to be able to write away from the piano. It is very useful, though, as you have a whole band under your hands with a piano, and it's the best thing for working on chord forms.

Progress in jazz can be made consciously—think of Sonny Rollins—he was back in November and we'll see something! Sonny "retired" before, and when he came back, he'd added quite a bit. I admire his tremendous powers of concentration. You have to do a lot of work consciously, then you can leave the rest to your subconscious later on.

Jazz is a companionable thing, and I like playing in smaller places, so that I can see what people feel. I would like my music to be part of the surroundings, part of the gaiety of a club atmosphere. I realize I'm in the entertainment business, and I'd like to be [the] sort of guy who can set audiences at ease. If you go about music without a smile, people think you're not happy. I don't make a habit of wishing for what I don't have, but I often wish I had a lighter nature. Dizzy has that beautiful gift—I can't say "Be happy, people"—it's something I can't command. But you have to be true to your own nature.

May I say, though, that when I go to hear a man, as long as he conducts himself properly, and moves me with his music, I am satisfied. If he should happen to smile, I consider it something added to what I have received already, if not, I don't worry because I know it is not wholly essential to the music.

"JOHN COLTRANE: A MODERN FAUST"

J.-C. Dargenpierre

This article provides a vivid account of the events of November 18, 1961, when the members of the Dizzy Gillespie and John Coltrane groups arrived in Paris for their concert at the Olympia. Coltrane is quoted extensively.

Orly, Carrefour du Monde, Saturday, November 18, 12:15.

Mr. John Birks finally arrives, pushing a cart piled with luggage. Just seeing him, one senses a humor-filled Dizzy; a humor free and joyous, as he would be showing us soon. What comedic gifts! A prodigious musician, he still inspires admiration as a man. With the look of a Barbary pirate, little beard flowing in the wind; here's Eric Dolphy, loaded down with many boxes and instrument bags. With him, a big guy wrapped up in a thick jacquard vest which makes him look like a polar explorer: Elvin Jones. A young man of distinguished appearance carefully handles a contrabass, it's Bob Cunningham. And still behind them: little Leo Wright, McCoy Tyner accompanied by his wife. Reggie Workman and two white men whose heads are covered by Tyrolean hats. The bigger one, who looks British and is wearing glasses, is Mel Lewis. The other speaks French well, with a slight Spanish accent, Lalo Schifrin. Once the customs formalities are fulfilled, everyone gets back together and heads toward the bus reserved for bringing the passengers to Paris. Oh! I forgot the one whose presence overshadows this J.A.T.P. [Jazz at the Philharmonic] 1961 with a particular prestige: John Coltrane. He is, good heavens, so sober, so discreet, that one would easily take him for a passenger just like all the others. On first contact, he establishes a certain distance, and weariness can be read on his face. Having gone to bed at 3 or 4 in the morning, after having played all evening and gotten up three hours later to wait in an airport is no fun. I tell him that his concerts are being awaited impatiently

From *Jazz Magazine* (France), January 1962, pages 21–25. Translated by John B. Garvey.

in Paris and that his recent records have been very successful. Being precise, he asks, "Has *My Favorite Things* come out? It hasn't come out in England yet." In fact, it's better to know the latest of Coltrane's recordings, or else it might happen that the public would announce their surprise vehemently. And Coltrane is the first to know it; later, I'll learn that he remembers very well the welcome that he received in Paris two years ago.

I find myself next to Lalo Schifrin: "I learned French during my stay in Paris from '54 to '57. I studied at the Conservatory." The Argentine pianist is clearly very happy to find himself in France again, and especially to be able to speak French. [. . .] From time to time bursts of laughter interrupt our conversation. Dizzy, who seems completely oblivious to fatigue, is having a good time. He even manages to mock Coltrane who is half asleep in his seat. When we arrive at the Porte d'Italie, Dizzy exclaims with a fake emotion and a sincere pleasure: "Ah! Paris." We arrive at the hotel at last. Coltrane goes to his room and expresses the desire to not move again before 5 p.m. The two drummers, who seem as thick as thieves, decide to take the air on the Champs (Elysées).

Coming out of the restaurant, Schifrin and Dolphy hurry off to a record store. Works by Erik Satie and Olivier Messiaen for Dolphy; Berg, Boulez and Messiaen too for Schifrin. The latter tells me about his attraction to this music; he is very interested in the studies of the dodecaphonists regarding composition. "What do I think of Coltrane? That's a hard question. He's a great musician, that goes without saying. But to claim that I understand exactly what he's doing would be lying. He is so personal. He works so much; I think he has preoccupations with the sound issues, in the sense that, in order to express himself better he must reach a rare mastery of the sonic element, which is both difficult and thankless. And as a listener, I appreciate what makes him greatly superior to other moderns—his musicality. I believe that it is very important to stay musical."

Coltrane is having problems with his shirt collar, one of whose buttons has just popped off. While he's changing, he shows me a letter, which he just received, on the table. A New York impresario is telling him that he has organized on his own an interview with Ravi Shankar. He's an Indian musician who recorded an album for World Pacific (WP 1248), bringing together his most famous compositions: *Raga pouria Danashri* or *Kafi Holi*. Trane, who takes great interest in every form of folk music, is happy and flattered by this meeting.[1] In the car which brings us to the Olympia, Coltrane tells me about his latest recordings produced for Impulse, live at the Village Vanguard, with the same personnel as the Parisian concerts.

I don't really know who graciously warned me that Trane was an unapproachable man, distracted, refusing to respond to his questioners. For a man reputed to be harsh, I found him rather talkative. Imagine that in a half-day, he was interviewed by a journalist from Radio-Beromunster, by Postif, and that he chatted with me for several hours, and that he finally had a conversation with the American critic Marc Crawford!

Trane recalled his last visit to the Olympia: "I was very uncomfortable. I don't see what they found so extraordinary in what I played; for me, it definitely wasn't." This reminded me of an interview with John Lewis. When I expressed to him the interest that everyone had in Thelonious Monk, the avant-garde musician, the musical director of M.J.Q. [Modern Jazz Quartet] smiled quietly: "Of the avant-garde? You seem to be unaware, young man, that Monk's music is not at all revolutionary; it is beautiful and classic, that's all." I then talked to Coltrane about Cannonball but that was, I realized, preaching to the choir, since I was aware of the admiration that he has for Johnny Hodges. We also discussed American critics. "I like what Bill Mathieu does in *Down Beat*," said Coltrane. "Of course, what he writes is fairly technical but, you know, that's what interests me." Then I asked him what direction he was looking to deepen especially if, for example, he was still working on harmonies. "Right now I don't have a very specific direction, but I think that I'm rather oriented toward melodies." I come back to the concert two years ago.[2] "They told me that it was Miles who asked you to play as 'modern' as possible, claiming that the audience liked novelty." Coltrane stifled a silent laugh: "Miles? Say something like that to me? That's a good one! No, Miles would never have said anything like that to me. I played exactly the way I wanted to." And I sincerely believe that even if he wanted to, Trane couldn't do anything but play what he felt he had to play.

While Dizzy played, in the second part of the first concert, I was privileged to attend an interview that Trane gave to the Radio-Beromunster reporter. Questioned on the classic problem of influences, he stated: "I think that the one who influenced me the most, at the beginning, was Lester Young. Much more than Hawkins. I didn't discover the latter until after Parker, in a way 'reviewed and corrected' by Parker."

I'm not quite sure if this is still important, since Trane is probably one of the most individualistic musicians around, which is different than certain individualists who wish to be musicians! Even when he talks about everything that Monk taught him, one must understand that it's a matter of technique. The source of his inspiration is deeply original and in direct relation to his synaesthesia. This explains why he sets himself up with so many questions. As for me, I suspect at least that Trane, throughout our conversations, had an accent of sincerity which is not inclined to trick.

Coltrane's personality, as far as I was able to approach him, is a vivid antithesis to the intellectualized portrait that some have tried to paint of him. There is nothing more natural, more instinctive than his preoccupations and the lenses that he views them through. And still, I recognize that if there is a music that lends itself to commentary, it is absolutely this one. Listening to the radio rebroadcasts of the concerts from the 18th of November, I was even more impressed by the flagrant contradiction between the music I heard and the man that I saw living through a good half-day. One might object that several hours aren't enough to claim to know the character or the personality of an individual. That's true, but I'm convinced that there is something originally organic in Trane's music. And, in this, I deeply disagree with the opinion of Jean-Louis Chautemps about the record *My Favorite Things*. Forgetful of the liberation of the individual through sound and musical projection from one's deep being, Coltrane? Without being a psychoanalyst, it seems to me that it's just the opposite. And when he shows himself preoccupied by the formal and technical sides, it is precisely in order to achieve a liberation and more complete expression. To the point where I wonder if one couldn't classify him as a musically modern Faust or Prometheus.

Between the two concerts, we returned to Trane's hotel. I asked Coltrane how he had reacted to all his "triumphs" in the international polls: "That's a question I have a hard time answering. In fact, I don't place any more importance than they deserve on those polls in terms of being liable to categorization. But, in any case, this makes me aware of being surrounded by a certain number of people who give me confidence and whom I mustn't disappoint, in order to, somehow, prove to them my gratitude. But since that happened to me without me wanting it personally, I can't sacrifice my personal researches for the satisfaction of my fans. Honestly, this isn't possible, that would be cheating. And really, I couldn't. I've had too many problems in following my evolution, on a technical level, to stop along the road under the pretext that it would make a pretty good number of people happy. There are still lots of things I want to do, everything I still have to want, and that's to find people who will like my music throughout my evolution. That way, they'll allow me to pursue my studies on the material level. I'll tell you again, I believe that it wouldn't be honest to stop just because I've found a broad enough audience to be well placed in the polls. And still, I've been very happy to see that I could 'touch' a broad public, since I've always had to resolve the problem of communication with my listeners. Regarding that, I suppose that it's pointless to tell you how much I admire Dizzy Gillespie. I have to prove to them that they're right to have confidence in me and, of course, that's all that I hope to be able to do."

John Coltrane's diet, at least in Paris, seemed austere to me: it is essentially vegetarian. He wants to lose weight. Thus it was over a cup of tea that we talked while we waited for François Postif, the king of the Parisian interviewers. Coltrane took a guitar out of a case and started playing chords. "I bought it in Glasgow, since my hotel neighbors complained that I was making too much noise when I practiced the saxophone. It's a lovely instrument. I really like what Wes Montgomery does. Do you know that he played in my group when we were in San Francisco? At the Monterey [Jazz] Festival, we also played with Wes. You can say that the people who heard us were really lucky, especially since I was the one who paid, but I don't regret it; it was really worth it!"

Then I bring up the question of his recordings. Among the first ones he made, he recalls a quartet session with Tadd Dameron, *Mating Call* (Prestige, 7070, unfortunately out of print). "I was very satisfied with *My Favorite Things* [Atlantic U.S. 1361, sold in France]. Right away, I was convinced that it would be impossible for us to ever do better; today, I don't claim that we will never take it back up again, at least not for now. Yes, I know the Jazzland album [*Thelonious Monk with John Coltrane*] on which you can find several tracks that I did with Monk in 1957; they're not bad but, unfortunately, they're nothing compared to what we did at that time at the Five Spot."

Trane then shows me a book that he brought with him, *Since Debussy* by André Hodeir in the original edition (Evergreen Books, Grove Press, NY; out in France from the Presses Universitaires de France). "This is a very good book. I regret that I don't have a very deep classical music culture, but I'm correcting that gap." I assure him that with Dolphy along in the stages of his education, he found a perfect initiator. I also talk to him about Schifrin: he respects him a lot, and he appreciates many of his musical qualities even if, as you might imagine, they're not the same ideas. As for Elvin Jones: "I'm very happy to have hired him; I think he's extraordinary and I hope to keep him with me for a long time, even more so because he is quite unknown and underestimated. And we get along very well. I'm also very happy with McCoy Tyner whom I've known for a long time; I noticed him when I was still in Philadelphia and I promised myself that I would get in touch with him if I ever formed my own group."

Enter Postif, tape recorder under his arm. Curtain . . .

Notes

1. Coltrane became friends with Ravi Shankar; they met on occasion, over the years, as their schedules allowed. Shankar told Yasuhiro Fujioka, "Each time [we met] he came to my hotel. For two to three hours we sat down, he asked me questions, he wrote notes. He never brought [his] instrument, I never had [my] sitar, but I was telling him basic things about raga, how we improvise, the meaning of raga, the spiritual quantity" (Ravi Shankar, interview by Yasuhiro Fujioka, Sankei Hall, Osaka, Japan, February 6, 1998).

2. The Miles Davis Quintet was at the Olympia on March 21, 1960.

"JOHN COLTRANE: AN INTERVIEW"

François Postif

Coltrane gave several interviews on November 18, 1961, in Paris (see the preceding article). In this interview he once again goes over his career, but he also drops a few interesting tidbits along the way.

John Coltrane is certainly the most modest and agreeable musician that I have ever had the pleasure of interviewing. His answers are direct, unemotional but also not evasive, and they are always presented objectively, as if there is nothing personal.

One thing that happened between us, a little adventure which I want to relate: John Coltrane is on a diet, and, what's more, a bit of a vegetarian. After the 6 o'clock concert, since he was hungry, we go into a grocery store on Rue Caumartin [a narrow street adjacent to the Olympia] that specializes in serving the stars between shows. John takes a few lettuce leaves here and there, a few hazelnuts, and breaks an egg to eat it right there. He also asks for some fresh spinach to get his strength back, but, faced with the canned variety, refuses. I turn back toward the street: the concert had just ended, and we were walled in by two or three hundred fans demanding that Coltrane come out of the shop. The grocer, a very admirable man for whom this wasn't the first such occasion, talks about kicking the fans' butts and draws the bolt on the door.

We barely got out of it, John and I, thanks to the calmness of the grocer whom I wish to publicly praise here. But I tell this story simply to say that a musician who was booed in 1959 [sic; March 21, 1960] during the Miles Davis tour might very well find himself two years later with several hundred fans waiting to demand his autograph. When I spoke to him about his previous tour, he tells me: "But there

From *Jazz Hot* (France), January 1962, pages 12–14. Translated by John B. Garvey; additional material translated by Lewis Porter.

were boos at this concert as well, I heard them perfectly; it's not pleasant, of course, but at least it proves that one is a musician being talked about."

I find him again, friendly and relaxed, in his room at Claridge, squeezing a few oranges and eating several lettuce leaves.

"I was born on the 23rd of September, 1926, in Hamlet, North Carolina. My family loved music and my father played the violin very well. I was an only child, but I was raised with one of my cousins whom I think of as a sister and for whom I wrote 'Mary's Blues' and especially 'Cousin Mary.' At first, I played alto, I'm not too sure why, especially because I admired Lester Young at that time. That was in 1944, but I wasn't planning on becoming a professional musician. I learned things bit by bit, almost by chance, without any planning, just enough to play one or two tunes. I wanted to jump ahead. In any case, our school didn't have an orchestra, but had a sort of community center where we went to spend our free time. That 'Youth Group' was the responsibility of a minister who knew how to play a bunch of instruments, but who didn't have a lot of time to teach us. However, we formed a group in which each of us played a piece that he knew well—which caused each of us to limit his familiarity to one or two pieces. Those were my first contacts—if one can say that—with music.

"This was something new for me, and I threw myself into it body and soul. This was in 1944, and my favorite instrumentalist was Johnny Hodges. I wonder if today I play the soprano saxophone simply to follow in the footsteps of Johnny Hodges, unconsciously, naturally.

"My first real 'job' was one I had in Philadelphia in 1945, where I played with a pianist and a guitarist. It was a kind of cocktail music, but it kept me alive! Then, after accompanying Big Maybelle for a time, I got in with King Kolax. It was a big band, and since Kolax had played trumpet in Billy Eckstein's big band with Dizzy Gillespie, you can imagine that we didn't play rhythm and blues.

"I really liked that band, which really was my 'school.' But at that time, I wanted to arrange. We even recorded one of my pieces, 'True Blues,' for a small label out of Los Angeles!

"I didn't stay with King Kolax very long; I moved on right away to Eddie 'Cleanhead' Vinson, the blues singer. Since he played alto, I started on tenor (I didn't take up the alto again until 1949, with Dizzy). That happened in 1947.

"When I left Eddie Vinson, in 1948,[1] I played in Harlem, in the Apollo band. We were part of a band that accompanied blues singers and vocal groups, but I also had the opportunity to solo, and I have to say that, since we were playing fairly modern things, the reactions of the audiences were quite favorable. Bop had been accepted very quickly by this exclusively black public.

"Before joining up with Dizzy, I played in Philadelphia with Howard McGhee, Jimmy Heath and Philly Joe Jones.[2] Then I joined up with Dizzy because of a recommendation from his pianist.

"I stayed with Diz for a year and a half or two years, from 1949 to 1951. This was Dizzy's crazy time, when he was trying to find a new public by playing a kind of rhythm and blues in his own way, with [singer] Joe Carroll. It was really fun, but I don't know if what we were doing was appreciated enough!

"See, I stayed in obscurity for a long time, because I was happy to play what was expected of me, without trying to add anything. I saw so many guys get fired from bands because they tried new things that I was somewhat disgusted to try anything else! I think that it was with Miles Davis, in 1955, that I started to realize what else I could do.

"Miles is sort of a strange guy: he doesn't talk a lot, and he rarely discusses music. You always have the impression that he's in a bad mood, and that he's not interested in or affected by what other people are doing. It's very hard, in a situation like that, to know exactly what you should do, and maybe it's because of that that I started to do what I wanted.

"Monk is the exact opposite of Miles: he talks about music all the time, and he wants you to understand so much that, if by chance, you ask him anything, he'll spend hours if necessary to explain it to you. But Miles' reactions are completely unpredictable; he'd play a few measures with us, then go off no one knew where, leaving us alone. And if I asked him anything about his music, I never knew how he was going to take it. I always had to listen to him attentively to stay in tune with him.

"Naturally, I was extremely happy to hear that I would play with Monk, in the summer of 1957. I had always wanted to play with him, and this opportunity was unique: I remember that I had been practicing with him four or five months before the opening of the Five Spot, or else at the home of the Baroness Nica de Koenigswarter; we stayed there for the whole night, Monk explained a phrase or two to me on the piano, we listened to records, and the scotch flowed.

"We didn't have an official recording contract with the Five Spot, and that's too bad, but I console myself with the ones that my wife made on our tape recorder. She came with me and recorded all night. I listen to those tapes from time to time, and I have a bit of nostalgia! The only recordings that we made during that time were done in the studio, for Riverside and Jazzland.

"The critics, at that time, were all wrapped up in what we were doing, but you know, for a musician, it's difficult to take a stand on that; really, the only thing that mattered for me wasn't so much what I played but being able to play, and with Monk as well! We played like crazy, all night, and it was really fantastic.

"I used to have the habit of using really stiff reeds, number nines, because I especially wanted to have a broad, solid sound. And it was before I started playing with Monk that I tried out number fours. I realized quickly that number nine limited my possibilities by reducing my volume; with the fours, I could show an expressiveness that the nines had kept me from. Little things mean a lot! Obviously, with Monk, I had a great deal of freedom; from time to time Monk went off to have a drink and left us alone, Wilbur Ware, Shadow Wilson and me, on the stage at the Five Spot. And we improvised without any constraints for fifteen or twenty minutes, exploring our different instruments like madmen. I did the same thing last year at the Half Note;[3] I left my musicians playing while I went off to eat spaghetti. With that diet, I got very fat . . .

"With Monk, I got into the habit of playing a long time on each piece. And the fact of playing the same piece for a long time brought us to a new concept of solos; we only improvised very rarely on certain pieces. I'll explain to you the mechanics of these solos that never end; we have a certain number of given reference points, which indicate to us what should happen next. Obviously, it's not a question of always placing these reference points in the same place, but simply moving them around or even leaving them out sometimes. That's what creates the suspense: my musicians never know when I'm going to give them the cues! If we have to keep it short, I arrive immediately at a certain spot near the end of the piece; when I know that we can take our time, I may sometimes come back to one of the reference points. This method of operating permits us to never lose touch with the moment in our pieces, and to never be caught by surprise.

"Here's how I play: I take off from a point and I go as far as possible. But, hopefully, I'll never lose my way. I say hopefully, because what especially interests me is to discover the ways that I never suspected were possible. My phrasing isn't a simple prolongation of my musical ideas, and I'm happy that my technique permits me to go very far in this domain, but I must add that it's always in a very conscious manner. I 'localize'—that is to say that I think always in a given area. It infrequently happens that I think of the totality of a solo, and very briefly: I always return to the little fraction of the solo that I'm involved in playing. Chords have become something of an obsession for me, which gives me the impression that I'm looking at the music through the wrong end of the binoculars.

"Many people think wrongly that 'My Favorite Things' is one of my compositions; I would love to have written it, but it's by Rodgers and Hammerstein. This piece is constructed, through several measures, on two harmonies, but we've drawn out those harmonies in order to perform it and make it last. In fact, we've stretched those two harmonies through the whole piece. (We did the same thing with another piece, 'Ev'ry Time We Say Goodbye.') 'My Favorite Things' is my favorite piece of everything we've recorded; I don't think I'd like to redo it in any other way, although all the other records I've done could be improved by a few details. This waltz is fantastic: when you play it slowly, it has a 'gospel' aspect, which is not at all unpleasant; when you play it fast, it has certain other undeniable qualities. It's very interesting to discover a terrain that renews itself according to the impulse that you give it; that's the reason why we don't always play this tune in the same tempo.

"You accuse my rhythm section of lacking a bit of cohesion; [you should] admit that the acoustics in the Olympia didn't particularly favor me. But you're right, in one sense; Miles Davis' rhythm section, with Wynton Kelly, Paul Chambers and Jimmy Cobb, certainly did better. See, a bassist of the stature of Paul Chambers is hard to find in New York, because he finds the groove; he listens to the piano and the drums, and all his work consists of improvising based on those instruments. His melodic line is a sort of result of the melodic lines of the two other musicians. And even though I can't particularly complain about my current bassist, Reggie Workman, he hasn't yet reached that level of maturity.

"At the beginning of my collaboration with Elvin, I was very disoriented by the way he was playing, which was completely different from other drummers. I had to accept it, and now I'm caught up in Elvin's playing. What he needs is a bassist who is a 'force of nature,' because he plays so loudly that if you don't respond to him with the same authority you're practically drowned out. With Elvin, you also have to have a flexible bassist, because he often plays ahead of the beat; you have to able to follow him and anticipate him at the same time. It's very hard, and right now I don't know of a single available bassist who can do that. Maybe Wilbur Ware, but he's so available that nobody knows what's happened to him!

"I have several problems with this quartet, but I think I can fix them pretty quickly. We rehearse very little, only for recording sessions, and that's not enough. As a rule, I prefer recording pieces that I'm used to playing live, because I know in advance the reactions of the audience and, on the other hand, everything comes together in the recording studio.

"What I'm going to tell you is maybe going to seem weird to you, but I don't like experiments that much. For example, I would really not like to make a record with Charlie Mingus right now simply because his music is not familiar to me, and I'm not sure I understand all his theories. I'm not saying that what we would do together would be a failure necessarily, no, and maybe the result would surprise both of us, but I have to say that the idea would not excite me, at least for the moment.

"Anyway, this kind of thing should happen by chance, without being planned out.

"On the other hand, there's a musician with whom I would love to make a record, an Indian [sitarist] named Ravi Shankar. I've been collecting his records, and his music excites me; I'm sure that, if I made a record with him, I would expand my possibilities to the tenth power, since I'm familiar with what he's done and I understand and appreciate his work. I plan to meet him once I'm back in the United States.

"See, if you want to achieve interesting things in the musical sphere, you have to be really familiar with and appreciate the people that you play with. I feel bad for Eric Dolphy, since I wrote all my arrangements to play them with a quartet and the addition of a fifth voice doesn't give him much opportunity, right now, to become a star. But I really like what Eric does, and I want him to shine in my quintet. Looking at it more closely, I should have kept my quartet the way you heard it in New York, and added a fifth voice after I had written some new arrangements.

"It bothers me to have done it this way, but I had to decide quickly for the European tour, and I thought that we would have more diversity with a fifth voice. I recently made an album for Impulse with the quintet, and you'll see that it's more intense than what you heard in concert.

"To get back to the musicians that interest you, the person with whom I would most like to make a record is Ornette Coleman. I've only played with him one time in my life; I went to hear him in a club and he asked me to join him. We played two pieces—exactly twelve minutes—but I think this was definitely the most intense moment of my life!

"I'm just starting to understand his work with four voices, without a piano. When I played with Monk, four years ago, I played many times without a piano: Monk, as I said before, after two pieces, would return to the dressing room or even stand looking out the window for two or three hours. So, we played without a piano; however, I personally prefer to play with a pianist, because he gives you a certain support, but not when the pianist is named Cecil Taylor! I've played with Cecil. It's much too complicated.

"My current pianist, McCoy Tyner, holds down the harmonies and that allows me to forget them. He's sort of the one who gives me wings and lets me take off from the ground from time to time."

Notes

1. Coltrane's dates are off a bit here; he joined Vinson in late 1948 and stayed with him well into 1949.
2. Coltrane played with Howard McGhee (who had taken over Jimmy Heath's big band) in 1948, before his stint with Eddie Vinson.
3. Coltrane is referring to an October 1960 Half Note gig in New York that Postif attended (see "New York in Jazz Time," by François Postif, *Jazz Hot*, December 1960, page 25).

INTERVIEW WITH JOHN COLTRANE

Claes Dahlgren

Not a lot is known about this interview fragment (the surviving tape is about 3 minutes and 45 seconds long). The interviewer is believed to be Claes Dahlgren, a Swedish journalist who wrote for *Orkester Journalen*. In this segment, Coltrane discusses his concept of rhythm and the use of two bassists in the band.

John Coltrane: Well that's just the way that I—I naturally feel that way, you know?

Claes Dahlgren: Uh huh.

Coltrane: There's very little I can do about it. [*laughs*] Couldn't change it if I wanted to. But it is necessary to have a firm beat going, but it's not necessary to have everyone playing 4/4—I mean, you know, *rigidly*. But, between the three men, or the two men in the rhythm section, it should be enough interplay to give you at every point of the song the same solidarity that you get in 4/4, but it won't—it'll be implied sometimes instead of actually played. This thing is—it can be done, you know, and sometimes it is done, but it has to be the right combination of individuals playing and if they really feel this way, and they have to have—very good sounds, they have to be, be able to produce good quality sounds on the instrument, so when they, when they *do* play, and what they play, it will sustain, will be sustained, you know, and thus, and thus create this level thing underneath, although it'll be broken, actually, as it's played.

Dahlgren: You said earlier that you first had to experiment with, with chords and so on—

Coltrane: Yeah, that was—

Dahlgren: —but then you wanted to get—go into the rhythm thing.

Coltrane: Yeah.

Dahlgren: And now maybe you've done it. Is that right?

Coltrane: Well, I don't know, when I was speaking of that, I was speaking as a solo-ist, I wanted to do this. And, as a soloist, I need to extend my playing some, and to play in different ways, instead of just one way—from a harmonic standpoint. I should also play from a rhythmic basis, and some, some things, in solos, should be based on melodic principles—I mean, you know, from melodic sources. And then there should be combinations of everything, you know, and to make every-thing richer and more full. And also, the *band itself* should be conducted like this, you know, like, good bands—and I've noticed they do some of everything, you know—they don't just play in one vein all the time; they cover the whole musical scope. And, well, I'm learning, you know, trying to learn as I go, and that's what I need to do: I need to be able to incorporate all of the—every facet in music.

Dahlgren: On the Stateside, I think you had two bassists at one time.

Coltrane: Sometimes. Yeah, there were times when I used two.

Dahlgren: And how does this, how does this thing work? You play—

Coltrane: Well, the bass, the other bass, is used in a percussive sense, you know. It's sort of like—used as a—it's a sound like between a drum and a bass. It's like a drum, but melodious, you know—little melodic thing going—and it fills in some of the spaces that are left open, you know? In some of these songs that we've played with a drone bass, you know, we use in some tunes a drone bass line. And the other bass, playin' in between, fills it in, and if they get the right counterplay and interplay going, it sounds, maybe sounds like one thing moving along—you know, you get a more solid pulse on it, you know. I've used Art Davis. Art Davis is a great rhythmic instrumentalist, because he can play against whatever Reggie's playing underneath. He plays high, in the high register and he's pretty good at it. On some of the songs, it's very effective.

"JAZZMAN OF THE YEAR: JOHN COLTRANE"

Barbara Gardner

This article appeared in *Down Beat*'s annual yearbook for 1962, after Coltrane topped several of the magazine's popularity polls for 1961. (The 1962 yearbook was published in late 1961 or early 1962, so Gardner probably interviewed Coltrane sometime in mid- or late 1961.) Despite an alarmingly melodramatic first paragraph, the article quickly shifts gears and becomes a particularly interesting overview of Coltrane's music and career. It also includes observations from a number of his musical associates.

He walked a fast trail of self-destruction for much of his early adulthood. By the time he was 31, he had about physically and spiritually burned himself out, and he just lay there, smoldering in deterioration. One day in 1957, he made up his mind to "get some fun out of life for a change." He rose out of the ashes of his life to become one of the most controversial contributors to modern jazz . . . John Coltrane.

John William Coltrane was born on September 23, 1926, in Hamlet, North Carolina. He was an only child. When he was still an infant, his parents moved to High Point, N.C. There was nothing spectacular about their life there. His father, a tailor, saw his son enjoying music as he himself did. The Coltrane home was filled with musical instruments. In time, young John learned to play clarinet, alto saxophone, and ukelele.[1]

When Coltrane was 12, his father died, leaving him little but a love of music. The high school he attended did not have a school band, but he played alto saxophone and clarinet in a community center band after school.

In 1943, Coltrane and his mother moved to Philadelphia.[2] He continued his studies at Granoff Studios and Ornstein School of Music. In 1945, he entered the

From *Down Beat's Music 1962—The 7th Annual Yearbook*, pages 66–69.

Navy, serving in Hawaii, where he played in a Navy Band. He was discharged in the middle of the following year.

A quiet, introspective musician of 21, who had never played the tenor saxophone in his life, John Coltrane was hired on tenor by Eddie (Cleanhead) Vinson. Pianist Red Garland, who was working with Vinson at the time, was instrumental in getting him the job. Coltrane objected mildly that he was an altoist but made the switch without trauma.

The multinote soloist of today is in direct contrast to the shy, reluctant instrumentalist of the late '40s.

"Yeah, little ol' Coltrane used to be in my band," Vinson remembers with a paternal smile. "He never wanted to play. I used to have to play all night long. I'd ask him, 'Man, why don't you play?' He'd say, 'I just want to hear you play.'"

It was partly sincere admiration that made the newcomer hesitate to play in the presence of the pros, but much of the reluctance could be attributed to the stage of his development, which he alone knew. There was little individuality or personal creation in his early playing.

"At that time, I was trying to play like Dexter Gordon and Wardell Gray," Coltrane said. "I liked what they were doing. I heard in them lots of the ideas of Lester Young, who was my first influence. So when I made the switch to tenor, I was trying to play like them."

In 1949, Coltrane began accumulating jazz experience with the giants. He joined the Dizzy Gillespie big band as an altoist. Later he was to work in a Gillespie combo playing tenor. About the time of his first Gillespie stay, the fleeting, biting tenor of Sonny Stitt caught his ear. Again, the exploring musician attempted to find his direction in another man's course.

"Sonny's playing sounded like something I would like to do," Coltrane recalled. "He sounded like something between Dexter and Wardell, an outgrowth of both of them. All the time, I thought I had been looking for something and then I heard Sonny and said, 'Damn! There it is! That's it!'"

And he thought it was and set about developing that brand of tenor playing that drew on Lester Young and Charlie Parker for its chief points of departure. He was more than competent in this style. Several jazzmen of stature kept an eye on him. In turn, he was snapped up by Earl Bostic, Johnny Hodges, Jimmy Smith, and in 1957 [sic; 1955], Miles Davis. He left Davis briefly to work with

Thelonious Monk in 1958 [*sic*; 1957] but returned later the same year [Coltrane probably rejoined Davis in January 1958].

With Davis, the bubble of false security burst, and Coltrane again was forced to view those repressed aspirations for musical freedom and individuality.

"I began trying to add to what I was playing because of Miles's group," he said. "Being there, I just couldn't be satisfied any longer with what I was doing. The standards were so high, and I felt that I wasn't really contributing like I should."

Then he added a thought that reflects his concern for musical truth:

"About this time, I got the recording contract with Prestige, and I decided that if I was going to put anything on record, then it ought to be me."

This was the beginning of the emergence of John Coltrane as one of the most individual of musicians.

Once the decision was made, Coltrane wasted no time in beginning at the core of his frustrations. He put his mental and physical health on the mend by stopping two destructive habits—alcoholism and narcotics addiction—simultaneously and immediately. Not only was this the turning point in John Coltrane's life, it reflected the great inner strength of the man.

"He never clarified his direction, verbally," remembers Cannonball Adderley, who worked with him in the Davis group. "He did suggest that he was going to change all around, both personally and musically.

"All of a sudden, he decided that he was going to change the John Coltrane image. Along with changing the physical and spiritual things, he encountered Monk along the way musically, and played with him for near a year. I'm sure that he heard a lot of things he's playing now, even back then."

Then Adderley expressed a prevalent admiration for the strength of conviction that led to Coltrane's musical direction:

"You've got to hand it to him, you know. In the middle of a successful career, Coltrane decided that he wasn't playing anything and made up his mind to go ahead and develop something that had been in the back of his mind all along."

There was no outside influence demanding that Coltrane move on from his comfortable, accepted position as a rising young tenor man in the pattern of Gordon, Gray, and Stitt. He was being accepted, even welcomed, on this basis. Adderley describes the Coltrane of the Miles Davis era as "not so much commercially successful, as commercially acceptable. He played quite a few solos back then that the hippie-in-the-street began to hum. I challenge them to hum some of his solos now."

Exactly what the spark was that ignited Coltrane into new flamboyant motion is yet unknown, even to the reed man himself. Adderley attributes part of the answer to the acceptance being given Sonny Rollins.

"Coltrane had appeared on most of the commercially successful records with Miles Davis, and his material was becoming more and more popular," Adderley said. "People were beginning to say 'John Coltrane' with some degree of serious feeling about it. At that time also, Sonny Rollins had broken through with a little thing of his own in vogue, and I guess John thought that the time was right for him to start fooling around with his own stuff."

If Sonny Rollins can be referred to as a fresh breath of wind in the static tenor scene, then the post-1958 Coltrane must be regarded as a tornado.

He bombarded the listener with a rapid-fire succession of 16th notes; long, apparently unrelated lines; interchanging, reversible five-note chords; and constantly altering tone. Some charged he was repetitious. He played an idea over and over, turning the notes around in every possible combination, summoning every imaginable tone from his instrument, trying to coax out of the horn the thing he felt, trying to attain that certain feeling that would tell him that he was on the right track.

"I work a lot by feeling," Coltrane still admits. "I just have to feel it. If I don't, then I keep trying."

This musical and physical renaissance was not without its outside problems and disappointments. Coltrane found that to be different and distinctive, to dare to step outside the pale of the accepted, overworked pattern of tenor playing was to inspire, most often, the wrath of those writers and listeners who complained loudest about the clichés and imitation existing in tenor playing at that time.

Coltrane's repetition and constant trial and error reaped criticism from within the charmed music circle as well. Musicians occasionally cloaked in criticism their admiration for his daring.

Adderley remembers that occasionally Miles Davis would question Coltrane about his long solos:

"Once in a while, Miles might say, 'Why you play so long, man?' and John would say, 'It took that long to get it all in.' And Miles would accept that, really. Miles never bothered anybody much about what to play or how to play it."

Initially, much of the jazz world laughed. This man could not be serious, was the attitude even though there perhaps never has been a jazzman with a greater reputation for sobriety about his work. Coltrane never deviated from his newly charted course.

"He was serious about everything—everything he played," Adderley says. "Where sometimes Miles would take on some humor in his playing—or lots of times I might feel lighter than usual—John was heavily involved with being just serious and musical, all the time."

Donald Garrett, a Chicago musician who works with Coltrane as the second bassist[3] occasionally, has said:

"He is a meticulous musician. He will often play a tune seven or eight different ways before he decides on just how he wants to play it."

Coltrane's wife, Juanita, remembers that during the early period of experimentation, Coltrane sometimes would woodshed for 24 hours straight without food or sleep. He stopped only when he was physically unable to practice anymore. And when he was too exhausted to play, he talked music.

Gradually, the first wave of critical laughter passed and was replaced by a general outrage or a sophisticated mockery. Writers articulate in their craft referred to him as an "angry young tenor," to his sound as "the bark of a dog," to his ideas as "epileptic fits of passion."

One compassionate writer, Ira Gitler, in 1958 described Coltrane's playing as "sheets of sound," and in *Jazz Review* Mimi Clar elaborated on this years later to describe the saxophonist's music as "yards of accordion-pleated fabric hastily flung from the bolt."

When Coltrane's name was breathed in the same context as Charlie Parker's, one writer retorted, "Charlie Parker's playing is like an electric fan being switched on and off; Coltrane's playing is like an electric fan being turned on and left."

There were a few Coltrane champions in those days, but they were almost consumed in the raging heat of controversy. By 1960, the general attitude of most jazz writers and listeners was succinctly expressed in a Martin Williams record review:

". . . Patience for all may be the best thing to suggest. When the plant is growing, it doesn't do to keep pulling it up to look at the roots."

Following this metaphoric admonition, most jazz listeners, professional and otherwise, settled back to await the maturation of the "angry young tenor." The wait has not been a quiet or uneventful one. In April 1960, Coltrane formed his own combo. Since that time, he has changed personnel and instrumentation often in his search for new sounds and new musical concepts.

"John is one of the most brilliant jazz musicians of all times because he has the rare combination of originality and the ability to make profound decisions, musically," Adderley said. "By profound decisions, I mean that he can think of so many things to play, a whole variety of things, before he plays anything; and he can instantly make a good selection from this wide choice. He is a brilliant soloist, but he is also a good, original, all-around musician. His concept is altogether different.

"He has a tremendous influence and will have on the young tenor players coming up now. He is a definite departure. I don't mean that he was a radical departure from the tenor played by, say, Coleman Hawkins because there were some radical departures before him. But there was a generally accepted, established style of play that was a mixture of Charlie Parker, Dexter Gordon, Lester Young, and some of Coleman Hawkins' style. And John decided, all of a sudden, that although he was one of the most successful of these modern jazz players, that wasn't good enough for him."

A well-discussed departure that Coltrane has made from the accepted jazz pattern has been the addition of a second bassist.

Young Garrett maintains that this is an idea Coltrane had toyed with for several years. Garrett himself takes credit for having interested Coltrane in the idea.

"Well, we have been friends since 1955, and whenever he is in town, he comes over to my house and we go over ideas," Garrett said.

"I had this tape where I was playing with another bass player. We were doing some things rhythmically, and Coltrane became excited about the sound. We got the same kind of sound you get from the East Indian water drum. One bass remains in the lower register and is the stabilizing, pulsating thing, while the other bass is free to improvise, like the right hand would be on the drum. So Coltrane liked the idea."

To Garrett, Coltrane represents more than a successful tenor man.

"Coltrane has individual freedom without sacrifice of musical message," he said. "He just proves that if you've really got something to say, you don't have to cheat."

The bassist is too good a musician not to recognize and acknowledge many of the early limitations of the renovated saxophonist. But Garrett has a simple and sympathetic explanation:

"He just had a sound in his head that he couldn't get out of his horn. His direction has always been the same. He is just getting able to express it better. Just like Sonny Rollins. When Sonny started, he used to squeak a lot. He was just trying to play what he heard in his head. Any time one is an innovator, there are lots of defects in the early playing because nobody's ever tried it before."

Coltrane says that he plans to continue extending his harmonic growth, but, at the same time, he does not turn his back on rhythmic developments. He wrote in 1960, "I want to be more flexible where rhythm is concerned. I feel I have to study rhythm some more. I haven't experimented too much with time; most of my experimenting has been in a harmonic form. I put time and rhythm to one side, in the past."

Others recognize rhythmic development as one of Coltrane's most fertile areas.

"His growth has to be basically rhythmic," said bassist Garrett. "His harmonic conception will be limited until his rhythmic concept is fully developed. This is one of the reasons for his success now. He is extending in all rhythmic directions which give him more area for climactic development."

For all practical purposes, Coltrane has arrived. No one is asking for further extension from him. Perfect that which you have introduced, he is asked today. Coltrane himself surveys his lot and answers in confusion:

"I haven't found it yet. I'm listening all the time, but I haven't found it."

Where is it? What is it? How will he know it when he has it?

"I don't know what I'm looking for," he answers frankly. "Something that hasn't been played before. I don't know what it is. I know I'll have that feeling when I get it. I'll just keep searching."

Two years ago, Coltrane said he had something "that I'm afraid to play. People won't let me get away with it."

"I don't remember what I was talking about specifically," he says now. "I guess I must have tried them already. I've gone through all the things I used to want to do. Some I liked and am still working on. Others I had to set aside."

Restless and discontented, he says he does not feel dissatisfied with his present contribution, but, at the same time, he does not feel completely satisfied. He still feels the tenacious tug of incompleteness that spurred him to walk away from his "commercial acceptance" in 1957 and begin moving in a more self-satisfying direction. But he knows no guaranteed answers to fulfillment.

"I just can't seem to find the right songs," he said. "I'm listening everywhere. I listen to other groups, records, the men I work with, trying to find what I'm looking for. I learn a lot from the fellows in the group. Eric Dolphy is a hell of a musician, and he plays a lot of horn. When he is up there searching and experimenting, I learn a lot from him, but I just haven't found exactly what I want yet."

There is the obvious solution a musician can employ when available material ceases to provide the musical stimulus or outlet for expression.

"I just have to write the tunes myself," he said flatly, without any show of arrogance. "And I don't really want to take the time away from my horn. Writing has always been a secondary thing for me, but I find that lately I am spending more and more time at it, because I can't find the proper tunes."

Friends and associates closest to the quiet, withdrawn reed man are holding their breath, hoping that he begins to catch a glimpse of his elusive rainbow. There is perhaps not a bolder, more aggressive, more volitant tenor player anywhere among the leading musicians of today. The Coltrane experimental and effectual use of the soprano saxophone is held by many to be a further step in modern-jazz coloration. Yet his personal acquaintances are waiting for some sign of that abrupt, venturesome departure that hurtled Coltrane into the spotlight almost two years ago.

Some remarks are clothed in blind faith, and some rare speculation, like Adderley's: "You never know what he's going to do next. He may come out in a few months with a whole new thing."

Garrett observes with admiration, "He's always going to be new and fresh and ahead of everything. He isn't going to sacrifice anything. He's always learning, trying new things."

Eddie Vinson remembers from years back and repeats today, "That ol' boy was something. He changed his playing every six months almost. Even now, you never can tell what he's going to be playing six months from now."

Constant change, this is the basic characteristic with which John Coltrane has impressed every person who knows him well. And dedication to music—he lives and breathes music. An interview with Coltrane must be something like intruding into a human being's soul. His honest love and respect for his work and his unembarrassed humility in his current dilemma gush forth, almost unasked for. He seems to want to share his stalemate with the world in the faint hope that someone someplace might have a key to unlock for him the entire world of music.

Beyond the ambition to find "something," he has no further plan. At the moment he has no new ideas for further direction. He wants to improve and refine those he has. His next album may contain only material written by him. He is not sure, but he may or may not return the alto saxophone to his horn kit. This may help him to extend his harmonic development. One thing of which he is certain, he will definitely have to write more, whether he wants to or not.

In the meantime, he continues to pour into his craft a dedication born of intimate knowledge of neglect and its devastation. He does so even knowing that he is marking time, at least according to his own criteria. That much of the world hasn't caught up to his work is its problem. He does not want to bask in belated glory. Coltrane says he very well may be looking into the sinking sun and cannot feed on the plaudits of the late risers.

"I just want to play all I can," he said, almost desperately. "Sometimes an entertainer just has a certain span of productivity. I hope that never happens to me, but you never know, so I want to keep playing as long as I possibly can."

Notes

1. In several interviews Coltrane mentioned that his father played ukelele, but he never gave any indication that he also played the instrument. From what's known about Coltrane's childhood, it also seems that Coltrane never studied any instrument seriously until after his father's death.

2. It's well established that Coltrane's mother moved to Philadelphia before her son did; he didn't join her until after he graduated high school.

3. Low-fidelity recordings of radio broadcasts exist from the March 1961 Sutherland Lounge gig in Chicago, including one tune, "Equinox," on which Donald Garrett joined Reggie Workman as the second bassist.

"JOHN COLTRANE AND ERIC DOLPHY ANSWER THE JAZZ CRITICS"

Don DeMicheal

Don DeMicheal was an editor at *Down Beat* from 1961 to 1967. He played the vibraphone and drums, helped initiate the Chicago Jazz Festival, and was one of the cofounders—along with Art Hodes, Muhal Richard Abrams, Joe Segal, and Bob Koester—of the Jazz Institute of Chicago.

From 1958 to 1962 *Down Beat* ran five feature articles on Coltrane. By the time this one, the fifth, was published, Eric Dolphy was no longer a member of Coltrane's group (although he sat in on gigs with Coltrane several times over the next two years). This feature article was the last *Down Beat* would publish on Coltrane until after his death.

JOHN COLTRANE has been the center of critical controversy ever since he unfurled his sheets of sound in his days with Miles Davis. At first disparaged for his some-times involved, multinoted solos, Coltrane paid little heed and continued explor-ing music. In time, his harmonic approach—for the sheets were really rapid chord running, in the main—was accepted, even praised, by most jazz critics.

By the time critics had caught up with Coltrane, the tenor saxophonist had gone on to another way of playing. Coltrane II, if you will, was much concerned with linear theme development that seemed sculptured or torn from great blocks of granite. Little critical carping was heard of this second, architectural, Coltrane.

But Coltrane, an inquisitive-minded, probing musician, seemingly has left architecture for less concrete, more abstract means of expression. This third and present Coltrane has encountered an ever-growing block of criticism, much of it marked by a holy-war fervor.

From *Down Beat*, April 12, 1962, pages 20–23.

Criticism of Coltrane III is almost always tied in with Coltrane's cohort Eric Dolphy, a member of that group of musicians who play what has been dubbed the "new thing."

Dolphy's playing has been praised and damned since his national-jazz-scene arrival about two years ago. Last summer Dolphy joined Coltrane's group for a tour. It was on this tour that Coltrane and Dolphy came under the withering fire of *Down Beat* associate editor John Tynan, the first critic to take a strong—and public—stand against what Coltrane and Dolphy were playing.

In the Nov. 23, 1961, *Down Beat* Tynan wrote, "At Hollywood's Renaissance Club recently, I listened to a horrifying demonstration of what appears to be a growing anti-jazz trend exemplified by these foremost proponents [Coltrane and Dolphy] of what is termed avant-garde music.

"I heard a good rhythm section . . . go to waste behind the nihilistic exercises of the two horns. . . . Coltrane and Dolphy seem intent on deliberately destroying [swing]. . . . They seem bent on pursuing an anarchistic course in their music that can but be termed anti-jazz."

The anti-jazz term was picked up by Leonard Feather and used as a basis for critical essays of Coltrane, Dolphy, Ornette Coleman, and the "new thing" in general in *Down Beat* and *Show*.

The reaction from readers to both Tynan's and Feather's remarks was immediate, heated, and about evenly divided.

Recently, Coltrane and Dolphy agreed to sit down and discuss their music and the criticism leveled at it.

One of the recurring charges is that their performances are stretched out over too long a time, that Coltrane and Dolphy play on and on, past inspiration and into monotony.

Coltrane answered, "They're long because all the soloists try to explore all the avenues that the tune offers. They try to use all their resources in their solos. Everybody has quite a bit to work on. Like when I'm playing, there are certain things I try to get done and so does Eric and McCoy Tyner [Coltrane's pianist]. By the time we finish, the song is spread out over a pretty long time.

"It's not planned that way; it just happens. The performances get longer and longer. It's sort of growing that way."

But, goes the criticism, there must be editing, just as a writer must edit his work so that it keeps to the point and does not ramble and become boring.

Coltrane agreed that editing must be done—but for essentially a different reason from what might be expected.

"There are times," he said, "when we play places opposite another group, and in order to play a certain number of sets a night, you can't play an hour and a half at one time. You've got to play 45 or 55 minutes and rotate sets with the other band. And for those reasons, for a necessity such as that, I think it's quite in order that you edit and shorten things.

"But when your set is unlimited, timewise, and everything is really together musically—if there's continuity—it really doesn't make any difference how long you play.

"On the other hand, if there're dead spots, then it's really not good to play anything too long."

One of the tunes that Coltrane's group plays at length is "My Favorite Things," a song, as played by the group, that can exert an intriguingly hypnotic effect, though sometimes it seems too long.

Upon listening closely to him play "Things" on the night before the interview, it seemed that he actually played two solos. He finished one, went back to the theme a bit, and then went into another improvisation.

"That's the way the song is constructed," Coltrane said. "It's divided into parts. We play both parts. There's a minor and a major part. We improvise in the minor, and we improvise in the major modes."

Is there a certain length to the two modes?

"It's entirely up to the artist—his choice," he answered. "We were playing it at one time with minor, then major, then minor modes, but it was *really* getting too long—it was about the only tune we had time to play in an average-length set."

But in playing extended solos, isn't there ever present the risk of running out of ideas? What happens when you've played all your ideas?

"It's easy to stop then," Coltrane said, grinning. "If I feel like I'm just playing notes . . . maybe I don't feel the rhythm or I'm not in the best shape that I should be in when this happens. When I become aware of it in the middle of a solo, I'll try to build things to the point where this inspiration is happening again, where things are spontaneous and not contrived. If it reaches that point again, I feel it can continue—it's alive again. But if it doesn't happen, I'll just quit, bow out."

Dolphy, who had been sitting pixie-like as Coltrane spoke, was in complete agreement about stopping when inspiration had flown.

Last fall at the Monterey Jazz Festival, the Coltrane-Dolphy group was featured opening night. In his playing that night Dolphy at times sounded as if he were imitating birds. On the night before the interview some of Dolphy's flute solos brought Monterey to mind. Did he do this on purpose?

Dolphy smiled and said it was purposeful and that he had always liked birds. Is bird imitation valid in jazz?

"I don't know if it's valid in jazz," he said, "but I enjoy it. It somehow comes in as part of the development of what I'm doing. Sometimes I can't do it.

"At home [in California] I used to play, and the birds always used to whistle with me. I would stop what I was working on and play with the birds."

He described how bird calls had been recorded and then slowed down in playback; the bird calls had a timbre similar to that of a flute. Conversely, he said, a symphony flutist recorded these bird calls, and when the recording was played at a fast speed, it sounded like birds.

Having made his point about the connection of bird whistles and flute playing, Dolphy explained his use of quarter tones when playing flute.

"That's the way birds do," he said. "Birds have notes in between our notes— you try to imitate something they do and, like, maybe it's between F and F#, and you'll have to go up or come down on the pitch. It's really something! And so, when you get playing, this comes. You try to do some things on it. Indian music has something of the same quality—different scales and quarter tones. I don't know how you label it, but it's pretty."

THE QUESTION in many critics' minds, though they don't often verbalize it, is: What are John Coltrane and Eric Dolphy trying to do? Or: What *are* they doing?

Following the question a 30-second silence was unbroken except by Dolphy's, "That's a good question." Dolphy was first to try to voice his aims in music:

"What I'm trying to do I find enjoyable. Inspiring—what it makes me do. It helps me play, this feel. It's like you have no idea what you're going to do next. You have an idea, but there's always that spontaneous thing that happens. This feeling, to me, leads the whole group. When John plays, it might lead into something you had no idea could be done. Or McCoy does something. Or the way Elvin [Jones, drummer with the group] or Jimmy [Garrison, the bassist] play; they solo, they do something. Or when the rhythm section is sitting on something a different way. I feel that is what it does for me."

Coltrane, who had sat in frowned contemplation while Dolphy elaborated, dug into the past for his answer:

"Eric and I have been talking music for quite a few years, since about 1954. We've been close for quite a while. We watched music. We always talked about it, discussed what was being done down through the years, because we love music. What we're doing now was started a few years ago.

"A few months ago Eric was in New York, where the group was working, and he felt like playing, wanted to come down and sit in. So I told him to come on down and play, and he did—and turned us all around. I'd felt at ease with just a quartet till then, but he came in, and it was like having another member of the family. He'd found another way to express the same thing we had found one way to do.

"After he sat in, we decided to see what it would grow into. We began to play some of the things we had only talked about before. Since he's been in the band, he's had a broadening effect on us. There are a lot of things we try now that we never tried before. This helped me, because I've started to write—it's necessary that we have things written so that we can play together. We're playing things that are freer than before.

"I would like for him to feel at home in the group and find a place to develop what he wants to do as an individualist and as a soloist—just as I hope everybody in the band will. And while we are doing this, I would also like the listener to be able to receive some of these good things—some of this beauty."

Coltrane paused, deep in thought. No one said anything. Finally he went on:

"It's more than beauty that I feel in music—that I think musicians feel in music. What we know we feel we'd like to convey to the listener. We hope that this can be shared by all. I think, basically, that's about what it is we're trying to do. We never talked about just what we were trying to do. If you ask me that question, I might say this today and tomorrow say something entirely different, because there are many things to do in music.

"But, overall, I think the main thing a musician would like to do is to give a picture to the listener of the many wonderful things he knows of and senses in the universe. That's what music is to me—it's just another way of saying this is a big, beautiful universe we live in, that's been given to us, and here's an example of just how magnificent and encompassing it is. That's what I would like to do. I think that's one of the greatest things you can do in life, and we all try to do it in some way. The musician's is through his music."

This philosophy about music, life, and the universe, Coltrane said, is "so important to music, and music is so important. Some realize it young and early in their careers. I didn't realize it as early as I should have, as early as I wish I had. Sometimes you have to take a thing when it comes and be glad."

When did he first begin to feel this way?

"I guess I was on my way in '57, when I started to get myself together musically, although at the time I was working academically and technically. It's just recently that I've tried to become even more aware of this other side—the life side of music. I feel I'm just beginning again. Which goes back to the group and what we're trying to do. I'm fortunate to be in the company I'm in now, because anything I'd like to do, I have a place to try. They respond so well that it's very easy to try new things."

Dolphy broke in with, "Music is a reflection of everything. And it's universal. Like, you can hear somebody from across the world, another country. You don't even know them, but they're in your back yard, you know?"

Two views of John Coltrane and Eric Dolphy. In *Down Beat's* artist rendition (left), we see a pair of humorless, almost sinister characters (especially Dolphy), lurking and vaguely menacing. A snapshot, on the other hand (right), shows a beaming Dolphy and a relaxed Coltrane outside Trane's home in Queens circa 1961.

COVER COURTESY OF *DOWN BEAT* MAGAZINE. PHOTOGRAPH PRINTED BY PERMISSION OF ANTONIA ANDREWS,
EXECUTRIX OF THE ESTATE OF JUANITA COLTRANE.

"It's a reflection of the universe," Coltrane said. "Like having life in miniature. You just take a situation in life or an emotion you know and put it into music. You take a scene you've seen, for instance, and put it to music."

Had he ever succeeded in re-creating a situation or scene?

"I was getting into it," he said, "but I haven't made it yet. But I'm beginning to see how to do it. I know a lot of musicians who have done it. It's just happening to me now. Actually, while a guy is soloing, there are many things that happen. Probably he himself doesn't know how many moods or themes he's created. But I think it really ends up with the listener. You know, you hear different people say, 'Man, I felt this while he was playing,' or 'I thought about this.' There's no telling what people are thinking. They take in what they have experienced. It's a sharing process—playing—for people."

"You can feel vibrations from the people," Dolphy added.

"The people can give you something too," Coltrane said. "If you play in a place where they really like you, like your group, they can make you play like you've *never* felt like playing before."

ANYONE WHO has heard the Coltrane group in person in such a situation knows the almost hypnotic effect the group can have on the audience and the audience's almost surging involvement in the music. But sometimes, it is said, the striving for excitement *per se* within the group leads to nonmusical effects. It was effects such as these that have led to the "anti-jazz" term.

Such a term is bound to arouse reaction in musicians like Coltrane and Dolphy.

Without a smile—or rancor—Coltrane said he would like the critics who have used the term in connection with him to tell him exactly what they mean. Then, he said, he could answer them.

One of the charges is that what Coltrane and Dolphy play doesn't swing.

"I don't know what to say about that," Dolphy said.

"Maybe it doesn't swing," Coltrane offered.

"I can't say that they're wrong," Dolphy said. "But I'm still playing."

Well, don't *you* feel that it swings? he was asked.

"Of course I do," Dolphy answered. "In fact, it swings so much I don't know what to do—it moves me so much. I'm with John; I'd like to know how they explain 'anti-jazz.' Maybe they can tell us something."

"There are various types of swing," Coltrane said. "There's straight 4/4, with heavy bass drum accents. Then there's the kind of thing that goes on in Count Basie's band. In fact, every group of individuals assembled has a different feeling—a different swing. It's the same with this band. It's a different feeling than in any other band. It's hard to answer a man who says it doesn't swing."

Later, when the first flush of defense had subsided, Coltrane allowed:

"Quite possibly a lot of things about the band need to be done. But everything has to be done in its own time. There are some things that you just grow into. Back to speaking about editing—things like that. I've felt a need for this, and I've felt a need for ensemble work—throughout the songs, a little cement between this block, a pillar here, some more cement there, etc. But as yet I don't know just how I would like to do it. So rather than make a move just because I know it needs to be done, a move that I've not arrived at through work, from what I naturally feel, I won't do it.

"There may be a lot of things missing from the music that are coming, if we stay together that long. When they come, they'll be things that will be built out of just what the group is. They will be unique to the group and *of* the group."

Coltrane said he felt that what he had said still did not answer his critics adequately, that in order to do so he would have to meet them and discuss what has been said so that he could see just what they mean.

Dolphy interjected that the critic should consult the musician when there is something the critic does not fully understand. "It's kind of alarming to the musician," he said, "when someone has written something bad about what the musician plays but never asks the musician anything about it. At least, the musician feels bad. But he doesn't feel so bad that he quits playing. The critic influences a lot of people. If something new has happened, something nobody knows what the musician is doing, he should ask the musician about it. Because somebody may like it; they might want to know something about it. Sometimes it really hurts, because a musician not only loves his work but depends on it for a living. If somebody writes something bad about musicians, people stay away. Not because the guys don't sound good but because somebody said something that has influence over a lot of people. They say, 'I read this, and I don't think he's so hot because so-and-so said so.'"

Dolphy had brought up a point that bothers most jazz critics: readers sometimes forget that criticism is what *one* man thinks. A critic is telling how he feels about, how he reacts to, what he hears in, a performance or a piece of music.

"The best thing a critic can do," Coltrane said, "is to thoroughly understand what he is writing about and then jump in. That's all he can do. I have even seen favorable criticism which revealed a lack of profound analysis, causing it to be little more than superficial.

"Understanding is what is needed. That is *all* you can do. Get all the understanding for what you're speaking of that you can get. That way you have done your best. It's the same with a musician who is trying to understand music as well as he can. Undoubtedly, none of us are going to be 100 percent—in either criticism or music. No percent near that, but we've all got to try.

"Understanding is the whole thing. In talking to a critic try to understand him, and he can try to understand the part of the game you are in. With this understanding, there's no telling what could be accomplished. Everybody would benefit."

Though he said he failed to answer his critics, John Coltrane perhaps had succeeded more than he thought.

LETTER TO DON DEMICHEAL

John Coltrane

This letter was published in C. O. Simpkins's *Coltrane: A Biography*. In it, Coltrane hints at his discomfort with the term "jazz," which he would make clear in an interview in Japan in 1966 (see page 266; for the full article, see page 265). The letter is dated June 2, 1962; Coltrane had started a two-week gig at Birdland a couple of days earlier. Don DeMicheal was *Down Beat*'s editor at the time.

June 2, 1962

Dear Don,

Many thanks for sending Aaron Copland's fine book, "Music and Imagination." I found it historically revealing and on the whole, quite informative. However, I do not feel that all of his tenets are *entirely* essential or applicable to the "jazz" musician. This book seems to be written more for the American classical or semi-classical composer who has the problem, as Copland sees it, of not finding himself an integral part of the musical community, or having difficulty in finding a positive philosophy or justification for his art. The "jazz" musician (You can have this term along with several others that have been foisted upon us.) does not have this problem at all. We have absolutely no reason to worry about lack of positive and affirmative philosophy. It's built in us. The phrasing, the sound of the music attest this fact. We are naturally endowed with it. You can believe all of us would have perished long ago if this were not so. As to community, the whole face of the globe is our community. You see, it is really easy for us to create. We are born with this feeling that just comes out no matter what conditions exist. Otherwise, how could our founding fathers have produced this music in the first place when they surely found themselves (as many of us do today) existing in hostile communities where there was everything to fear and damn few to trust. Any music which could grow and propagate itself as our music has, must have a hell of an affirmative belief inherent in it. Any person who claims to doubt this, or claims to believe that the exponents of our music of freedom are not guided by this same entity, is either prejudiced, musically sterile, just plain stupid or scheming. Believe me, Don, we all know that this word which so many seem to fear today, "Freedom," has a hell of a lot to do with this music. Anyway, I did find in Copland's book many fine points. For example: "I cannot imagine an art work without implied convictions." —Neither can I. I am sure that you and many others have enjoyed and garnered much of value from this well written book.

If I may, I would like to express a sincere hope that in the near future, a vigorous investigation of the materials presented in this book and others related will help cause an opening up of the ears that are still closed to the progressive music created by the independent thinking artist of today. When this is accomplished, I am certain that the owners of such ears will easily recognize the very vital and highly enjoyable qualities that exist in this music. I also feel that through such an honest endeavor, the contributions of future creators will be more easily recognized, appreciated and enjoyed; particularly by the listener who may otherwise miss the point (intellectually, emotionally, socially, etc.) because of inhibitions, a lack of understanding, limited means of association or other reasons.

You know, Don, I was reading a book on the life of Van Gogh today, and I had to pause and think of that wonderful and persistent force—the creative urge. The creative urge was in this man who found himself so much at odds with the world he lived in, and in spite of all the adversity, frustrations, rejections and so forth—beautiful and living art came forth abundantly . . . if only he could be here today. Truth is indestructible. It seems history shows (and it's the same way today) that the innovator is more often than not met with some degree of condemnation; usually according to the degree of his departure from the prevailing modes of expression or what have you. Change is always so hard to accept. We also see that these innovators always seek to revitalize, extend and reconstruct the status quo in their given fields, wherever it is needed. Quite often they are the rejects, outcasts, sub-citizens, etc. of the very societies to which they bring so much sustenance. Often they are people who endure great personal tragedy in their lives. Whatever the case, whether accepted or rejected, rich or poor, they are forever guided by that great and eternal constant—the creative urge. Let us cherish it and give all praise to God. Thank you and best wishes to all.

Sincerely,

[John Coltrane]

P.S. Congratulations to the writer of [the] article, "Thunder in the Wings." I think it was Bill Mathieu. He is constantly proving himself one of the best in music theory. Thanks also to Martin Williams for his very fine discourse in the same issue.

"ON THE TOWN: COLTRANE'S BACK BETTER THAN EVER"

Tony Gieske

This brief review/interview is almost as dense as a Coltrane solo, packing a wide range of information about Coltrane into a small space.

CAPACITY CROWDS are jamming a dark, low-ceilinged Washington nightclub this week to hear John Coltrane, a man who has been called the world's greatest saxophonist but who characteristically won't admit it.

The Bohemian Caverns, at 2001 11th St. NW., has raised its prices to formidable levels for the special one-week stand celebrating the beginning of its second year. Even so, customers are being turned away.

Coltrane, whose facial expression ranges from glum to glum, was surprised to hear how much people were paying to hear him. "I'm not sure I like all that pressure on me. I wish I had more to offer the people," he said.

"There are so many other saxophone players who say more than I do," said Coltrane.

A weight-watcher, he was having a supper consisting of a glass of iced clam juice, washed down with a glass of orange juice, washed down with a glass of pineapple juice and anchored with some salted walnuts, which he carried in a can.

A DEMONIC whirlwind on the stand, Coltrane is placidity itself when he's not playing. After a solo, he will seat himself quietly in a dark corner behind the bass player, out of sight.

He said he almost never loses his temper. "When something drags me, I go off and sulk, that's about all. After a while, whatever it is that's bothering me goes away. But that doesn't happen very much.

From the *Washington Post*, August 31, 1962, page B11.

"As a matter of fact the whole band's kind of that way. They're very even-tempered. We've been together more than a year and there's never been a personal argument. I've never been in a band like that," he said.

THE SMOOTH glassy temper of the band's relationships off the stand present a sharp contrast to their playing, to say the least.

Elvin Jones, his devilish little eyes burning, attacks the drums like a prize fighter and can be heard for blocks. Pianist McCoy Tyner sets up a pedal point in the left hand that makes the tension created by Ravel's "Bolero" seem quite mild. Jimmy Garrison, bass, digs in with a primordial counterpoint to both.

The men travel together, live together, and play together almost constantly, and after it was suggested to him—Coltrane is rather literal minded—the saxophonist said it was somewhat like being in a family.

"Elvin is the most emotional—the one who might get drug, I guess," Coltrane said. "You can hear it in his playing, and somebody will turn around and say what's the matter? But after a couple of sets that all goes away.

"But after work we all split up and do different things," the leader added.

HIS VICTORIES in critics' polls seem to please him—"the plaques make the wall look kind of nice"—but he is not at all vain about them.

It could be said that Coltrane puts all his color in his music, which is relentlessly demanding—loud, fierce and enormously fast-moving. He himself is not like a band-leader at all. He doesn't smile at the audience, tell jokes, engage in gymnastics or even speak much.

Neither does he take the other tack, currently fashionable, and snarl and glare at his listeners. After he has played a 40-minute solo that has gripped the deeper reaches of a rapt assembly, he will give a polite little nod and go back to his corner amid deafening applause.

In the year since he last played in Washington, Coltrane has kept moving further and further along his unique musical path. The pedal-points that he was beginning to use then have become almost unbearably moving, and the rhythm section moves in and around the time with exhilarating freedom. Tyner, in particular, has improved spectacularly, making explicit many of the ideas that he was a little subtle about before.

A MAN who seems totally and continually absorbed in his music, Coltrane was asked if he ever got bored and wanted to go into some other line of work.

"Music is about the best thing I can think of to do," he replied. "If there were something better, it would have to be very wonderful."

The group is appearing through Sunday.

DUKE ELLINGTON & JOHN COLTRANE LINER NOTES

Stanley Dance

Stanley Dance interviewed Coltrane for these liner notes, probably sometime in October 1962 (the album was recorded on September 26, 1962, and released around January 1963).

Three of the major stylistic influences in jazz have been Louis Armstrong, Coleman Hawkins, and John Coltrane. In introducing each by turn to Duke Ellington, producer Bob Thiele has convincingly demonstrated the significance of Duke's position. [. . .]

"I'd really like to get into all Duke's songs," John said some weeks after the session heard here. "I have a feeling there's a lot to find out in his music. He has covered so much ground, and if you could work at it you maybe could really relate to it in five years or so. I once worked with Johnny Hodges, and that was the closest I'd been to Duke before this date. They're both kings in my book." [. . .]

For Coltrane, this occasion carried considerable musical obligations. "I was really honored," he said afterward with characteristic modesty, "to have the opportunity of working with Duke. It was a wonderful experience. He has set standards I haven't caught up with yet. I would have liked to have worked over all those numbers again, but then I guess the performances wouldn't have had the same spontaneity. And they mightn't have been any better!"

Duke certainly esteemed that spontaneity. When there was a question of another take of one number, he said, "Don't ask him to do another. He'll end up imitating himself."

They got on well together. Each arrived with his own rhythm men. The two drummers soon went off to a nearby bar in search of fuel; the bassists fell into friendly conversation; and the two leaders planned the program. Then, while Duke sat at the piano and mapped out the routines for the first numbers, John lit up the first of several long, brown cigars. A very promising, relaxed atmosphere was established—and maintained. [. . .]

On the opener, "In a Sentimental Mood," Coltrane immediately proves his ability to play a pretty melody expressively. He gives it a wistful, meditative quality that is absolutely right, that conveys respect and affection for the music and its composer. It is as though he had dedicated himself to seek—and to sound— the most possible in it. Duke's solo and introduction seem very much of a piece with Coltrane's conception. [. . .]

"Big Nick" is for [George] "Big Nick" Nicholas, an excellent tenor saxophonist whom Coltrane remembers from his days with Dizzy Gillespie. "In thinking back," John said, "it seemed to have something that would suit the style he liked to play in. But maybe not?" His decision to play it on soprano certainly left the field open to Big Nick! [. . .] As for the number's suitability for Ellington, John was in no doubt. "The way he plays," he said, "he can play anything!" [. . .]

In an article[1] by Gene Lees in the monthly magazine *Jazz*, there is an intimation that Coltrane's playing may have "undergone another spurt of rapid evolution" as a result of this relatively brief association with Ellington. It is more than possible, for Duke's catalytic influence is unique in jazz. The one certainty is that there is warm, exciting music here which will pleasantly surprise Ellington and Coltrane fans both.

Note

1. "Consider Coltrane," by Gene Lees, *Jazz*, February 1963, page 7.

INTERVIEW WITH JOHN COLTRANE

Jean Clouzet and Michel Delorme

This interview took place on November 17, 1962, in Paris. Michel Delorme
reports that Jean Clouzet's introduction is a bit exaggerated; Clouzet states
that the interview started at noon and "didn't finish until the next day
toward 5 in the morning." However, Delorme says that they met Coltrane at
the airport around noon to request the interview, which Coltrane agreed to.
They then joined Coltrane later that afternoon in his hotel room, around 3:00
or 4:00 P.M., and began the interview, which was concluded that evening
after the 6:00 P.M. concert.

In any event, this is one of the most interesting interviews Coltrane ever
gave.

The following interview is extracted from a long conversation that we had with
John Coltrane, Michel Delorme and I; a long conversation because, even though it
started at noon on the 18th [sic; 17th] of November, it didn't finish until the next
day toward 5 in the morning, somewhere between the Blue Note and the Mars
Club, only interrupted by the two hours of rest that John allowed himself and, of
course, by the two concerts that he gave at the Olympia.

This interview does not propose to lay out any important revelations about the
musician or the man; his ambition, as far as there is one, would place him rather
in the opposite perspective. Coltrane's response to the questions that I had prepared confirmed in fact what certain American and European critics are forced,
with growing success, to admit: where some have thought themselves able to discuss a free technical virtuosity, an irrationality and madness more or less deliberate, he teaches us, to the contrary, to find exceptional logic, rigor and self-control.
The performer of "My Favorite Things" gave in to the most fascinating temptation

From *Les Cahiers du Jazz*, number 8, 1963, pages 1–14. Translated by John B. Garvey.

that could present itself to an artist, whatever might be his mode of expression: a total plunge into his own depths, a methodical, obstinate, hopeless exploration, because it had no end, of his resources and possibilities. But this revelation of his interior landscape, this frenetic will to never look at what had already been achieved but only at what could be, what should be accomplished, expresses a clarity at every moment which is precisely the opposite of delirium. In fact, Coltrane views this voyage into the unknown as a downward climb rather than as a fall. He never proceeds blindly but only when the problems have been foreseen, the risk evaluated—that is to say, only when "success" has been assured.

Some of his answers may surprise or even shock through the apparent false modesty that they seem to reveal (if you believe, in fact, all the musicians whose names are put forward, whether Eric Dolphy or Charlie Mingus or Ornette Coleman or Art Blakey, are men whose attempts have been more original and more convincing than his). Let's not fool ourselves; we are in the presence of a *true* sincerity, that of a creator who's fully aware of the separation between what he's achieved already and what he feels capable of. This dissatisfaction, this refusal to stop, even for a moment, on one level, represents one of the essential characteristics of the greatest personality of the present in Negro-American music.

The Parisian concerts of November 1962 showed a clear evolution of the reaction of the audience who came to hear Coltrane. The spectators at the Olympia seemed to have passed from incomprehension and hostility into that sort of ambiguous feeling, which, while still not yet being love, is already more than liking. But at the same moment when one could believe that the public was filling up bit by bit the ditch that had been dug between themselves and Coltrane, it is very possible that the trench was widening more and more. Just because, this time, there was no booing to disturb the Coltranian solos, can we really, in good faith, decide that the game was won and the discomfort dissipated? You would have to be quite unaware or very optimistic to see a definitive step toward comprehension in what is just, doubtless, the beginning of a habit. The royal road on which Coltrane has launched his music is *first* the result of a personal experience, selfish, if one dare use the word, since it tends toward the full realization of what draws him, and only secondarily—nearly by chance, since one can imagine in the extreme that it is sufficient unto itself—toward a drawing closer to the individuals who might be the participants in its eventual fruits. John, as he has already confided to us, would hope that the dialogue would be possible. But if

Coltrane backstage at the Olympia, Paris, November 17, 1962.
PHOTOGRAPH BY ROGER KASPARIAN. COURTESY OF THE YASUHIRO "FUJI" FUJIOKA COLLECTION.

he took the first step, he would betray himself. And if he slowed his pace forward to let us catch up with him, the Grail that he pursues would certainly disappear over the horizon. So Coltrane, to repeat a comment by Jean Wagner, has taken on building a "cathedral," but we are ignorant of everything relating to the means he's using and the goal that he wants to attain.

Whether one wants it or not, a music like John Coltrane's cannot be, today, grasped in its entire essence. We must remember that we are only approaching it in a subjective manner. According to our temperament, our sensitivity or our facilities for adaptation, we listen to it either fascinated or quite hostile. A French jazz musician confided the other night to whoever would listen his irritation regarding certain young fans who claimed to appreciate the Coltranian improvisations while he, in spite of his deep musical knowledge, stayed sealed off from that form of music. Putting the question this way is certainly the best way of drawing back from what one claims to want to approach. Having great musical knowledge does not increase one's chances of entering into John Coltrane's universe. From the moment at which it gets complex, the Coltranian discourse gets away from us nearly totally. We have the feeling that it corresponds to an internal logic, but we don't know what it is.

Of course, works like "West End Blues" or "Ko-Ko" met with, on their release, an identical incomprehension, and in a few years "Africa" or "Chasin' the Trane" will probably be considered as the most solid links in the history of jazz. All the same, the effort that we make today should be more important than it's ever been at any point in this history. Bop, to take just one example, was not the work of one man but rather the putting in common of certain musical conceptions, of certain disciplines which were able to be rapidly assimilated by musicians and then by fans. So, let us repeat it one more time: the works by Coltrane, by Coleman or other Minguses, if they have many points in common, if they sometimes seem to be following parallel tracks, or aiming at an identical point, can still not be grouped under the same standard. On the other hand, if some of the elements provided by bop have dominated our musical habits so completely that we're no longer surprised that the majority of variety music draws, every day more so, from the springs of modern jazz, it is still quite unlikely that the fireworks set off by John Coltrane will soon become familiar to the average mortal or that song or dance music will be inspired by them; Coltrane's music, at least in the form in which it is presented today, brings in elements which would frighten off the most intrepid of popular music arrangers.

Thus, trying to judge the Coltranian discourse strictly in musical terms, confronting it according to our usual scale of values, is a heresy. The only ones who have a chance to grasp its meaning are those who will be faithful to its spirit and not to the letter, to its intentions and not to its language, since at the moment the latter has not yet delivered most of its secrets to us. If we're lucky enough to be attracted to all the richness that the Coltranian improvisations let us perceive—including among others a self-confidence and dizzying ambition, a discipline which approaches asceticism, a care that is more and more pronounced to approach that which, beyond appearances, represents the true essence of music and that manner of expressing man's anguish which is nowhere better expressed than in a few works of this century—if we are sensitive to all that and to many other things as well, only then may we accompany Coltrane in his progression; if not, we will probably never catch up to him. We must bring ourselves to him alone, naked, without habits, without prejudices, without memories. The reward that we obtain will be according to our efforts. Coltrane apparently does not know yet how far he will be able to go. Let's trust him. Even if he should reach an impasse, we will at least keep the memory of a magnificent and enriching journey through landscapes that, without him, we would certainly not have imagined existed.

JEAN CLOUZET

Here are some of the questions asked of John Coltrane:

In a recent edition of Down Beat, *the American critic John Tynan grouped together, under the name "New Thing," the music performed by Eric Dolphy, Ornette Coleman, and yourself. Do approve of this grouping? And, if so, what do you think are your points of commonality with those two musicians?*

John Coltrane: It's difficult for me to answer that question precisely. There is without doubt an origin, a common foundation for our music, but I think that Ornette, of the three of us, is the one who has been the furthest; he has essentially broken off from the structures that most of us still use. He has rejected the assumed notions, and, through that alone, he has led his music in a very unique direction since it is deeply different from that which has been done up to now; but, in spite of that, I feel that I'm capable of playing along with him, and even, as you probably know, I've already had that experience. Eric as well has made spectacular efforts to escape from the conventional improvisational schemes. As for me, my attempts have been identical, but I don't know yet if I've succeeded. I think sincerely that Ornette and Eric have been more successful in their attempts than I. I even feel like I'm rather behind. I haven't made the same kind of jump forward since I keep using the same structures based on chords. Working with Miles Davis, I started to appreciate the substitute chords, to feel the suggested chords, but these are still chords; that's why I don't feel that I'm very far ahead. In reality, Eric is here, and Ornette is there, and I'm somewhere else. They've gone past the regular means of expression to attain a particular idiom in which they excel. As for me, I am going nearly as far as anyone who wants to. What I've tried is to modify the manner in which I played. They've accomplished this, but also many other things: they've changed the complete structure of their music. Dolphy has also modified the composition of his group, since he's quit the piano.

On the American jacket for Olé, *you can read a sentence taken from a conversation that you had in 1961 with Ralph J. Gleason that I'll try to give you from memory: "During an engagement at the Apollo, I was obliged to shorten my solos and I had to play in ten minutes what I usually played in thirty, so it occurred to me that I could maybe improvise for a shorter time, add another melodic voice, and get a different thing." Where are you now regarding this project and why, after the Dolphy experiment, have you come back to the quartet formula?*

John Coltrane: I don't remember very well the words that you just quoted, but I can tell you this: I much prefer playing alone and being able to improvise for a longer time; that's the main reason why I didn't hire anyone else after Eric Dolphy left. Another important reason is that nobody showed up who suited me perfectly; that's why I prefer to play in a quartet while waiting for another Dolphy. He was perfect. He's the only soloist who gave me total satisfaction. When he arrived in my group, we didn't need to write parts or whatever. He played his own ideas and everything fell into place naturally. That's the kind of musician I'd like to have again. I'd take any trumpeter at all who could play that way but, in fact, I don't know of anyone at the moment whom I really like; I like all the young trumpeters right now, but I don't know of any of them whom I'd want to have in my group. While waiting to find one, I prefer to play in a quartet; but, I repeat, sincerely, my tastes lead me to play long solos rather than to cut my improvisations short. Whenever I'm required to, it's always for a particular reason required by the situation of the moment; that's what we had to do at the Apollo where, only having a limited time to improvise, we were required to limit ourselves. But some nights, when we start playing, we feel the inspiration and foresee the possibility of accomplishing good things, and then it seems illogical and unreasonable to us to cut our solos short. The way I play yields with difficulty to time limitations. My ideas have to develop naturally in one long solo. I can't do much about that; I have to accept it that way.

Your concept of music is so profoundly personal that it seems like it must isolate you, creating a sort of wall between the other greats of our day in the jazz scene and you. Is this just an impression? Could you, for example, become part of Charlie Mingus' group as a soloist?

John Coltrane: Well, I think so. I haven't had the opportunity up to now, but that experience would interest me a lot. Our meeting would certainly be delicate, since Mingus is working outside of the usual forms and structures and I don't think I've gone as far as he has, no really I don't think so.

Let's take a more . . . traditional group. Could you take the place of the tenor saxophonist with the Messengers and play what Blakey wants?

John Coltrane: Here too I would tell you yes. See, what Art wants more than anything is enthusiasm. That's really what all band leaders want. Take a young musician; if he has enthusiasm, that "drive" that means so many things for us, be indulgent with him even if his technique is hesitant; wait patiently while he makes this better, since he holds in him much more promise than the one who has technique but is lacking in enthusiasm, conviction and punch. I met Art during several recording sessions, and I can assure you that he likes saxophonists who put strength and enthusiasm in their playing.

The various musicians who have been part of your group were always colored musicians; is that by chance, or do you feel that the white sensitivity is incapable of adapting itself to the musical form that you created?

John Coltrane: In my opinion, this problem of facing sensitivities is not at the racial level but only on the individual level. I don't know any criteria that can differentiate a white musician from a black one; in any case, I don't believe they exist. If a man knows his instrument well, if he feels the kind of things that we're doing and if he likes our music, there's no problem at all and from that point on he can play with us without any problems. There are musicians who feel more easily than others the strength, the "feeling" of a band. These people who have the impression that they understand what's happening and who can blend their feeling naturally into the band's are quite often young musicians who came to listen to their elders from whom they want to learn something. At first, they're drawn by the music that they feel themselves, then, in the second case, they start to be influenced by it, and finally, when they've reached a certain maturity, they become part of this or that band of the same type. It's just a problem of comprehension, and has nothing to do with questions of skin color.

You seem to admire Sidney Bechet a lot, you've even dedicated a piece to him; still, your ideas about the soprano sax are apparently diametrically opposed. Isn't that your impression?

John Coltrane: You're right—our ideas are very different, but that doesn't keep me from liking Sidney for his perfect mastery of the instrument and for everything he's brought us. Of course it's a different age, but, in five or ten years another musician will show up on the jazz scene who will completely turn over our current idea since, if there are men who stay attached to the tradition of their time, there are others whose playing prefigures an era to come.

When you choose a new theme, what criteria do you use to decide to interpret it on the soprano rather than the tenor, or vice versa?

John Coltrane: It's difficult to express. It's something indefinable; a certain sonoric quality to get, a balance to establish between the specific atmosphere of the piece and the sound able to produce it as faithfully as possible. That's the objective that suggests the use of the tenor or the soprano.

So, you couldn't perform "My Favorite Things" on the tenor?

John Coltrane: [*laughing*] No, definitely not!

You said once that you would have to decide one day between the soprano and the tenor. Might one know what will be your decision?

John Coltrane: I haven't solved that problem yet. The soprano requires a particular way of holding the lips; it requires more muscles than the tenor, and, because of that, one's lips get hurt quickly. If I develop the habit of playing very "tight," my embouchure will maybe become too tight for the tenor; that's the problem. That could happen soon; in fact, I'm sure that it will happen. I've been playing the soprano for about two years and the first symptoms are already appearing. It's these technical difficulties, and only them, that will require me to choose the instrument that I will have to play in the future. Clearly the soprano is well worth the loss of my embouchure for the tenor, but it's nevertheless possible that finally I'll choose the tenor. No, really, I can't answer your question with any certainty.

Why don't you play as many harmonics as you did several months ago?

John Coltrane: For the moment, I've had enough. Harmonics are too difficult; they always end up "squeaking."

They've written that your sound sometimes took the aspect of the human voice. Is that what you want, or is it just the consequence of the way you play sharply?

John Coltrane: The two hypotheses that you just raised take into account one of the aspects of my style of playing. I like listening to certain sounds and I try to reproduce them in my music.

Your concert interpretations bring out, it seems, a tendency to abandon certain of the usual jazz structures—for example, the 4/4s and a certain thinning of the bass and drum solos. What is that exactly?

John Coltrane: No, I don't think that the claim you made can find its justification in my current conception of music. You mustn't forget that, last year, there was another musical voice in my group, and thus Eric and my solos left nearly no time for the bassist and the drummer to express themselves freely; but, this evening, it's an entirely different thing and I can assure you that soon, on stage at the Olympia, Jimmy and Elvin will play solos. As for the 4/4, I have nothing against it, and we do play it sometimes.

Why, in some of your recent records, did you use two bassists rather than just one?

John Coltrane: For some of my recent interpretations, I sought the possibility of hearing more rhythmic variety behind me than usual, and I think I achieved this with two bassists. But, right now, I don't plan to continue in that direction and to try that experiment again. I'm certainly going to try get an identical effect with a single bassist or maybe even—why not?—no bassist at all. You could in fact imagine a trio in which the rhythmic continuity would only be suggested by the tapping of our feet. But, if I keep a bassist, I hope that he could play without any constraint; that's to say, to not stay locked into an unchangeable rhythmic line.

Is it because of this problem that Steve Davis, Art Davis, Reggie Workman and Jimmy Garrison succeeded each other in your band while McCoy Tyner and Elvin Jones kept their respective places?

John Coltrane: In a rhythm section, what matters most of all is getting a certain consistency in the group's sound, a certain unity of timbres; that's why the relationship between the pianist, bassist, and drummer should be as perfect as possible. Art, Steve, Reggie and Jimmy played very well, and I don't mean to make any distinction between them, but it seems to me that Jimmy's the one who integrates himself the most perfectly between McCoy and Elvin. See, it's just a question of timbres, of getting a sound, and it doesn't concern at all technique or musical ideas of the bassists who succeeded each other in my group.

Do you feel comfortable within a big band? On Africa/Brass, *the band serves just as background for you. Is that your idea of a big band, or else would you see yourself in a more classically formed group, that is to say a band where the musician is only a part of the group and not an "accompanied soloist." Dialogue or background sound—where are your preferences headed?*

John Coltrane: Right now I don't think I want this soloist-band dialogue that you're talking about. I've already made several attempts in this direction. I know that you're often paid back playing this way, and that you can get a lot of satisfaction from it, but still I'm not thinking about it right now. *Africa/Brass* arose from a different idea. *Africa/Brass* was the quartet supported by a big band. We took what McCoy was supposed to play on the piano and arranged it for the band, so that it wasn't anything more than a "big piano" playing a musical background.

That way, I didn't have to adapt myself, to try to play according to what the band was doing. Maybe someday I'll manage something with a more orthodox big band, but I haven't yet figured out how that could be done.

Do you think that an attempt like that helps you to express yourself?

John Coltrane: No, that could only be an experiment, since small bands give me much more freedom to improvise, that's for sure. Anyway, that's the reason why I don't want a different grouping right now.

But if you had to do another session with a big band, which arranger would you like to work with? A man like Gil Evans, for example?

John Coltrane: I don't know. I don't have a very clear idea about the way things should take place. Gil is clearly a great composer and also a great arranger, so there wouldn't be any problem with him. If I knew exactly what I want to do, if I had a precise idea in my head, I would lead Gil in that direction and he would succeed very easily; that's how he works with Miles. He writes everything that Miles asks him for and he gets the right sound right away since he particularly excels in balancing the instruments. So he could very probably get everything I asked him for, but, I say again, I haven't reached this level yet.

Were you satisfied with your record with George Russell, New York, N.Y.?

John Coltrane: I only listened to it again once, so I can't say much about it to you. I can only tell you that the suite is very pleasant and I like its group sound.

Don't you feel yourself a bit restrained by this type of conception?

John Coltrane: Yes, of course, and that's not the way I prefer playing, but I can't do anything about it. When I accept a recording session, I am committed to accomplishing everything that they ask me to do, even if my ideas on the matter are different and if the soloists who have to play with me don't particularly suit me.

Would a session with strings attract you?

John Coltrane: No, at least not right now. I just finished a studio session and I have two more to do this year. Usually, as soon as I've finished a recording, I start thinking about the next one right away, but right now I don't have a specific idea about my next record.

Do you feel as comfortable, in order to develop your current improvisational style, with the standards, the jazz classics, as with your own compositions?

John Coltrane: Yes, sincerely yes. Naturally, when you write a piece yourself, you're sure it's adapted exactly to your ideas, to your style of playing, but it's possible as well to find standards that perfectly fit your way of looking at things. The author of the composition that you're going to play hardly matters as long as it's good. There are standards that put you at ease, and there are others that irritate you. The problem is finding the theme that lends itself exactly to the expression of your personality and your feeling. But the choice of material is not predominant and, really, in this area we're very conservative. We were talking a little while ago about the Messengers; well, Blakey uses those themes in 3/4, 6/8 or 4/4 that we play. Some groups frequently call on themes in 5/4 even though we haven't done anything with this yet. The majority of our repertoire is built on standards, ballads and blues. We're not trying to draw too far away from the traditional structures of jazz music. It's only during my improvisations that I try to go as far out as possible, musically speaking, and I want the people who play with me to do the same in the framework of their conception.

With you, ballads seem to go in two opposite directions. Sometimes, as in "Ev'ry Time We Say Goodbye," your improvisation diverges very little from the initial line; on the contrary, in "Greensleeves," for example, you transform the ballad completely, making it literally explode. Which way are your preferences going right now?

John Coltrane: Certain pieces suit us just as they were written and don't need to be modified. That's strictly a personal problem; it's a question of conception. In my repertoire, there are pieces that satisfy me just as they are, since the beauty of their melodic line doesn't need anything exterior to be brought to them, and others that need to be enriched since they're just a point of departure for improvisation. There too, everything depends on your feelings and on what you feel at the moment of playing.

What are the exact importance and placement of African and Oriental elements in your music?

John Coltrane: What attracts me in the music you mention are the colors and rhythms that they bring to me.

Is it for reasons of color and rhythm that you like Ravi Shankar?

John Coltrane: [*laughing*] In fact, I *really* like Ravi Shankar. When I hear his music, I want to copy it—not note for note, of course, but in its spirit. What draws me closest to Ravi is the modal aspect of his art. Right now, at the particular level where I find myself, I feel like I'm going through a modal phase. I've gone through several periods, you know. There was a point when I was going through a "chord" phase, back when I recorded *Giant Steps*; now I'm in my modal phase. There's a lot of modal music that's played every day throughout the world. It's particularly evident in Africa but, whether you look at Spain or Scotland, India or China, that's what you'll find every moment. If you really want to look beyond differences of style, you'll realize that there is a common base. That's very important. Sure, British popular music is not the same as South American, but take away their purely ethnic characteristics—that is to say, their folk aspects—and you'll find yourself in the presence of the same pentatonic sound, of comparable modal structures. It's that universal side of music which interests and draws me, and that's where I want to go.

A very important question, John. For you, does playing only signify an attempt to resolve certain harmonic, melodic and rhythmic problems, or are you also looking for a way to provoke certain reactions from your audience, to create a particular atmosphere; some critics have gone so far as to suggest hypnosis; what's it all about, exactly?

John Coltrane: The moment we start to play, we find ourselves faced with the majority of problems inherent in any musical creation, no matter what form it takes. It's inevitable, and I think that it's the same for all musicians. But, on the other hand, we're playing for the public. I try to reach people who come to hear me and I think that the other members of my group have the same concern. We're really not trying to provoke a state of hypnosis or anything else like that; we just want to reach the audience, to communicate with them, to make them feel what we do. I play what I feel in me, and I hope that what I feel in me says something to the audience. It's easy to get up and say "I have a message for you" and to express this message in words, but it's not so easy when your means of expression is music. Even so, we shouldn't stay isolated. What we feel deep in ourselves should be communicated to others. But, in fact, I'm not always sure what people want exactly, and I'm afraid of being wrong when I try to guess. In any case, does everyone, taken individually, really want the same thing as his neighbor? To be sure of reaching the greatest number, I now present a varied program, allowing me to explore the emotional terrain that is the most complete possible. That way, I increase my chances of speaking to the majority and I improve myself while I remain myself. Definitely, everyone finds his own preferences. I want to be able to bring something to people that feels like happiness. I would love to discover a process such that if I wanted it to rain, it would start raining. If one of my friends were sick, I would play a certain tune and he would get better; if he were broke, I would play another tune and immediately he would receive all the money he needed. But what those pieces are, and what way do you have to go to arrive at knowing them, I don't know. The true powers of music are still unknown. To be able to control them should be, I think, the ambition of every musician. The knowledge of these forces fascinates me. I would like to provoke reactions in my audience, to create a real atmosphere. That's the direction that I want to go in, and to go as far as possible. I hope that everything I've done up to now is just the beginning. Two and a half years ago, I got my own group. Before that all I had for my recordings were musicians taken from here and there and, for the first time, I had my own band. Then we developed several projects, and I believe sincerely that the things we accomplished after that were really the things that we were thinking of then. But the point that we find ourselves at now is marking the end of that first phase. Maybe the moment has come for another approach, and I even believe that it *has* come. We're ready.

(Conversation recorded by Jean Clouzet and Michel Delorme)

Note

The audio recording of this interview has been lost, and Michel Delorme would greatly appreciate any information regarding its whereabouts. If you have any leads, please contact the editor at ChrisPFDeVito@gmail.com. Interestingly, a fragment of the audio does survive, but it's not from the interview itself: Coltrane received a telephone call during the interview, and the surviving tape fragment captures Coltrane's side of the phone conversation. He speaks to Ben Benjamin, owner of the Blue Note club in Paris, about a possible gig there that seems to have never happened.

INTERVIEW WITH JOHN COLTRANE

Benoît Quersin

This interview was held between shows at the Paris concert on November 17, 1962. In it, Coltrane mentions his intent to do an "exhaustive" study of twelve-tone music. When asked sometime later if it's possible to improvise serially, he replied, "Damn the rules, it's the feeling that counts. You play all twelve notes in your solo anyway" (Joe Goldberg, *Jazz Masters of the Fifties*, page 210).

Benoît Quersin: Did anything new happen for you in the meantime [since Coltrane was interviewed by Quersin in 1961]?

John Coltrane: Well, no, just—I'm continuing to—*trying* to evolve, [*laughs*] I'll say, you know, there's nothing new happening. We're trying to bring some of the things that we started to a conclusion, and hoping that there will be something else waiting after that.

Quersin: Some extensions.

Coltrane: Yeah. I hope so, yeah.

Quersin: And professionally, it has been improving a lot, yes?

Coltrane: Well, we have been trying to extend our scope a little bit as far as the places that we work. We've worked in a few different clubs up in New York State. We've widened our circuit a little. It's a problem we've had; our circuit is small, we've played the same clubs over and over now. It kind of tires the listener, you

185

know, so we've been trying to broaden our—get around more to more distant places and—

Quersin: Have you been trying to get some new material together?

Coltrane: I have. I've been trying, but I haven't—it hasn't come in a rush, yet. I've had a few things here and there but I haven't done any—I haven't gotten a—I think I need a new approach to the tunes that we get, and then I can use a whole lot of things that have been done before. But they'll be different, you know, have a different approach.

Quersin: Have you been thinking of expanding your group, I mean the instrumentation?

Coltrane: Well, I'm always thinking of that, but I can't do it until I better my writin' ability. That's something that has to be done before I can use another horn. Yeah.

Quersin: Yeah, because—

Coltrane: Unless I have somebody like Eric Dolphy, you see. Yeah, he can fit in, he can—a lot of time, makes his own parts, you know, or he just . . .

Quersin: What happened—

Coltrane: . . . fills in so well, you know.

Quersin: What happened to him, man?

Coltrane: Oh, he has a quintet now. He has his own group.

Quersin: *Africa/Brass* was the first experience in some new orchestra sounds. Are you going to try something again in that field?

Coltrane: Maybe for recording, but as far as actual roadwork, I'm quite certain that I couldn't ever be—it costs too much to employ a group of musicians like that. But for recording, I may try something with maybe nine, or eight or nine pieces. There were some things which arc—we started in *Africa/Brass,* which I'd like to maybe, you know, take a little further, but I have to work on it a little bit more till I see clearly.

Quersin: With what instruments? What kind of colors?

Coltrane: Hm?

Quersin: What instruments? What colors?

Coltrane: On *Africa?*

Quersin: No, I mean in your—

Coltrane: Oh.

Quersin: —you're thinking about.

Coltrane: Oh, well I don't know yet. Because I'm—

Quersin: Oh, just thinking about it.

Coltrane: I don't know. Well, just thinking about it. It would probably be something like that. Probably heavy on the lower brass instruments and woodwinds. Not too many of the higher brass like trumpets or cornets. Few, very few, but more of the lower brasses and woodwinds. I think something like that I might—you know—might be able to get the sound of the thing that I want.

Quersin: Are you interested in contemporary music [*unintelligible*]?

Coltrane: Of what nature?

Quersin: Well so-called classical field.

Coltrane: Well, I've—I'm beginning now to listen to it more than I have in the past. I'm going to study some of the twelve-tone things. In fact, I have a few of them, but I haven't really studied them yet. Actually, if I hear the sound, I usu-ally—if there's—if I hear a sound or something that I like, you know, it doesn't matter what era it's from, I just like *that*, you know? So, I don't know, I haven't—like I say, I haven't studied much of the contemporary music, but I do intend to do an exhaustive study of the twelve-tone works.

Quersin: Do you think it can be integrated into jazz, the twelve-tone technique?

Coltrane: Well, it is being—I would say that Ornette Coleman is doin' it. Well, he's not—

Quersin: Consciously?

Coltrane: —actually doin' it, he's not doin' it, like, say, "I want to do this because someone else is doing it," he's doing it because he feels this, see? So, he's doing it in what I consider the right way, the natural way, in other words, the way which is—one arrives at through his own natural evolution. And not just because he just consciously wants to do something like that. That's why I, I mean, I haven't actually studied this so much, because I haven't actually evolved, myself, to the point where I'm—I want to play consistently just in a manner of twelve tones. I still like to play over a chord base, although I do like to play passages which do contain twelve tones, but I build them in my own way of structure, you know? Sequential structure.

Quersin: Well, it's kind of a very slow technique, I mean, it takes a lot of work to follow.

Unknown voice: Let's go, John.

Coltrane: Yeah, well it has to—

Unknown voice: John.

Coltrane: Yeah, OK. [*continues to Quersin*] It has to come naturally, you know. And then this, because you've got to do it just like you talk and walk, where you have to do it instantly, you know. It's not—you don't want it to be a thing that you've got to think out at home and work out like that, or sit down and work out, you want it so you just do it, you know, in a moment. That's the way it's got to happen. So you have to [*laughs*]—it has to happen that way. You have to work through it. Well, I guess we better run.

Quersin: Thank you.

INTERVIEW WITH JOHN COLTRANE

Michiel de Ruyter

In these excerpts from an interview conducted in Amsterdam on December 1, 1962, Coltrane touches on many of the recurring topics in his interviews (soprano vs. tenor, mouthpiece difficulties, and others) and expresses his appreciation for the creativity of the members of his quartet. The audio is available at http://mdr.jazzarchief.nl/interviews/coltrane/.

Soprano vs. Tenor

Michiel de Ruyter: One of the things we talked about last year was that you said, "One day or another, I have to make a choice between the soprano and the tenor."

John Coltrane: [*laughs*] You know, I'd forgotten I'd said that. But I guess it was very fresh in my mind then, and it's still a problem and it hasn't been solved. It seems now that I'm fightin' to stay with the tenor because I don't want to lose it. But the soprano is so easy to pick up and play, and I—like in my room or when I'm traveling, I find it's the easiest one to have at hand, you know?

de Ruyter: Mm hmm.

Coltrane: And more often than not I find myself playing it. And most of the ideas that I get come from the sound of that and the range of that instrument. And I still like it very much, but I feel that I want to go back to the tenor, more or less, because actually the soprano is about my favorite instrument ever since I picked it up. And now I'm beginning to get used to it and I want to go and strengthen myself on the tenor again. I've got to change on tenor because it's about time to change mouthpieces, you know, and when the tour is over I'm going to Paris and

191

go down to Selmer company. And if things work as I hope they might, I might find a new combination of mouthpiece and horn which will give me something which will rekindle a new interest in the tenor, you know? At least, that's what I'm hoping for.[1] [*chuckles*] [. . .]

It [the soprano saxophone] has really begun to be my favorite, but I don't think it can take the place of the tenor in my life because it doesn't have the *power* that the tenor has, you know?

de Ruyter: Mm hmm.

Coltrane: And I've got to have that power to, you know, get across certain ideas. So actually I'm gonna need 'em both. I'm sure of that.

The Quartet

Coltrane: Yeah, well, they're doing *beautifully*, you know, and it's just a natural thing. They're just going into it. And it's very spontaneous. I'll try to, I'll only give a skeleton or a framework for a song and from then on it's up to them to create their own parts to it. And that way it's—well it's better, you know? [. . .]

It sort of shapes itself, see, through individual contribution and effort. That way everybody can kind of develop, you know, and develop in their own sense of musicianship, too, because they have to make their own choices and decisions, you know, musical decisions. Which gives me ideas, see [*laughs*], because I can't think drums like Elvin Jones, I can't think bass like Jimmy Garrison, nor can I think piano like McCoy, you know? I can't do it. They know much more about those instruments than I do. Much more. So it's better for me not to try to impose too many of my ideas on them.

Guitar, Sitar, and Harp

de Ruyter: Are you still fooling around with the guitar?

Coltrane: No, no, man. I got it at home. [*laughs*] I don't have time, man, for that. It was sort of a companion for me before, you know?

Coltrane in Milan, December 2, 1962. COURTESY OF GIOVANNI TOMMASO.

de Ruyter: Yeah.

Coltrane: Mm hmm. But I still have it, it's—I think eventually I'll probably get into it because, like, after I've started composing then I'll know what I'm lookin' for and I'll be able to use the different instruments which I have around the house to help me compose, see? I bought a sitar since I saw you last, too. And—well I still got the harp around there, and after I get my several modes of composing, compositions together then I'll be able to go to these different instruments with something definitely in mind.

Giant Steps

Coltrane: Yeah, but my approach was so limited then. But I was trying to, I was trying, you know, but it's—

de Ruyter: Limited in what way?

Coltrane: Well, melodically, melodically. Those, uh, *Giant Steps,* everything I did on there was kind of harmonic exploration—for *me* exploration, you know?

There were some harmonic sequences which I wasn't familiar with prior to that, you know, and I'd just been workin' on it and it was kind of new to me, and I was workin' strictly from a chordal, sequential progression pattern, you know? And not melodically. And it was easy to soon exhaust that, you know, harmonic thing. But to write melodically is really the best way because that—then you are not going by just a set rule here, a set rule there; it takes in everything. It's much more flexible and more far reaching for me to write like that than it is just to write from a harmonic basis.

Melody

Coltrane: But now that I'm trying to write from the melody first, the melody will be more important, and so eventually I might derive some melodies which are, uh, maybe have some quality or some lasting value of some sort. Melodies that can be worked into interludes or introductions or passages, you know, like maybe it'll be time to add a horn in, maybe really get a band, see—

de Ruyter: What kind of horn will it be?

Coltrane: Well, I guess a trumpet, you know? I don't want a trumpet alone. I'd like to have somebody like Eric Dolphy, but [*laughs*] that's impossible.

de Ruyter: There's nobody that plays trumpet that way.

Coltrane: No, you know that. I'd like to have Eric, really, I'd like to have Eric Dolphy and a trumpeter but Eric, he's got his own band now. But maybe I could find some young man who plays more than one reed, see. If I get somebody that plays several reeds, and a trumpeter, see? [. . .] I think by the time I [*laughs*], I learn to write, there won't be any problem [*laughs*], there'll probably be too many of 'em around like that. It's gonna take me a year—I think, you know, I'm not sure, but I think it's gonna take me six months to a year to get something good out of this. 'Cause I'm at the first step now, you know, and unless it snowballs real fast it's gonna take me a little while to get it really strong, but it will be a beginning, soon, I'm gonna make a beginning soon. I don't know whether I'll add that trumpeter until six months or maybe eight months or a year, or something like that. By that time my ideas might be strong enough to be able to write arrangements, you know—not write 'em, to set, to construct—or anyway, I'd like to develop these things with the quartet, and then when the hornman comes in we'll be so well set with 'em until all he'll have to do is just play what he hears, see? Which would be better.

Note

1. The following year, on October 26, 1963, de Ruyter asked Coltrane if he'd replaced his mouthpiece. Coltrane answered, "No I didn't. I bought around five, six of 'em. Mouthpieces that is. But I couldn't find what I wanted, so I'm still using the old one. Which is still better than any of the new ones I found, although it's not giving me the type of thing I want. But it's still the best one I have, so I have to use it." The audio is available at http://rndr.jazzarchief.nl/interviews/coltrane/.

PART III

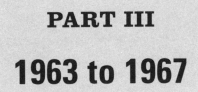

1963 to 1967

"AFTER DARK: HIS SOLOS RUN 45 MINUTES LONG"

Ken Barnard

In April 1963 Coltrane was on the road, spending a week in Detroit at the Minor Key and still battling his mouthpiece. (The mouthpiece won.)

When sax man John Coltrane decides to do something, he likes to go about it in an unhurried manner.

For relaxation, "Trane" smokes long, long Brazilian cigars; and on stage he's been known to do 45-minute solos.

When he and his quartet opened their current engagement at the Minor Key Tuesday night, Trane had a patient struggle with a new mouthpiece.

"It had some kinks in it," Trane said, "and you're not going to be happy unless you get just the right sound. I had to be the master of that thing and so we had a battle. I said to it, 'We'll just see now,' but it won!"

When he's home in St. Albans, N.Y., with his wife, Juanita, and 13-year-old daughter, Toni, Trane spends hours contentedly listening to his collection of records by classical harpist Carlos Salzedo.

Trane also showed his unhurried style in the way that he shaped his career. The son of a musical tailor in Hamlet, N.C., he studied saxophone in high school and later in Philadelphia, then began a gradual upward movement with many instrumental units.

"I accepted work," says Trane, "with all kinds of groups—even if I didn't agree with their musical tenets, because I could learn something while I made a living."

He's worked with Dizzy Gillespie, Earl Bostic and Miles Davis, and has won two *Down Beat* awards in the last couple of years.

From the *Detroit Free Press*, April 12, 1963, page B-5.

Detroiter Elvin Jones has been Trane's drummer for three years. Says Trane of Jones: "He's the only drummer for me. He's a unique talent, highly individual, and nobody in the world plays like him."

Trane, 37, listens when he can to younger jazz men to pick up trends. "What I hear now," he says, "is a movement to freer forms of expression. There's a challenge in this.

"But I never feel jazz is going in any one direction; it's going in all directions. Jazz is tied up with emotion, and there are all kinds of emotion to be expressed."

"THE TRANE ROLLS IN TO CREATE A MINIATURE UN"

Bob Hunter

The John Coltrane Quartet spent the first two weeks of May 1963 at McKie's in Chicago. The occasional "mysterious" absences of Elvin Jones noted in this article were caused by Jones's problems related to narcotics addiction. He left this gig to begin his stay at the Lexington Narcotics Hospital/Clinical Research Center in Lexington, Kentucky (Roy Haynes filled in for him).

A night at McKie's Disc Jockey Lounge (especially opening night) with John Coltrane is something else.

It is a weird scene. 'Trane and crew arrive at approximately 10 p.m. The quarter—minus John—runs through one fast tune while Coltrane is in the process of putting his horns (tenor and soprano saxophones) together.

Over at the door Lulu, McKie Fitzhugh's girl Friday of 15 years, is telling all customers that tonight, and every night of Coltrane's stay, there will be a cover charge of $1.

A few supposed 'Trane fans balk at the price. A traffic jam at the door occurs. The bar fills; the booths fill, and all the while the jazz great that everyone has come to see is still in the process of assembling his axe.

Set Underway

Pretty soon he completes the job and the set is underway. And more people pile in. And now, with the mixture of races, McKie's is transformed into a miniature United Nations. At last America is truly the melting pot of the world. The swinging world that is.

From the *Chicago Daily Defender*, May 16, 1963, page 16.

Backstage at Newport, July
7, 1963. PHOTOGRAPH BY JOE ALPER.
COURTESY OF JACKIE ALPER.

By now 'Trane is really on the track. The house listens with rapt attention, but nobody pats their foot. They can't.

The bartender, John, leans over and asks: "Do you dig Coltrane?"

"I used to—when he was playing with Miles Davis—," is the reply, "but now his music is so advanced it's bringing far out back in."

It is difficult to describe the music being played by John Coltrane. His solos are sharp, crisp and precise. His runs come as waves do during a typhoon or hurricane. Yet, his sounds tend to convey the impression that John Coltrane is at least 10 years ahead of the most progressive jazz fan.

Old Fashioned Tune

Every now and then he will slip in an old fashioned 4/4 tune as a sort of compromise. It is a concession but, after all, he must let the would-be hip paying customers seem a little hip to the rest of the crowd.

There are no adjectives in Webster's dictionary that can portray what Coltrane is trying to say. Such words as exuberant, furious, impassioned and thundering are not fit to be linked with his playing.

Just as Bell Telephone is preparing for the future, so is our hero. [. . .] To see and hear John Coltrane in person is to take a peek at the year 1984. His convoluting and exhortative phrases sound like sinners do when they know they are doomed for hell.

Great that he is, Coltrane cannot carry a gig alone. He must have other musicians with like ideas. And in drummer Elvin Jones he has just that.

Jones has been with John for over two years. Sometimes he takes a short leave of absence for mysterious reasons, but he always returns.

Jones contributes more than just support to a performance by the Coltrane quartet. He has an ability to construct drum solos of sometimes amazing complexity and rhythmic daring that, nonetheless, retain form, and form is the ingredient often missing from most drum solos.

Jones Talks

"I follow the improvisation the soloist has taken," he says, "and when he's through I pick up the last phrase he's played and use this as the beginning to my improvisation on the melodic pattern of the composition. It can be very simple or very complicated, and you can get into unlimited rhythmic and polyrhythmic patterns and phrases.

"Actually, a lot of solos I have taken have drum phrases, just as a saxophonist or trumpeter will play with his instrument. I make drums live." Coltrane doesn't believe in one-tempoed solos. To him it's natural to change the speed when he comes to a new movement. At times he will go from double into triple meter. The rest go right along with him. The rest, of course, [are] McCoy Tyner on piano and Jimmy Garrison on bass, plus Jones.

Until 1955 John Coltrane was never heard of. Then he joined Miles Davis' group and made a name for himself. Midway through "'Round Midnight," the flag waver of the first album he cut with Miles after becoming a part of the quintet, Coltrane burst forth with the zest of a runaway locomotive. All over America jazz lovers began asking: "Who's that?" He made them sit up and take notice.

"JOHN COLTRANE—'TRANE'" (PART 1)

Randi Hultin

Norwegian journalist Randi Hultin met Coltrane in Oslo on October 23, 1963, where the John Coltrane Quartet was performing. She interviewed Coltrane before the evening concert and invited him to her home afterward.

My first encounter with John Coltrane in 1963 made a big impression on me. Both his name and his music evoked awesome respect. He was an innovator whose tenor sax playing was nothing less than sensational. He was a trailblazer who left his own indelible traces on the history of jazz in the same way Louis Armstrong, Charlie Parker, and Lester Young had done before him. In Oslo, there was excited anticipation awaiting Coltrane's quartet—McCoy Tyner on piano, Elvin Jones on drums, and Jimmy Garrison on bass—on 23 October [1963]. The concert was to be given at Njårdhallen, and the musicians were booked in at the Continental.

Jan Erik Vold was a critic for *Dagbladet* at that time, and I also planned to do an interview. Coltrane was a little skeptical at first when I phoned and asked if I could come over as soon as I had finished my day at work. He said he was tired and needed to rest. I asked him when they were planning to rehearse, and in the midst of the conversation, he suddenly changed his mind and said that I could come over any time. I don't know what caused this sudden change of heart—perhaps he felt somehow I had a rapport with jazz musicians. When I got to the hotel, it didn't take long before we were in deep conversation. He was very personable, but he had an aura that inspired great respect at the same time, somewhat serious mannered—and shy in a way. It is always fascinating to meet the person behind the music and Coltrane seemed so much gentler than

From *Born Under the Sign of Jazz*, by Randi Hultin (London: Sanctuary, 1998, 2000), pages 157–162.

his output, but that of course only belied a deeper personality. He became lost in conversation and practically forgot the time.

"Music can't be easy to understand—you have to come to the music yourself, gradually. You can't accept everything with open arms."

"One can hear that you are inspired by Indian music."

"That's right. I've been interested in Ravi Shankar a long time, and I hope that I'll meet him one day.[1] There's another musician I admire a lot—harpist Carlos Salzedo. He plays Spanish music, but he's really a universal musician. I like strings, but the tenor is my living."

"Which saxophonist did you admire first?"

"First Johnny Hodges, but Lester Young has always had a big place in my heart. Later, it was Dexter Gordon. I really hope to meet Dexter while I'm in Copenhagen."

"How were the years with Miles Davis?"

"I played with Miles for five years, and that was a very inspiring period. It was the first time I changed my style, but I've changed again since then."

"Do you ever play at jam sessions?"

"No, preferably not."

"What about outdoor concerts?"

"If the weather is nice, it's all right. I get really inspired if I can find a deserted stretch of shoreline to play on. When there's no wind, the horn sounds good, and I can practice for hours. I like silence—there's nothing like driving long stretches of country road. I always travel by car when I'm on tour at home."

Welcome

When I asked Coltrane if he liked pop music, he answered that some of it is all right, "but they don't write any great melodies anymore. Not like Rodgers and Hart—that was great music. Everything recorded today is ruined by those aggravating pop rhythms and guitar amplifiers. I take notice right away when a good melody is produced, and I think it will happen again soon. In America, everybody's got to have pop music on radio and TV. Even kids two and three years old can dance the twist. Pop music will last a while—it's up to the individual just how long lasting it will be. Maybe it will lead to an interest in jazz—who knows?" [. . .]

Coltrane had just released his record *Impressions* when he was in Oslo, as well as an album with singer Johnny Hartman. "Don't ask me how Hartman sings," he said. "I can't explain it. He's a baritone. You don't have to explain music."

"It's too bad you couldn't play at the Metropol, because then we could have listened to you for a whole week, like we did with Cecil Taylor."

"I would love to be here a whole week. The way we travel, we never feel like we are in touch with the people at each place. We live in a hotel, and outside of that, we only see the concert hall. We don't even know if people like our music."

Since I had turned the subject to Cecil Taylor, I mentioned that I had just received a letter from this modernistic pianist who had been the object of so much attention in Europe. "You can read it. It's personal, while at the same time it could have been written to anyone. It's been a year since he was in Oslo—his first meeting with Scandinavia. His language is difficult to understand, and it's written in the third person."

Cecil had ruled off the letter's pages in squares, four per page, sixteen in all. Coltrane read intently.

"You're right. These are interesting thoughts, and this is a very intellectual letter. I'm glad you showed it to me—it tells me a lot about Cecil. I always feel refreshed when I hear him in concert, but I have never talked to him. I like his music."

Coltrane talked eagerly, but I found it best to end our conversation so that he could get some rest before the concert.

"Do you promise to come to the dressing room during intermission?" he asked.

"Of course. And if all of you want to come home with me afterwards, you're welcome to."

No Drums

The Njårdhallen concert hall was filled to capacity and the excitement was almost tangible. But when the musicians walked onstage they found that Elvin's drums hadn't arrived yet. Eventually they were brought up, and Elvin had to unpack and set up his kit, not only in front of the audience—but with Coltrane looking on as well. He leaned relaxedly against the grand piano and waited patiently while Elvin set up. Not a word was spoken.

The acoustics were peculiar. I sat on one side of the hall at first, and the drums drowned out everything else. After the intermission, I chose to sit directly in front of Elvin, deciding to concentrate on the drumming, which seemed like a band in itself. During the intermission, I went downstairs and took a picture of each of the musicians. The pictures were all good—another lucky break—and all four of them were later reproduced on a page of the Coltrane biography *Chasin' the Trane* [by J. C. Thomas]. Before I left Coltrane during intermission, he asked if my earlier invitation still stood. McCoy preferred to go off on his own, and Jimmy and Elvin were going out on the town, but Coltrane wanted to go with me.

"Can I take along a record?" he asked. "In Stockholm I got a record by Albert Ayler that I want to listen to."[2]

I set out goat cheese and frozen fish when we came home, and asked if John wanted a beer. He declined.

"It's been ten years since I last tasted alcohol. I prefer tea."

He wanted to hear Norwegian folk music and Norwegian jazz, and the hours went by quickly. In the end we forgot to play Albert Ayler. At that time, I had no idea who Ayler was and, in retrospect, it would have been interesting to hear Coltrane's opinion of his music. Ayler was very controversial, and I must admit that when I listened to the record later, I found it to be the longest LP I'd ever heard in my life.

I spent some fine hours with Coltrane. He opened up, he showed a warm sense of humor, and he seemed to enjoy himself. When I asked him to sign my guest book, he leafed through and glanced at what others had written.

"Would you write a few bars of your favorite composition?" I asked.

"Okay," he said, and he notated the first bars of "Naima," the tune he had written to his first wife.

When he was about to leave, Coltrane gallantly kissed my hand and asked if he could give my regards to Cecil Taylor. "Then I'll have an excuse to talk to him," he said. The thought of John Coltrane needing the pretext of bringing greetings from Norway just to talk to Cecil Taylor bemused me, but Cecil told me later that Coltrane actually had greeted him from me when the two men met in New York. Even stranger, I learned later that Taylor and Coltrane had made a record together *before* John visited me in Oslo. But, according to Cecil, they hadn't said a word to each other during the entire recording session. Coltrane had never mentioned any of this to me when we talked about Taylor.

Notes

1. Coltrane is believed to have already met Shankar by this time (see pages 124 and 128). He may have been referring to an upcoming meeting with the sitarist.
2. This must have been *Something Different*, Ayler's first record (Bird Notes BNLP 1), recorded by Swedish musician Bengt "Frippe" Nordstrom and released on his private record label.

INTERVIEW WITH JOHN COLTRANE

Michel Delorme and Jean Clouzet

This interview combines a direct transcription from the audiotape with written material translated from Michel Delorme's *Jazz Hot* article, "Coltrane 1963: Vers la Composition."

John Coltrane, has your style evolved since last year?

John Coltrane: No. This year, I'm going to see, uh—feature my writing, you know? Composing. In the next coming months, I think I'm gonna do something then. I hope to, anyway, I'm trying to, you know?

Are you going to write new compositions for the quartet?

John Coltrane: Yeah, for the quartet, for anybody wants to play it! [*laughs*] But for the quartet primarily because we need new material, see. And, I just haven't gotten around to doing it yet, you know, but now I'm workin' on it.[1] I'm workin' on my approaches to the problem of writing for a group, see? And I've almost— I've gotten enough solved to do a few things which I think might be up to the standard of the things that we have done so far, you know?

Does this need to write come from the fact that you've played your tunes for too long?

John Coltrane: Well, definitely, yeah, mm hmm.

From "Coltrane 1963: Vers la Composition," by Michel Delorme, *Jazz Hot*, December 1963, pages 10–11. Transcribed from the audio recording by the editor; additional written material translated from French by John B. Garvey.

So it's not just to write.

John Coltrane: No, there's a need for it, see. And also I have recording commitments, I mean, I have to record at least three times a year, and after you look around you can't always find the tunes out in the market, from the theater or from the shows, from Tin Pan Alley or what have you. You can't always find the kind of songs that suit your own individual taste and so forth. And there are not that many good ones that come along; they come along once in a while. So, actually, a man with a band is left to—he really has to write for himself.

And when you do a record you have to do something original, you see.

John Coltrane: Yeah, I have to do something different, see, and I hate to go back. But recently I've done this; I've made a few things that I've done before. But I don't intend to do that in the future.

After your "chordal" and "modal" phases, you said you wanted to go further. Where are you at with this now?

John Coltrane: Well, I think I'm gonna let the nature of the songs determine just what I play. So that's what I'm concentrating on now, developing the ability to write, and then after I write I'm gonna take the nature of the songs and just play them as I feel them. And this may call for any type of playing; it might be modal, it might be chord progressions, or it might be just playing in areas, tonal areas.

Atonal music?

John Coltrane: Well, I don't know, I don't know how you'd say it, but I just call it "playing in tonal areas." It might be that, I don't know.

Don't you think that every year you come nearer from atonal music?

John Coltrane: Nearer to it, or nearer—from it, or what?

Nearer to it, yes, excuse me.

John Coltrane: That's all right. You should hear my French—*none*, I have *none*. [*all laugh*] You're lucky.

I don't know; probably so. I think so. But I don't know if—I don't know whether I can call it that because I don't know just what it'll be, you know? I think the thing that I'm gonna do will eventually be called more—nearer a modal thing than atonal. But I'm not sure, you know? Because it's probably gonna be shades of each; it's gonna overlap, you know, it's not gonna be something where you can say "this is this" because there's never gonna—it's not gonna always be the same thing. In other words, I think that every piece of music demands a certain type of interpretation, just by the nature of the song itself. And that's what I'm gonna try to make myself—rely on myself to be governed by, just what I feel the song calls for.

Do you think that it's important to be a good composer, like Monk, for example?

John Coltrane: Yep, that's great! That's just what a musician should do: write his own.

On tunes such as "Chasin' the Trane" you are only accompanied by bass and drums, without the piano. Do you want to go in this way, or is it only on occasion?

John Coltrane: Sometimes, sometimes. Only on occasion.

Does it open new fields?

John Coltrane: Without a piano?

Yeah, without the piano.

John Coltrane: Of course. Or you could do the same thing with it, you know, you could do the same with it. It's according to how you're thinking.

Do you feel freer, or no?

John Coltrane: Sometimes. Sometimes I do, sometimes I don't. I feel, you know—sometimes I do, sometimes I don't. Sometimes I feel a need for it, sometimes I feel that I'd like to play without it.

[At this point, Coltrane receives a phone call that interrupts the interview—the tape recorder, however, continues recording. After he hangs up, they discuss whether to continue the interview later, either during intermission or after that evening's concert. During this discussion, someone knocks on the door. The knocking happens several times, and it gets progressively louder each time. When they finally let in the unidentified person—whose voice sounds like a man's—Coltrane initiates a financial discussion:]

Coltrane: Are you the man with the money?

Unidentified man: What?

Coltrane: Are you the man with the money?

Unidentified man: What? Why? No, I don't have it, what do you mean?

Coltrane: I'm broke!

Unidentified man: You're broke?

Coltrane: Yeah, I'm trying to get money from the States. I paid some advances [*unintelligible*] Frankfurt . . .

[The man says that he'll try to get Coltrane his money so he "can concentrate," presumably on music. Coltrane says, "All right well we'll see, you know we gotta have some for {unintelligible}. . . . So I'm waitin' on a call from New York at eight o'clock. So we'll try that."

The tape ends shortly after this, but in the published article Delorme added some of their later discussion, which follows:]

John Coltrane: This evening, I'm going to play two or three themes which I didn't used to play regularly but which aren't really new themes. I really like playing some of my themes which, for me, are really pretty like "Aisha" or "Syeeda's Song Flute," but I want to compose another one for my daughter, an even prettier one. What I consider my best composition is "Naima," but I can't play it at this concert.[2]

So it's time for the concert, and we're heading to the Pleyel Hall. As we go along, Coltrane asks me lots of questions—it's certainly his turn.

John Coltrane: Is Bud Powell doing better? Who's playing right now in Paris? Who was at the Antibes Festival? Have you heard Tony Williams, Miles' young drummer, he's great, isn't he? Who's going to be performing the next Parisian concerts? Roland Kirk! You're really going to hear something. How many seats does Pleyel have compared to the Olympia? Are the acoustics good? Hey, here you don't keep out the agents either?

(This last following a sudden turnabout on sighting a police hat! This man who is all calm, all restrained in his demeanor, almost timid, has his moments of humor.)
After a concert which can only be described (in the non-pejorative use of the term) as a "group hallucination," we find Coltrane again, as dynamic now as he was worn out earlier.

John Coltrane, how can you not be worn out after such an expense of energy?

John Coltrane: Did you like it? Do you think I played well? I really enjoyed playing this evening, and I think my music showed it. The audience was great, and that encouraged me even more. No, really, I feel very good now; the fatigue is gone. The most important thing is to not eat before a concert, that gets in the way a lot. I would really like to hear the broadcast of this concert; I really think I gave my best.[3]

Yes, we noticed how far your knees kept sinking to the ground, and by your smile, a rare enough thing, after a piece.

John Coltrane: Yes, I was really happy, and the quartet was in great form.

On that topic, why do you sometimes draw closer to the rhythm section?

John Coltrane: The quartet has become so solid that I like to get as close as possible to it, if that's what you mean. I'm happy that that's evident and that the audience understands.

(Collected by Michel Delorme)

Notes
1. Over the next few months Coltrane would write some of his most beautiful and personal songs, including "Alabama," "Crescent," and "Wise One."
2. It would be interesting to know why "Naima" couldn't be played at this concert. It was played at other concerts during this tour; some of these concerts were broadcast and recordings exist.
3. Part of the broadcast recording survives, including a particularly intense version of "My Favorite Things"; Coltrane's opening solo is stunning. ("My Favorite Things" was released on *Live Trane—The European Tours* [Pablo 7PACD-4433-2], disc 3, track 2, misdated November 17, 1962.)

"COLTRANE: NEXT THING FOR ME—AFRICAN RHYTHMS"

Ray Coleman

The John Coltrane Quartet appeared at the Half Note in New York from May 22 to June 4, 1964. Ray Coleman interviewed Coltrane in the early hours of Friday, June 5, after the last set (Coleman says it was 4:15 A.M. and that Coltrane was "ending his stint"). Coltrane discusses his increasing interest in drums and rhythm, an interest he would explore more fully the following year.

At 4:15 one morning, after an incredible five-hour session at New York's famous Half Note jazz center, John Coltrane sat down. Perspiration was pouring from his brow.

Understandably, because the final tune took an hour to play, and this was nothing unusual. Earlier, "Greensleeves" had lasted an hour and a quarter.

The waiter delivered "the usual" to Coltrane, who was ending his stint at the club. It was a big cup of hot water. The poll-winning tenorist drank it feverishly then relaxed with a cigarette as the crowds trickled out in search of taxis.

Contrast

His music depicts him as a man of fervor and intensity, but in person he shows few, if any, moments of drama. He is quiet and retiring, and speaks softly, in direct contrast to his instrumental tone.

Two years ago he came to Britain and admitted that he was not sure which direction his playing was taking. Is he any more certain today"Yes, I am," he told me. "If anything, I think it is going back a little. For the past few years we have

From *Melody Maker*, July 11, 1964, page 6.

been playing a more modern form of jazz, rather than progressive. The next thing for me is for more rhythmic aspirations.

"I may do some work with some more drums—on record, anyway. Not necessarily featuring any one drummer more, but featuring more than one drummer. If this works out in the early stages, I may extend it to stage work.

"I am beginning to get more interested in the drum itself. I feel that since we have used fewer chordal progressions, we need more rhythm, and I want to experiment."

Evident

Coltrane's music has often been said to have some Eastern influences at work, and during the session that night with his regular quartet—McCoy Tyner (piano), Jimmy Garrison (bass) and Elvin Jones (drums)—it was again evident. Did he agree?

"Yes. I find that my moods in music sometimes have that flavor, and I am often influenced by what sort of sounds I am listening to privately.

"At the moment, I am listening to records featuring an African drummer and a Chinese flute player—two different works entirely—but to me it sounds like they made the records together!

"Right now I am very concerned with African rhythms. But I do listen to all kinds of music all the time."

Which album by the Coltrane Quartet had given him most satisfaction?

"None. I like parts of all of them, but not one of them entirely."

Was John ever dissatisfied with his playing to the point of thinking that he had been wasting his time?

"Oh yes, sometimes. I can feel when things have not gone properly. Not that anything I do is regulated. If I feel something coming on during a performance, I just let it go and it just goes on. Then it's not a case of 'did it work out,' but 'it took its course.'

"Sometimes I start a tune with a set pattern, sometimes not. It depends on how I feel at the time."

Coltrane made no announcements that night at the Half Note, and I asked him for his comments on the perennial "presentation" controversy.

John and Alice Coltrane at the Half Note. PHOTOGRAPH BY RAYMOND ROSS. COURTESY OF YASUHIRO "FUJI" FUJIOKA COLLECTION.

Public

"I don't announce things because—well, over here they've got used to it. They know most of the things we are doing, anyway, I think it would be superfluous."

What was his answer to critics who attacked him for "practicing in public"?

"They are right," he answered. "But they should remember that I have been playing for almost 25 years. I have always practiced in public.

"But then, that's the wrong word. If you are playing jazz, you have to play what comes out at any moment—something you have never said before. So the word should not be practice, but improvise."

There was certainly some wild improvising going on earlier, and from my vantage point underneath McCoy Tyner's piano, some of it sounded very exciting.

Packed

It is asking a lot of any audience to have their attention for more than an hour at a time, but the group achieved it. And in Tyner, Garrison and Jones, John Coltrane has musicians with uncanny rapport.

"John is one of the hardest workers around," said one of the managers of the Greenwich Village venue. "Sometimes he'll take an hour's break, then come back and play one number for as long as two and a half hours."

And he must have something, because the place is usually packed.

"THE JAZZ BIT: A CHAT WITH JOHN COLTRANE"

Louise Davis Stone

Coltrane seems almost playful here—when asked yet again about the length of his tunes, he replies, "Well, if you like something for ten minutes, why shouldn't you like it for 45 minutes?" Then again, maybe he was just tired of being asked the same questions year after year.

The Quartet was in Chicago at McKie's from July 15 to July 26, 1964. This interview probably took place on the night of Saturday, July 25.

There is nothing quite like going to the horse's mouth when you want to clarify a situation. Right? Right!

Some folks say jazz is dying, some say it is a crucial stage, some say it is dead and John Coltrane says "I don't know."

Now that is about the most honest comment I've yet encountered. If you don't know the name John Coltrane, multiple saxophonist and great giant in Jazz, don't read any further, we've lost you.

Coltrane and group (Elvin Jones, McCoy Tyner and Jimmy Garrison) closed a short engagement at McKie's (63rd and Cottage Grove) Sunday night.

For one hassle or another I wasn't able to go before Saturday but when I finally dug Coltrane, I dug him.

I reaffirmed my attitude that in order to hear him, you must listen.

Even though Coltrane is always swinging you can't get his jazz by osmosis. McKie's was packed—and rather interestingly—about 60 percent white fans by 1:30 A.M.

From the *Chicago Defender*, August 1, 1964, page 10.

When I approached Coltrane during intermission with a question in reference to the introspective nature of modern jazz and the decline of interest, seemingly, in jazz, he pondered for a good three minutes and let me sweat.

"I don't know whether jazz is dying or not. My records are selling well and I'm happy about that. I have no fear about my music being too way out. You are not going to find something new by doing the same thing over and over again. You add something new to the old. You have to give up something to get something."

It is a common thing to pick on Coltrane for playing a 45 minute tune.

Coltrane defended himself and his group simply by saying, Well, if you like something for ten minutes, why shouldn't you like it for 45 minutes.

Elvin Jones is one of the top if not the top drummer of the current jazz scene.

In spite of his virtuoso and his complex drum thinking, he is a loud drummer. Personally it has been my experience to sit entirely too near Elvin everytime I have seen Coltrane, so one of my questions concerned the what-seems-like imbalance of instruments with Jones cancelling out the others on occasion.

In one way Coltrane ignored my question but commented that he has noticed the imbalance problem in clubs where the P.A. system was faulty.

He recognized that it was his place to press for a better amplifying system, but he had so much on his mind worrying about what they and he were going to play that he neglected this area.

No one seemed concerned that night in McKie's—especially yours truly. I thoroughly enjoyed this modal period Coltrane finds himself in—he played "My Favorite Things" (breezier than usual) and "Afro-Blue," among other things.

Sonny Stitt opens at McKie's this week.

"COLTRANE SHAPING MUSICAL REVOLT"

Leonard Feather

The Quartet appeared at Shelly's Manne Hole in Hollywood from September 24 to October 4, 1964, and Leonard Feather interviewed Coltrane during the gig. In the *Newsweek* article on pages 91–92, Coltrane tells the story of how he started playing soprano sax; here he identifies "a writer named Chip Bayen" as the person involved.

The path of the avant-gardist in jazz is a precarious one, strewn with critical contumely and with esthetic decisions that lead to economic hazards.

John Coltrane is one of the handful of new wave performers who can claim artistic and commercial success. His quartet, formed soon after he left Miles Davis in 1960, is widely accepted in nightclubs, recordings and overseas tours.

Though a real understanding of his music demands technical knowledge and intense attention, Coltrane's most devoted followers are young listeners, many of whom may be musically illiterate. Recently, at Shelly's Manne Hole in Hollywood, he discussed his audiences.

"I never even thought about whether or not they understand what I'm doing," he said. "The emotional reaction is all that matters; as long as there is some feeling of communication, it isn't necessary that it be understood. After all, I used to love music myself long before I could even identify a G Minor Seventh chord.

"Audiences haven't changed much. They say Dizzy and Bird had to face a lot of hostility; but they had their good audiences too. Eventually, the listeners move right along with the musicians.

"Jazz is so much a music of individuality that every new artist with any originality effects a change in the overall scene. Lester Young represented as

From *Melody Maker*, December 19, 1964, page 6.

great a change, in his time, as some of the things that are happening now. So did Bird."

The ethos of Coltrane's music is a hypnotic quality, achieved through variations on a simple modal or harmonic basis. He has moved into areas that were once the exclusive preserve of Indian music. I asked him how he hoped to extend the audience for this process of acculturation:

"You've had no television exposure at all. How long do you think it will be before the layman is ready for what you're doing?"

"I don't know . . . do you think they ever will be? Anyhow, you can't really do what you want to do in television. You're restricted."

His meaning soon became clear: In the next set it took Coltrane an hour and 15 minutes to play two tunes. Both were framed by a 20-second theme; everything in between was improvised. The first tune ran 50 minutes, with Coltrane playing tenor sax mercurially and uninterruptedly, with unbelievably complex ideas and execution, for the first half-hour. The second tune, which included a 13-minute drum solo by the phenomenal Elvin Jones, featured Coltrane on soprano saxophone, an instrument he rescued from limbo almost single-handedly.

"It's a beautiful horn," he said later. "A friend of mine, a writer named Chip Bayen, had one, and I tried it out one day in 1960."

Since that chance discovery, saxophonists from Paris to Tokyo have taken to doubling on soprano, in the Coltrane style. But the cult is modestly shrugged off by its leader:

"I don't think people are necessarily copying me. In any art, there may be certain things in the air at certain times. Another musician may come along with a concept independently, and a number of people reach the same end by making a similar discovery at the same time."

Despite this disclaimer, Coltrane is shaping a musical revolution. For a while it will seem as unpalatable to the masses as was Goodman in 1934 or Gillespie in 1944, but Coltrane's time, as his already substantial audiences make abundantly clear, has just arrived.

ALBUM OF THE WEEK: John Coltrane—"Black Pearls" (Prestige, 7316). Adventurous musicianship in three long tracks, taped in 1957 with Donald Byrd, Red Garland, Paul Chambers, and Art Taylor.

A LOVE SUPREME LINER NOTES

John Coltrane

Coltrane's own liner notes for his iconic album, *A Love Supreme*, state that "Psalm" is "a musical narration of the theme, 'A Love Supreme.'" As analyzed in detail by Lewis Porter in *John Coltrane: His Life and Music* (pages 244–249), Coltrane plays the poem on his saxophone, a fact first noted in print by reviewer Doug Pringle in *CODA* magazine's October/ November 1965 issue: "[In] 'Psalm' [. . .] Coltrane [. . .] sets to music the text in the liner, phrase-by-phrase, in the manner of liturgical plainsong. The true power of his performance can only be felt by following the text with the music. The vocal quality of Coltrane's playing is moving, and in this context he can best communicate his feelings about the spiritual realities he has found in his musical life" (from page 32 of *CODA*).

DEAR LISTENER:

All Praise Be To God To Whom All Praise Is Due.

Let us pursue Him in the righteous path. Yes it is true; "seek and ye shall find". Only through Him can we know the most wondrous bequeathal.

During the year 1957, I experienced, by the grace of God, a spiritual awakening which was to lead me to a richer, fuller, more productive life. At that time, in gratitude, I humbly asked to be given the means and privilege to make others happy through music. I feel this has been granted through His grace. ALL PRAISE TO GOD.

As time and events moved on, a period of irresolution did prevail. I entered into a phase which was contradictory to the pledge and away from the esteemed path; but thankfully, now and again through the unerring and merciful hand of God, I do perceive and have been duly re-informed of His OMNIPOTENCE, and of our need for, and dependence on Him. At this time I would like to tell you that NO MATTER WHAT . . . IT IS WITH GOD. HE IS GRACIOUS AND MERCIFUL. HIS WAY IS IN LOVE, THROUGH WHICH WE ALL ARE. IT IS TRULY—A LOVE SUPREME—.

This album is a humble offering to Him. An attempt to say "THANK YOU GOD" through our work, even as we do in our hearts and with our tongues. May He help and strengthen all men in every good endeavor.

The music herein is presented in four parts. The first is entitled "ACKNOWLEDGE-MENT", the second, "RESOLUTION", the third, "PURSUANCE", and the fourth and last part is a musical narration of the theme, "A LOVE SUPREME" which is written in the context; it is entitled "PSALM".

In closing, I would like to thank the musicians who have contributed their much appreciated talents to the making of this album and all previous engagements.

To Elvin, James and McCoy, I would like to thank you for that which you give each time you perform on your instruments. Also, to Archie Shepp (tenor saxist) and to Art Davis (bassist) who both recorded on a track that regrettably will not be released at this time; my deepest appreciation for your work in music past and present. In the near future, I hope that we will be able to further the work that was started here.

Thanks to producer Bob Thiele; to recording engineer, Rudy Van Gelder; and the staff of ABC-Paramount records. Our appreciation and thanks to all people of good will and good works the world over, for in the bank of life is not good that investment which surely pays the highest and most cherished dividends.

May we never forget that in the sunshine of our lives, through the storm and after the rain—it is all with God—in all ways and forever.

ALL PRAISE TO GOD.

With love to all, I thank you,

[*signed*] John Coltrane

A Love Supreme

I will do all I can to be worthy of Thee O Lord.
It all has to do with it.
Thank you God.
Peace.
There is none other.
God is. It is so beautiful.
Thank you God. God is all.

Help us to resolve our fears and weaknesses.

Thank you God.

In You all things are possible.

We know. God made us so.

Keep your eye on God.

God is. He always was. He always will be.

No matter what . . . it is God.

He is gracious and merciful.

It is most important that I know Thee.

Words, sounds, speech, men, memory, thoughts,
  fears and emotions—time—all related . . .
  all made from one . . . all made in one.

Blessed be His name.

Thought waves—heat waves—all vibrations—
  all paths lead to God. Thank you God.

His way . . . it is so lovely . . . it is gracious.

It is merciful—thank you God.

One thought can produce millions of vibrations
  and they all go back to God . . . everything does.

Thank you God.

Have no fear . . . believe . . . thank you God.

The universe has many wonders. God is all.

His way . . . it is so wonderful.

Thoughts—deeds—vibrations, etc.

They all go back to God and He cleanses all.

He is gracious and merciful . . . thank you God.

Glory to God . . . God is so alive.

God is.

God loves.

May I be acceptable in Thy sight.

We are all one in His grace.

The fact that we do exist is acknowledgement
  of Thee O Lord.

Thank you God.

God will wash away all our tears . . .

He always has . . .

He always will.

Seek Him everyday. In all ways seek God everyday.

Let us sing all songs to God

To whom all praise is due . . . praise God.

No road is an easy one, but they all
    go back to God.

With all we share God.

It is all with God.

It is all with Thee.

Obey the Lord.

Blessed is He.

We are from one thing . . . the will of God . . .
    thank you God.

I have seen God—I have seen ungodly—
    none can be greater—none can compare to God.

Thank you God.

He will remake us . . . He always has and He
    always will.

It is true—blessed be His name—thank you God.

God breathes through us so completely . . .
    so gently we hardly feel it . . . yet,
    it is our everything.

Thank you God.

ELATION—ELEGANCE—EXALTATION—

All from God.

Thank you God. Amen.

                    JOHN COLTRANE—December, 1964

"JOHN COLTRANE"

Joe Goldberg

This is an abridged version of a long and thoughtful chapter in Joe Goldberg's book *Jazz Masters of the Fifties* (Macmillan, 1965).

A writer in the December 1960 issue of the men's magazine *Nugget* remarked that "One of the best things that ever happened to John Coltrane was the discovery of Ornette Coleman by the jazz avant garde . . . Coltrane . . . has been able to continue his search for his own musical personality without the onus of having everything he does, missteps and all, hailed as evidence of genius." It would have been nice had it been true. By comparison, the Ornette Coleman controversy was an argument carried on by physicists on the blackboard of the Princeton Institute for Advanced Study; discussions about Coltrane can take on some of the truculent, hysterical aspects of political arguments in neighborhood bars.

Often, the participants in arguments about Coltrane have about the same amount of accurate information as barroom philosophers. Coltrane is as undecided about his music as those who discuss it. Since 1959, he has run through several musical ideas so rapidly that a given Coltrane record may be obsolete before its release; it will almost surely be outdated before reviews of it are published. He therefore identifies with very little of what he reads about himself.

Very little is known about Coltrane's personal life; on the face of it, there is not much to tell. As his wife Juanita, who is an avid partisan of her husband and his playing, puts it, "He doesn't think about anything else but his music."

I once questioned him about an album he had recorded, one side of which was a trio with only bass and drum accompaniment. When I first heard these performances, I wondered why he had chosen to record that way. Did he feel

From *Jazz Masters of the Fifties* by Joe Goldberg (New York: MacMillan, 1965), pages 189–212 (abridged).

more freedom, or was there constriction? Sonny Rollins had made considerable impact by recording and playing personal appearances without piano; was Coltrane challenging Rollins? His answer was brief and to the point: "The piano player didn't show up." Another time, he was speaking of the writers who were nearly unanimous in their dislike of his first widely-heard efforts, seeming to feel that he did not know how to play. "I was hurt by it," he says, "but I was surprised. I don't know why they talked about me the way they did. I wasn't original then; I wasn't playing anything new or different."

Of his role as everybody's recording sideman [circa 1956–1958], Coltrane says, "I wouldn't do it now." At the time, he needed the money. The major turning point in Coltrane's career seems to have come in the summer of 1957, when he left Davis, who was temporarily dissatisfied with his group,[1] to join Thelonious Monk. [By the early 1960s] Coltrane had become deeply involved with the music of India, going so far as to study briefly with the Indian musician Ravi Shankar. Although he is not what he calls "an astute observer of the music," he has found much of what he has learned of it applicable to the sort of jazz he wants to play. Indian music is based on ragas, Indian scales which ascend differently than they descend. There are countless ragas, and each has a particular significance, concerned with religion, time of day, etc. Coltrane had found that "My Favorite Things" could be played almost as a raga. His next soprano recording, "Greensleeves," also played on principles of the raga, was an even more eerily hypnotic performance. Coltrane had been fascinated by the Indian water drum, essentially a drone instrument which keeps a steady tone going while others improvise around it. To simulate this, he used two bassists ("I like music to be heavy on the bottom"). Coltrane was quite pleased when he later discovered that Ali Akbar Khan, considered the greatest Indian musician, likes to play "Greensleeves." "I wish I could hear him do it," was his disarming remark. "Then I'd know if I was playing it right.

"Most of what we play in jazz," he continues, "has the feeling of just that one raga. The Indian musicians don't play the melody, they just play their scales. But maybe that's the melody to them. But what they do with it, the little differences, that's the improvisation." For a time, Coltrane pursued this so far that he would call off a chord sequence for his sidemen to play on, rather than an actual tune. They would then improvise on the mood suggested by the chord sequence and the tempo. "Yeah, I did that," he admits somewhat ruefully.

To be able to keep the feeling of the raga, but yet not play just chord changes ("I want to play tunes," he says, "I want to play the feeling of the song"), he began looking through old song books for folk tunes, perhaps turning to folios rather than recordings so that he would not be influenced by another's interpretation. He came up with "Olé," based on the Spanish folk song "Venga Vallejo." It is a remarkable synthesis of Indian elements, ideas propounded by Miles Davis in *Sketches of Spain*, and a growing concern with multiples of 3/4 time. Coltrane contributes one of his most furious solos, and Art Davis plays some of the most intricate, superbly musical bass that has ever been heard on a jazz record. In another song book, he found a piece he calls "Spiritual," which he plays with the irreducible minimum of one chord.

Coltrane's approach may owe as much to Miles Davis as to India. Davis had become preoccupied with "modal" jazz, based on scales rather than chords. Davis thus predicts the development of both Coltrane[2] and, to a lesser degree, the more extreme, more melodic Ornette Coleman.

Coleman, who is also interested in the music of India, has, conversely, been an influence on Coltrane. It is not surprising that Coltrane's insatiable curiosity and insistence on fewer and fewer chords should have led him to Coleman's music. For Coleman, who has all but done away with traditional harmony, had taken the step which Coltrane's deeply harmonic sensibilities might not allow him to take.

Coltrane and Coleman are good friends, and when they were working a few blocks from one another in New York, each would leave his own club between sets to hear the other man play. It was quite likely Coltrane's interest in Coleman which led him, in 1961, to invite the late Eric Dolphy to "come on in and work" in his band. Although Coltrane was delighted with the association, there was such a storm of critical protest that Coltrane's advisors eventually convinced him to ask Dolphy to leave. Coltrane had tremendous respect for Dolphy's formal education ("I'm into scales right now," he said one evening, and when asked if Dolphy was doing the same, replied proudly, "Eric's into everything"), and, when his explorations led him into a new area, traces of Dolphy's work began to show up in his own playing. Dolphy, for his part, felt that "I can't say in words what I've learned from John, the way he handles things. He's such a pro."

A synthesized recorded statement of Coltrane's musical ideas was made after [Jimmy] Garrison joined the group. This is not surprising, since each of his musical discoveries has immediately been reflected in changing personnel. Adding, subtracting, changing players, he gathered around him an impressive cadre of young musicians. "I keep looking," he explains, "for different ways to present my music. I don't think it's as presentable as it could be." He once mentioned that "I'd like to add an instrument that can play melody and percussion, maybe a guitar." Thus, Wes Montgomery joined the band, but the guitarist soon noted that the spaces between his solos were longer than the intervals between sets, and left. For a time, the second bassist was Art Davis, a brilliant young musician from Harrisburg, Pennsylvania. When Coltrane became involved with his new ideas about the use of the bass, he got into the habit of driving over to Davis' home and picking him up for a practice session. But Davis will not travel, preferring to remain in New York, where he often works in a non-jazz context. Coltrane uses Davis when he can. "I don't think Trane thinks of anything but music," Davis says. "He'll come back off the road and call me up to say, 'We're opening at the Vanguard tonight.' I say, 'We are?' and then I have to tell him that I'm working somewhere else. He never seems to think to let me know in advance, so I can stay free." Asked one night during a one-bass engagement in New York, why Davis was not with the group, Coltrane replied with some puzzlement, "Art's a very busy guy." For such reasons, he generally bills himself as "John Coltrane and his Group." "I'm playing it safe," he says.

Long permanent fixtures were the heavily chordal pianist McCoy Tyner ("McCoy has a beautiful lyric concept that is essential to complement the rest of us") and Elvin Jones, the most fiery, compulsively brilliant of modern drummers, in many ways the finest now playing. "Even I can't play with him," Coltrane says bemusedly. "He uses so many accents."

Coltrane is puzzled by the fact that one critic may praise him for exactly the same qualities another writer uses to damn him. Too often, the opposition to his work has assumed a hysterical cast, his detractors employing words like *anarchistic*, *nihilistic*, *gobbledegook*, *confusion*, *amorphism*, *nonsense*, and the dread epithet, *antijazz*. More reasoned questioning of his approach dealt with the extreme length of his solos, his use of suspensions ("vamps," he calls them) and the essential emotional sameness of his performances, no matter what the material.

With this in mind, it is extremely enlightening to listen to a Miles Davis album, *Someday My Prince Will Come*, recorded during the time that Coltrane was making such controversial music. Coltrane appears on two of the selections ("I sneaked down one afternoon and made it," he says of the record), the title track and a Spanish-influenced piece called "Teo." In the stricter, long-familiar setting of the Davis group, Coltrane contributes not only the most exciting, impassioned music on the set, but two of the best solos he had played in a long time. There were rumors that Davis wanted Coltrane to rejoin him, but even though Davis consistently outdrew Coltrane in the same clubs ("He has a wonderful name," Coltrane says, "he'd hire Sonny, he'd hire me, he'd hire all of us, just to hear us play. He's got a lot of money, and he loves to listen to music"), it seemed unlikely that the merger would ever come to pass.

For "everybody's sideman" is now indisputably a leader himself. He has created a music which is identifiably his, even during the long stretches of any selection when he is not soloing. How he has arrived at this new status is a fascinating question.

To see Coltrane in action is only to increase one's puzzlement about him. A quiet, pleasant, shyly friendly man who dresses simply and speaks softly, he is likely to be found between sets seated on his horncase, reading and eating an apple. At the conclusion of a solo, he wanders off-stage, Miles Davis fashion. He may talk to friends who have come to hear him, Ornette Coleman, for instance, or Davis or he may sit quietly at the far end of the club, listening to his band. But on the stand, he becomes impassioned and engrossed; it is as if setting the instrument to his lips completed an electrical circuit. As the music takes hold, he leans far back, eyes tight shut as if possessed with instant frenzy. Then, after the solo, he may move to the side of the stage, light one of the long, thin cigars he has begun to affect, and adjust a reed.

In a little over a year, he passed rapidly through several different styles of music, a man with a sudden thirst for knowledge, and each new thing he tries only opens up wider areas to explore. Basically a romantic player—the rage in his playing is only the reverse side of the lyricism—he has accumulated in his search, as most romantics do, an ever-growing list of what he knows he does not want. It may be pertinent that he has retained his original slow ballad style. When playing other music, though, he is in a dangerous position. The first attempt at any new thing inevitably involves awkwardness, and the listener on any given night may find Coltrane struggling through his own musical vocabulary. This has caused many to turn away in exasperation, but the saxophonist is apparently willing to take that chance. All he can offer his audience on such occasions is the excitement of participating in the creative process. It is a thrilling thing to be able to share, but obviously not everyone is willing to share it.

This concern with pure music is easily understood. Jazz began as music-at-home, in which almost anyone could participate. Today, when many jazz musicians can in some respects outplay their symphonic counterparts, it has become a virtuoso's music, a music in which one begins as a virtuoso and goes on from there. But technical facility is not Coltrane's only concern. He would like, he says, for his music to have "strong emotional content."

Some of that emotion comes out in his compositions. Now determined to play songs instead of chords, he has found none that completely satisfy him, and has turned to writing his own, more from necessity than a desire to compose. One night at the Jazz Gallery, he premiered a new untitled piece (now called "Big Nick"), so simple and charming that several members of the audience immediately began whistling it. Coltrane was unable to believe he had been successful. "I'd like to know what the hell they were whistling," he said, puzzled. "I thought it was mine." Some of his pieces do sound familiar. His "Blue Train" is the prototype of much of his work, and some of his blues sound like classic lines from the thirties.

Coltrane has expressed a desire to write in the twelve-tone system. Asked about the seeming impossibility of improvising serially, he replies, "Damn the rules, it's the feeling that counts. You play all twelve notes in your solo anyway."

Despite the increased emphasis on composition, improvising remains the primary vehicle of Coltrane's emotions. If we are, in [critic-saxophonist Don] Heckman's words, to "meet the music on its own terms," to understand the menace of its almost crushing energy, then some attempt must be made to understand Coltrane himself.

One clue is in his Jamaica, Long Island, home. There are few records in his library, but what he has is almost all folk music from India. For a long time, occupying a considerable part of the livingroom was a large rented harp, which he was learning to play "because it helps me with harmony." His only apparent hobby is a telescope in the back yard, which he looks through on the rare occasions when he has the chance. His group works constantly. "I don't know what you mean by a dedicated musician," his wife says, "but all he does is practice. Many nights he'd fall asleep with the horn still in his mouth."

Scant attention has been paid to furnishing; ceramic wall plaques provide almost the only decor. Coltrane, the most pleasant of men, seems almost naïve; his musical sophistication is not hinted at by his manner. ("A lot of 'literary' people say that," comments Cecil Taylor. "I always feel good about being with John *after* I've talked to him.") "White Americans," James Baldwin has written, "find it as difficult as white people elsewhere to divest themselves of the notion that they are in possession of some intrinsic value that black people need, or want." In that remark may lie the ultimate significance of the power and danger of the jazz of quiet, naïve John Coltrane, who has taken his musical imagination from India, from Africa, and from the blues.

While displaying an ever more voracious appetite for all things new (Coltrane does not tend to think of himself as a leader, but as a student of music who is in the remarkable position of being paid to do what obsesses him), he has still managed to combine commerce and art. Though his playing is basically the same on both his instruments ("I think you have to have musical conviction, rather than let the instrument dictate to you"), his soprano sax is primarily responsible for a popularity that, in 1961, enabled him to appear at all four of New York's major jazz clubs. He has judiciously combined the elements of his success. Early in an evening, he will feature the soprano on pieces like "My Favorite Things" and "Greensleeves." Afterwards, he might say to a friend, "The next set will be different. The next set I'll play all my nonhits." The soprano disappears, to be replaced by the tenor and long, furiously impassioned and basic blues.

Off the stand again, he once more becomes the shy, friendly man whose cigar is the only indication that he knows he is a success. His main concern with his constant work on the road is the protracted absence from his wife ("She really knows me, and understands the problems I have as a leader"). Perhaps he takes his preeminence with such equanimity because, having made it the hard way, he has an extremely realistic view of the business he is in. "Every time I talk about jazz," he says, "I think of prizefighters. One year it's your year, like it's mine now, and the next year everybody's forgotten you. You only have a few years, and you have to stay up there as long as you can, and do the best you can, and be graceful about it when it's someone else's turn."

I was interested to know what John Coltrane would do when the young musicians who are learning so much from him overtook him.

"I'd just keep playing," he said. "It's all I know."

Notes

1. Davis disbanded in April 1957, a week or so into what was scheduled to be a much longer engagement at the Café Bohemia in New York. *Down Beat* ("Miles Davis Disbands," May 30, 1957, page 9) reported that Davis broke up the band because he was "dissatisfied at the conduct of two of the members of his combo": "Miles Davis has broken up his quintet. Davis explains that he has been increasingly dissatisfied at the conduct of two of the members of his combo. He walked off a Baltimore date toward the beginning of a week stay, and then was fired along with his band by the owner of [Café] Bohemia in New York for leaving at 2 A.M. one morning during the first week of a long booking. Miles' story is that two of his men were not in optimum playing condition, and he didn't want to be held responsible by the audience for what they were doing onstand." Although there's no definitive proof, it's generally accepted that the two band members who provoked Davis's ire were Coltrane and Philly Joe Jones.

2. Coltrane himself explicitly credited Davis (as well as Ornette Coleman) for this. For examples, see pages 100 and 117.

"DROPPING THE BALL AND CHAIN FROM JAZZ"

Michael Hennessey

On July 26 and 27, 1965, the Quartet appeared at the Antibes Jazz Festival in Juan-les-Pins, France. Fortunately these powerful performances were recorded on both videotape and audiotape (though only the first part of the July 26 performance survives on video). Several journalists also interviewed Coltrane during the festival. This interview was conducted on July 27.

Of all the jazz musicians currently exploring new directions, John Coltrane has always seemed to me to be the only one with a map and compass.

To begin with, Coltrane was way-in before he became way-out. His evolution from rhythm and blues has been constant and logical.

He is a musician of many virtues. He has a passionate sincerity, a simple dignity and a command of the tenor saxophone which, in my view, is without equal in the jazz world.

No other musician to my mind has broken away with such consummate success from the "theme-solos-fours-theme" format over 12 or 32 bars which has, for many, become the ball and chain of jazz.

If you want a contemporary equivalent of Charlie Parker, then you need look no further than Coltrane. As his bass player, Jimmy Garrison, says: "Now that Ornette don't come out, John is the only one who's keeping things alive."

When I met Coltrane in his hotel room during the Antibes Jazz Festival, I was immediately impressed by the apparent contrast between the man and his music. He is a big, slow-moving man with an extremely gentle disposition and an economy of conversation. You have the impression that he expresses himself so completely and comprehensively in his music that when it comes to interviews there is little left to say. In the music of Coltrane you can find anger, bitterness, anguish, sadness. In the man you are conscious only of a great inner peace and serenity.

From *Melody Maker*, August 14, 1965, page 6.

It was a fascinating meeting. Because for the first hour and a half Coltrane expressed himself through his tenor and soprano. He stood at the table, blowing into a portable tape recorder and then playing it back. Unhurriedly he changed reeds, adjusted mouthpieces, tore off characteristically intricate and extended runs. He was practicing for the concert that evening.

When he finally laid down the tenor I asked him how long his reeds lasted. "A good reed lasts me three weeks—but it doesn't seem too easy to get a good one these days." Then he picked up the soprano and practiced for another half an hour.

My appointment had been for 4 o'clock. By the time we got to talk it was 6:30 p.m. . . . and even then I somehow felt that Coltrane would much rather have played than talked. But as he touched into a slightly bizarre dinner of two raw egg yolks, clear soup, milk, iced water and fresh peaches (he's trying to keep his weight down) he answered my questions amiably and thoughtfully.

"How often do you practice like that?"

"Not as often as I should. I have been thinking about writing so much recently that I haven't done too much practicing. I think four hours' practice a day would be good for me. That little bit of practicing just then—well, I didn't play a thing I didn't know. But after four hours I would get through all that and then maybe I'd break into something new."

"What were you listening for on the playback?"

"Just to see how the notes were coming out—whether they were coming through clear and in tune."

"Do you have intonation problems with the soprano?"

"Funnily enough, I have more problems with the tenor than with soprano. I was lucky with my soprano. I've had it five years—it was the first one I bought. It was a good one, but it's beginning to go off a little now."

"How do you think your playing now compares with your work with Miles Davis five years ago?"

"I don't think it has changed basically—though I suppose I've grown a little, musically. But then in some respects I think I might have been a little more inventive in those days."

"What would you say were the faults in your playing—do you feel there is anything missing?"

"That's hard to answer. I don't know if you can ever be a complete musician. I'm not. But I don't think I'll know what's missing from my playing until I find it—if you understand me. Perhaps my main fault at the moment is that I have a natural feeling for the minor. I'd like to do more things in the major. I want to work to bring that up—and there are many other modes I've got to learn."

I asked him if, in his search for new directions, he ever found himself in a musical dead end.

He laughed. "I doubt if there are any dead ends." Then, on reflection, he added: "There may be, though, I suppose I've had some things which didn't work out. But usually if you get on a new thing you just keep on playing it until you get it together. I'm very lucky—I work with very fine musicians. They are very inventive. I don't have to tell anybody what to do. When we have a new thing, I just define the different sections and leave the rest to them.

"We have great confidence in one another. That's essential—that's how it hangs together. They're with me in always wanting the band to move into a new area. We generally don't believe in standing still."

A philosophy which, while thoroughly commendable, also raises an audience problem. At the first Coltrane concert at Antibes, the audience was a little puzzled and disappointed to hear just one piece, "A Love Supreme," played for 47 minutes.

"What about giving the audiences a chance to catch up?" I asked Coltrane.

"This always frightens me," he said candidly. "Whenever I make a change, I'm a little worried that it may puzzle people. And sometimes I deliberately delay things for this reason. But after a while I find that there is nothing else I can do but go ahead." (In fact—and this underlines Coltrane's anxiety to carry his audiences along with him—he changed the program for the second concert and featured some more established pieces like "Impressions" and "My Favorite Things"—but without sacrificing any of his individuality or inventiveness.)

Coltrane says he hasn't yet composed anything he is completely satisfied with. "I plan to do more extended works—I have sketches of them in my head. I want to get to a point where I can feel the vibrations of a particular place at a particular moment and compose a song right there, on the spot—then throw it away. I try to avoid repeating things as much as I can."

It has been said that Coltrane has recently discovered God. I asked him about this.

"Rediscovered would be a better word. Religion has always been with me since I was a kid. I was raised in a religious atmosphere and it has stuck with me throughout my life. Sometimes I feel it more strongly than others."

"Do you listen very often to your own records?"

He smiled. "No. Perhaps two or three times a year I'll take them out and evaluate them—but I'm more concerned with how I'm playing right now."

More often Coltrane listens to African and Indian music. "There's a harp record I play quite a lot, too. I got very interested in harp for a while. But now I think when I get tired of blowing, I'll take up guitar or piano."

"How far have you extended the range of the tenor?"

"Well, you can't get below B-flat. But there's at least another octave above the normal top limit which can be fingered."

"And talking of extending limits, which musicians do you think are making important contributions in seeking new jazz expressions?"

"I think the Jazz Composers' Guild are doing good things—I admire Albert Ayler, Archie Shepp, Dewey Johnson, Pharoah Sanders and John Tchicai."

Has Coltrane definitely abandoned the more orthodox jazz frameworks?

"Not necessarily. I've been thinking of doing another album of ballads—just playing them straight. Though generally I do feel that normal forms have pretty well been used up. I'm also thinking of doing an album with a couple of horns and Latin percussion."

"COLTRANE, STAR OF ANTIBES: 'I CAN'T GO FARTHER'"

Michel Delorme and Claude Lenissois

Michel Delorme attended the Antibes Jazz Festival and interviewed
Coltrane, probably on July 27, 1965, the second day of the festival.
Intriguingly, Coltrane mentions that the songs "Wise One," "Lonnie's
Lament," and "The Drum Thing"—from the album *Crescent*—are based on
poems he had written.

In his prescient introduction to this interview, Delorme speculates on the
future of the Quartet: "Even more than the surprise of hearing a single work
[. . .] is the feeling of not getting the flow of the music. [. . .] I will always see
Elvin Jones, clearly out of the loop, standing behind his drum kit at the
beginning of the second concert, not being able to decide what he should
do. It seems therefore quite clear that, if Coltrane is humanly and musically
at a turning point in his career, the quartet itself is approaching a dangerous
curve. And yet, each member is giving his best, like their leader." Within six
months both McCoy Tyner and Elvin Jones would leave the band.

Coltrane at His Culmination, or the Most Thrilling Failure of the Festival

It's the third time that I've met John Coltrane. In Paris, in 1962, Jean Clouzet and I
had a long, very interesting conversation with him. In 1963, after the two extraordinary concerts which he performed for us at Pleyel, I asked him several additional questions. How were we going to find him in Antibes this year? I was quite
sure that the fairly euphoric atmosphere of the festival would have no impact on
this impenetrable man, despite excellent precedents (Miles Davis in particular).
I was nevertheless far from suspecting that his behavior, up to that point balanced between reservedly serious and politely amiable, would so generally feed
the polemics usually reserved for other musicians. To tell the truth, I don't know

From *Jazz Hot*, September 1965, pages 5–6. Translated by John B. Garvey.

what to think about Coltrane's stage manner this year. Almost not acknowledging his audience, he always left the stage immediately after his last note, and didn't return. Even more serious was the discomfort caused by the music itself. Of course, it was a mistake to offer "A Love Supreme," which no one knew, on the first evening, instead of yesterday's classics like "Naima," "My Favorite Things," and "So What" [Coltrane's working title for "Impressions"]; nevertheless, this winning over the public is not primary from my perspective, and I was personally fascinated by the music that Coltrane played during that long set. What seems much more important, and which explains the discomfort felt by many, is the relationship between this music and the stage manner, not just Coltrane's, but of the whole quartet, shown continuously throughout both concerts.

Actually, as soon as John had finished his last phrase, the rhythm continued by itself for another moment, giving the impression that it didn't know if it was all over or not. Several threads of themes during the second concert confirmed the impression the audience had the first evening. Even more than the surprise of hearing a single work (which, for that matter, included several very lovely themes, lasting nearly forty-five minutes) is the feeling of not getting the flow of the music, of not getting the beginning or the ending, which sidetracked the audience more than anything else. I will always see Elvin Jones, clearly out of the loop, standing behind his drum kit at the beginning of the second concert, not being able to decide what he should do. It seems therefore quite clear that, if Coltrane is humanly and musically at a turning point in his career, the quartet itself is approaching a dangerous curve. And yet, each member is giving his best, like their leader. Who would continue to doubt Coltrane's sincerity after having seen him at Antibes pushing himself to his physical limits? Who didn't feel the interior strength, the total self-denial that this exceptional being communicates through his music? John Coltrane was not satisfied with his first concert. Having forgotten the little rubber gaskets that he puts on the upper part of his tenor sax in New York handicapped him a great deal. He replaced them as well as he could with make-dos, the second evening.

The personal contacts I've had with him during these two days he spent in Juan allowed no expectations of a change in attitude. He came across very agreeably, took a sharp interest in listening to Ravel's "Bolero," which he already knew but which I wished to encourage him to record a complete, textual version of with his quartet (he responded to me, laughing, that after all it was probably

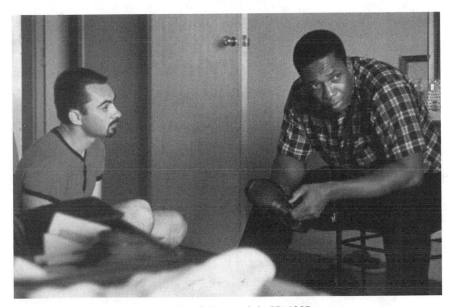

Michel Delorme interviewing John Coltrane, July 27, 1965.

better to leave the masterpieces the way they were, despite however much one might want to give one's own interpretation), played back on his soprano sax certain themes from the first album of Spanish organs which he appreciated a great deal, declared that the photographs by Jean-Pierre Leloir were the best that he had ever seen of his quartet, and gave in gracefully to the usual interviews, including the one which follows, and which I now let you read through:

The last time we met was in November of 1963, and you told me that you wanted to dedicate yourself to composing.

Coltrane: I'm still looking; I think that we're nearly at the point of finding.

What records have you made since 1963?

Coltrane: I think there have been four. *Live at Birdland, Impressions, Crescent, A Love Supreme.* Since then, we have recorded three or four more, either as a quartet or with a large ensemble with seven winds including Archie Shepp; I especially appreciated that session with seven winds.

Do you want to keep this style of composing or would you rather return to the formula of such short works as "Crescent"?

Coltrane: There it involved short pieces, but I am soon going to record longer pieces on which I'm currently working, a set we haven't started working on yet where, this time, the melody will play a more important role.

Yesterday, we were talking about Archie Shepp and Albert Ayler; someone said to me that next to them, you were "corny"; what do you think about that?

Coltrane: [*laughing*] They didn't lie to you . . . I'll play you a track from the Albert Ayler concert with Don Ayler and Sonny Murray in a little while.

We don't know them very well here. Can you talk to us about them?

Coltrane: Archie Shepp has already been playing with Cecil Taylor for a while. As for Albert Ayler—I don't remember exactly when—but when I went to Copenhagen a few years ago, he was playing with Cecil Taylor. It's when he came back to the United States that he started to become known in New York, two or three years ago.

About the album A Love Supreme; *do you think that the text and the poem that you wrote help with understanding the music?*

Coltrane: Not necessarily. I just wanted to express something that I felt; I had to write it.

Do you often write poems?

Coltrane: From time to time—I try. This one is the longest I've ever written, but certain pieces from the album *Crescent* are also poems, like "Wise One," "Lonnie's Lament," "The Drum Thing." Sometimes I do it this way because it's a good approach to musical composition. I'm also interested in languages, in architecture. I'd like to get to the point where I can capture the essence of a precise moment in a given place, compose the work and perform it immediately in a natural way.

Your latest record is to the glory of God. Why?

Coltrane: I refound my faith several years ago. I had already found it and lost it several times. I was brought up in a religious family, I had the seeds of it in me, and, at certain moments, I find my faith again. All of that is connected to the life one leads.

Does religion help you in living, in playing?

Coltrane: It's everything for me; my music is a way of giving thanks to God.

Do you have any plans to return to a more conventional musical structure (32 measures, for example) or are—do you think that everything has been said about these structures?

Coltrane: I've thought about it; but it is possible that really everything has been said in a conventional way. In spite of everything, I've recently done several pieces with traditional form and harmonies.

Your record of ballads is very traditional. Are you thinking of doing that again?

Coltrane: Yes. I'm planning a new album where I'll play the melodies simply, just as they are. After that I'll go back to composition.

Do you listen to your own records?

Coltrane: I work mostly with a tape recorder, which lets me oversee my experiments, but it does happen that I listen to my records two or three times a year to keep up to date.

Since you left Miles, do you have the feeling that your style has changed?

Coltrane: No. It's still the same music, more or less. In a way, I think I can control my technique better but, in two hours of work, I'm not doing anything that I don't already know.

What criteria did you use to choose your musicians?

Coltrane: I never have to tell them anything. They always know what they're supposed to do and are constantly inspired. I know that I can always count on them, and that gives me confidence. There is a perfect musical communion between us that doesn't take human values into account. Even in the case of *Love Supreme*, without discussion, I don't go any further than to set the layout of the work. It's just twelve minor measures, developed, which has, for the framework of the last part, a minor blues. The first part doesn't contain a set number of measures, and the central part is composed of three groups of eight measures. For me, when I go from a calm moment to extreme tension, it's only the emotional factors that drive me, to the exclusion of all musical considerations. For Elvin, I think that the musical considerations are the most important.

John Coltrane, can I ask you in conclusion what you're planning for in the future?

Coltrane: I don't know yet. I'm looking for new ground to explore. Physically, I can't go beyond what I'm doing right now in the form that I'm practicing. It always scares me a little to think that I'm going to have to change again. Very often, when I'm at a turning point, I put off the decision so that everyone might understand me before I've already changed.

(Material collected by Michel Delorme and Claude Lenissois.)

INTERVIEW WITH JOHN COLTRANE

Michiel de Ruyter

In this interview—another from Antibes (July 27, 1965)—Coltrane discusses Albert Ayler, *A Love Supreme*, *Ascension*, open-air jazz festivals, and his ability to block out distractions such as photographers and noisy audiences ("The problems that I have in music [are] always there, you know? They take my time pretty completely").

Michiel de Ruyter: On the, ah—as far as private things—

John Coltrane: Mm hmm.

de Ruyter: —for myself. On the cover of an Albert Ayler record, released in Denmark, was a story that you once should have had a dream in which you were playing like Albert Ayler.

Coltrane: Hmm.

de Ruyter: That's, that's what a story said.

Coltrane: No kiddin'! Who wrote that?

de Ruyter: I don't know, just, just somebody who wrote a liner note.

Coltrane: Well, it's, it's kinda true. It's, it's really true. Because I had a dream, I had a dream once and the whole band was playin' like that. You know? And I don't know whether I was in the band but I—either I felt the band was mine or I was in it but I was *watchin'* this band, you know? I'd had a dream like that around, around nineteen fifty . . . fifty-seven. You know? And the whole band, man, had that kinda sound.

de Ruyter: Also—

Coltrane: So that's really true. [*There's a pause. Then Coltrane begins to speak, but de Ruyter interrupts.*]

de Ruyter: No, it was—it was more or less suggested that you had that dream *after* you had heard Albert Ayler.

Coltrane: Well—

de Ruyter: You see?

Coltrane: Well it happened before, I had it before then.

de Ruyter: [*unintelligible*] Yeah.

Coltrane: Yeah, I had it before then.

de Ruyter: It's different.

Coltrane: I knew, I knew this was coming. See? I knew this was coming, I just—I *felt* it was comin', I didn't *know*, [*chuckles*] I don't know the future, but I felt this was coming.

de Ruyter: We heard *Love Supreme* yesterday—

Coltrane: Mm hmm.

de Ruyter: —and, I know the record of course, I played it on my program.

Coltrane: Mm hmm.

de Ruyter: [*unintelligible*] And in the liner notes, if I may call them so, on *A Love Supreme*, you said it's not the complete work which is on the record. For instance when I compared the record with what I heard yesterday, there is no bass solo—not *that* long, anyway—on the, on the record. And you talked about a part that Archie Shepp was playing and it was left out.

Coltrane: Yeah. Well the first part of it, uh, we—Archie Shepp played on it, and I think I had another bass on there, but ah—I didn't use this, this part. Because I had, I had two parts, I had one part that I was singing on, and I had another part—well not singing, chanting—then I had another part that Archie and the other bass was on. And when I—in editing, editing and I, I felt that I wanted to use the part that I had the, uh, the singing on, see. So that's the one we did use. . . . But I made a thing recently with Archie.

de Ruyter: Oh yeah?

Coltrane: And, also another young tenor man named Ferrell Sanders, who is some-thin' to hear too. And Freddie Hubbard, and um . . . trumpeter Dewey Johnson, and, uh . . . Marion Brown on alto, John Tchicai—a big band thing, you know—which is—

de Ruyter: From the way you smile, it [*unintelligible*]—

Coltrane: I like—well, it—you know, it's something. It's something that, there's something in it I like. [*trails off; says something like* "Yeah, somethin' that I like."] Is this carbonated water here?

de Ruyter: Uh . . .

Coltrane: Or is it—well I'll taste it and see. Oh, this is lemonade.

de Ruyter: Yeah, it's uh . . .

Coltrane: Hm. I dig.

de Ruyter: Anyway . . .

Coltrane dominated the polls in 1965. COURTESY OF *DOWN BEAT.*

Coltrane: OK. [*chuckles*]

[*Unintelligible exchange; glass clinking*]

de Ruyter: Ah, just one other thing. [*clears throat*] I've—in fact, I've never been at, uh, open-air jazzival—jazz festivals like this one. But you've played Newport several times I guess, and [*unintelligible*] festival in the, in the States. Can you compare them to the, this affair here?

Coltrane: How do I compare the festivals in the States to this?

de Ruyter: Yeah, I mean, uh, the reaction from the crowd; was the crowd noisier, or, or, or—

Coltrane: Well, I th—they compare, they're about the same. You know, it's about the same as the ones I've been on. It's about the same.

de Ruyter: Because for, for ten thousand people that are here in this park, they're pretty quiet when they're listening—

Coltrane: Ten thousand?

de Ruyter: Yeah.

Coltrane: When were there ten thousand there?

de Ruyter: That's what, what they say that the park can hold [*unintelligible*].

Coltrane: The park that we played last night?

de Ruyter: Yeah.

Coltrane: This thing can hold ten thousand? It didn't look that big to me.

de Ruyter: It didn't look that big to me either [*Coltrane laughs*], but uh, somebody who had to do something with the organization—

Coltrane: I don't know.

de Ruyter: —said it can hold ten thousand people!

Coltrane: They should know.

de Ruyter: But they're pretty quiet.

Coltrane: For ten thousand.

de Ruyter: You like, like [*stutters*] to play affairs like this—open-air things?

Coltrane: No, I don't prefer 'em, because usually the acoustics are kinda horrible, you know. I prefer a certain type of club, but I don't al—we can't always get that, either. Or, or a concert hall, you know. Good—I've found the smaller places, the more compact they are the better we, our sound is held together, you know? And we can hear and feel each other better, the smaller the place is.

de Ruyter: Do you like the, the Concertgebouw in Amsterdam?

Coltrane: Hm?

de Ruyter: The Concertgebouw in Amsterdam, you know that concert hall [*unintelligible*].

Coltrane: Yeah, we get a good sound there, I can hear, I can hear.

de Ruyter: [*interrupting; hard to make out, something like:* "Is, is, is it good to play there?"]

Coltrane: Yeah, I can hear pretty well there. I can hear everything, you know? Some places as soon as you hit the first note it goes all over the place and [*unintelligible word*] you can't feel the flow of the thing, you know.

de Ruyter: Are you distracted very much by, by outside interference? I mean noisy crowds, people walking around, people taking pictures? Because—

Coltrane: No.

de Ruyter: —I ask that because, because you don't look like it, see.

Coltrane: Mm mm. [*negative*]

de Ruyter: You're not too much disturbed by it.

Coltrane: Mm mm. Mm mm. [*negative*]

de Ruyter: Too concentrated on the, the music.

Coltrane: Oh, yeah, well the, you know, the problems that I have in music that—they're always there, you know? They take my time pretty completely.

de Ruyter: OK, that's it.

Coltrane: Mm hmm.

"JOHN COLTRANE—'TRANE'" (PART 2)

Randi Hultin

Norwegian journalist Randi Hultin met Coltrane at the Antibes Jazz Festival and then again in Paris, where the Quartet appeared at Salle Pleyel. Hultin's encounters with Coltrane were particularly interesting in that she spent time with him—going to dinner and to jazz clubs—rather than just interviewing him.

Encounter in Antibes

In 1965, I was again in Juan-les-Pins, and I was looking forward to seeing Coltrane. At his hotel I was stopped at the reception desk, but when they called his room and announced "Randi from Norway," they got the green light. When I entered his room, there were two gentlemen sitting on the floor, awaiting an interview, one of them Mike Hennessey, an excellent jazz journalist. Coltrane was standing with his back towards them, practicing and recording everything he played on a tape recorder. "I want to check my pitch," he said.

"Would you like something to eat?" he asked me politely. I declined, and decided to write some postcards while we were waiting for him to finish playing. The other two were just sitting there, waiting patiently. Finally, Hennessey asked if he could start the interview. "Go ahead," Trane said. He was then asked about his plans for the future. Did he have any special musician in mind that he wanted to use? While Coltrane was pondering the answer, I remarked that the next time he was making a record, it ought to be with an accordion player. A dead silence followed until John suddenly started laughing. He alone had understood that I was trying to break the tension.

After finishing the interview, we had dinner in his hotel room. What a scrumptious meal—and what service! That evening, I went with John to the concert.

From *Born Under the Sign of Jazz*, by Randi Hultin, pages 162–172.

Elvin had arrived at the last minute in the company of a blonde lady, and even though Coltrane didn't utter a word, he had been very nervous. I asked John if Elvin's friend was French. "I have no idea," he said. "The musicians never tell me anything."

The atmosphere when Coltrane and his band walked on stage was similar to that at a Beatles concert, he was so tremendously popular. For forty-eight minutes, he played a version of *A Love Supreme*, intensely and aggressively, and without a break. It was very demanding, but the audience cheered and everybody acknowledged his genius. His playing was obviously influenced by Indian music, but at times it would sound like the lowing of cattle, or the barking of angry dogs. Whatever its inspiration, the musicians in the audience were chuckling with exhilaration, and not just with Trane. McCoy, too, played a marvelous solo, having obviously developed a great deal rhythmically since the last time I had heard him, and Garrison played a ten-minute bass solo that was anything but dull.

After the concert, I invited John over to my hotel. As usual I was staying at Les Pergolas, where I had a refrigerator, kitchen, bathroom, and bedroom. We walked from the festival grounds in the park named La Pinede, to my hotel, located just a few yards away from the Grand Hotel. Four or five fans were walking on each side of Coltrane, asking him the strangest questions. One of them said, "Mr. Coltrane, do you have a record player with you? I would love to hear some of your records . . ."

"Randi, what is he saying?" The fellow was speaking English, but I'm sure that John thought, like I did, that he must not have heard right.

Just before we reached Les Pergolas, I observed some Swedish musicians at the street corner. Later they told me that when they saw Coltrane coming down the street, they nearly collapsed. They wanted to meet him, but the two of us had suddenly disappeared up a flight of stairs—at the time, I didn't know who these Swedes were.

I was boiling an egg, and I asked Trane how he wanted it. "Five minutes," he said, so I timed it very carefully, but it still turned almost green. "This egg must have been pretty hot already when it came out of that French chicken," I observed. We relaxed and talked. I think Coltrane appreciated getting away from the big hotel, where the journalists—especially the photographers—would be lurking in the bushes. At the time, I did not consider myself in either of those professional categories. I was merely a friend.

We talked about everything, including our families. He had recently split up with Naima. It happened that we even talked about a new French lighter named "Cricket" for about a quarter of an hour. It is strange to be remembering such details, but I'll never forget how we examined this lighter, which had just come out on the market. I also remember how John would all of a sudden start singing "O Sole Mio"—only the first bars. I don't know if he was even aware of it.

Dissatisfied

Naturally, we talked about music. John asked me what I thought about the concert. I told him what I felt to be true—that to me, it sounded "too coarse." "You played so angrily it sounded like you were irritated at something."

"I sure was! I can get pretty irritated with Elvin sometimes. At the same time, I worry that I won't be able to keep the quartet together, and without them I wouldn't have the guts to come back to Europe. I'm really afraid of losing Elvin, he's really special. It always takes some time before he gets going, but when that happens, there's nobody like him. I wasn't too pleased with the concert myself— it didn't take off the way I wanted it to. It isn't always that easy. I'm constantly trying to move one step further."

"Are you playing a lot of concerts in America?"

"Mostly clubs. I also have a contract to make three records every year, which isn't easy either. The company always expects me to come up with something new."

"Have you thought about the responsibility you have? If you mixed your music with, say, Finnish jenka, a whole lot of saxophone players all over the world would try to do the same thing."

"I never thought of myself in that way."

"When you made that record with Johnny Hartman, was that to prove that you could play beautiful ballads if you wanted to?"

"Sometimes I get the urge to play something more commercial. He's a fine singer, and I wanted him to make a comeback. A recording like that is also relaxing for my musicians. I'm not always up to presenting something new. I want to give everything I've got, and I want it to be good."

I understood John when it came to self-expectations. I explained to him my own feelings about modern art. If I were to paint in a modernist style, I would have to learn more about life—perhaps attend more schools. It was easier to paint nice portraits.

"Strange you should be saying that. That's exactly the way I feel. I would like to go back to school to learn more. Not necessarily about music, but about things in general . . . that way, I could express it all in my music. Actually, though, I think I'm too lazy for that. I really had planned to practice four hours a day. I need to do that, but I'm always skipping it. I've gained a little too much weight lately, and that dulls your will and your physique. A musician has to be in shape in order to perform at his best."

"What do you think about the Albert Ayler record? A lot of people say he doesn't even know his horn."

"I don't agree, I have a lot of faith in Ayler. He's developing all the time, and he does know his horn."

"What about the concert tomorrow—couldn't you play a few more melodies, so that people can have a few breathers? A few ballads, perhaps? What about that beautiful 'Naima'?—it's very popular in France. Les Double Six have arranged that one in their own way. And what about 'Blue Valse'[1] or 'My Favorite Things.'"

"We'll see," John said. The next day, he played "Naima," followed by "Blue Valse," before going directly into "My Favorite Things." It was beautiful and lyrical, and I felt very proud and happy. As a matter of fact, he got even more applause than the previous night. A record was released in France from that first concert, with *Love Supreme* on it, and many years later, a double album came out including "Impressions," "Naima," and "Blue Valse." A bit stunned, I read in the liner notes that Randi Hultin from Norway had persuaded him to play those particular melodies. The last day in Juan-Les-Pins, John actually did rent a record player, because I had brought a couple of Norwegian records along on the trip. Karin Krog wanted me to let Coltrane hear her version of "My Favorite Things" from the Metropol record, because in it she had written a lyric about Coltrane. I had also procured some authentic Norwegian folk music, with mouth harp, harding fiddle, and stev.

"That's an interesting vocalist," John said, "she's into the right thing when it comes to improvising." Aside from the vocalizing, he was particularly intrigued by the mouth harp.

With Trane in Paris

I caught an earlier plane to Paris than John, and I took advantage of the opportunity to work in flight, writing captions for frames of the film I had developed at the hotel, and putting the finishing touches on my article. Coltrane had told me where he would be staying in Paris, but when I contacted the hotel, I was told the musicians had been moved elsewhere. I called Salle Pleyel, where they were supposed to play, and learned that they were staying at the Mac Mahou. Coltrane was pleased when I phoned.

"Can you buy some hamburgers, eggs, and milk? They don't have any food at all here!"

I got hold of Nathan Davis, the saxophonist, who lived in Paris at that time, and he went along with me to shop for eggs and milk. We could buy hamburgers and French fries at a local kiosk. I asked Nathan if he was planning on going to the concert that night, but he said he couldn't afford the price of the ticket. "Ask for me," I said, "and I'll let you know."

The first person I met at the old hotel was McCoy [Tyner]—as aloof as always, but polite—who told me where I could find John. McCoy and I eventually became good friends, but it always takes time before he accepts new acquaintances. Coltrane was famished, but he wanted first to check with his manager that his airline tickets were in order, as well as check on Elvin. Elvin was flat out on his back in bed, obviously dead to the world for the time being. In front of the bed stood the manager, who never had a sober moment after noon each day. It was late afternoon now. No one knew where the plane tickets were, and Elvin was sleeping.

"Let's get out of here," John said to me, "let's go eat."

We sat on the edge of the bed and had our simple meal on a pile of newspapers. The food tasted good. After that, we were driven to Salle Pleyel. Even Elvin got there on time. In the dressing room, a gypsy lady appeared, offering bulls with red ribbons tied around their necks—only ten francs. Coltrane bought one. Elvin then barged into the room.

"Mister, you buy a bull?" the gypsy supplicated. "Louis Armstrong buy one from me, you use it as a piggy bank."

Elvin grinned broadly: "Bullshit. No, no."

Coltrane was wearing new shoes, and they were hurting his feet. He slipped out of them for a second and wiggled his toes.

"Put the shoes in water, Mister, it helps," advised the gypsy woman.

In the middle of the concert, Elvin got mad at the drum pedal and walked off the stage, leaving Jimmy Garrison standing there alone. Elvin went out and picked up a whole bag of drum equipment, which he then dumped unceremoniously all over the stage, nuts, screws, and bolts clattering onto the floor. Coltrane stood in the wings, calm as usual.

When the drums were repaired, Elvin began to play with Jimmy, but after a short while, the audience began to clamor for Coltrane: "We want Trane, we want Trane."

"You'd better go on," I said, "you'll cause a riot."

"These people are impolite. They can listen to the people who are already playing."

John and McCoy did eventually go on again, and when the concert was over, the audience shouted and clapped for an encore. Coltrane said, however, that we were leaving.

"The last time I played here, they threw tomatoes at me. I don't have much respect for French audiences."

After we had left the stage, the manager opened a side stage door and yelled in to the audience, "He's not going to play any more for you, so you can just go home!"

In Jazzland

When the young Frenchman who had driven us to Salle Pleyel came to pick us up, I tried to explain to him that we were going out to see some of the Paris jazz clubs. Coltrane had promised to keep me company until my flight to Molde early the next morning, when I would have the honor of Donald Byrd's company on the plane. Byrd also lived in Paris.

I asked the young French driver to take Coltrane's tenor and soprano saxophones and drop them off at his hotel. "Take them there directly," I said, trying to sound authoritative. What I was thinking of mainly, was that John wouldn't have to drag around the instruments.

Before we went to the clubs, we ate at a Japanese restaurant where Japanese music was played and Oriental ladies tiptoed daintily about. The place positively oozed with authentic Japanese atmosphere—and we ordered two plain omelettes. We had to laugh, because we definitely showed no deference to the Japanese decor and traditional cuisine. But we had a pleasant meal there.

Afterwards, we went to Jazzland, where Art Taylor and Johnny Griffin were playing. They were very surprised to see us. Griffin even accompanied us, to show us the way to Le Chat Qui Pêche. On the way to the club, we met Elvin— big, stocky Elvin, who got so excited when he saw Griffin that he lifted him high over his head and grinned his pearly-toothed smile. He was in high spirits, and meandered on his way.

Inside Le Chat Qui Pêche, Don Cherry was playing with his international quintet. I had heard the group before I went to Antibes. Don had invited me to a musicians' party, but I didn't have the cab fare and told him that I would return after Antibes. When Coltrane and I came through the club, each of us carrying a stool that we plopped down three feet in front of the bandstand, Don was astounded.

"I told you I'd be back," I said.

Coltrane was very interested in the music and said that it sounded exactly as I had described it when we talked about Don back in Antibes. As the night dragged into the wee small hours, it was soon time to pick up my luggage from Coltrane's hotel. As we got out of the taxi, he rushed into the reception area ahead of me.

"Did you get my instruments?" he enquired.

Poor John. He had sat thinking about his horns all evening. I regret that he didn't simply stop me from sending them back to the hotel. None of us knew the Frenchman who had driven us—and I am almost naively trusting. But yes, they had received the saxophones.

Suddenly there was a phone call for Coltrane at the reception desk. Elvin had fallen asleep in a club—what should they do?

"He'll have to handle it himself," said Coltrane. Shortly afterwards, John stood on the front steps of the hotel, waving goodbye to me as I left for the airport. That was the last time I saw John Coltrane, but I did receive several greetings, and some wonderful letters.

Note

1. "Blue Valse" is actually a quartet version of "Ascension" (the title "Blue Valse" appears to have resulted from a misunderstanding). This tune would have been unfamiliar

to Randi Hultin and the rest of the audience at that time. In an early version of
this article, Hultin wrote that she suggested "Naima" and "My Favorite Things" ("I
Remember 'Trane," by Randi Hultin, *Down Beat Music '68*, page 104); the mention of
"Blue Valse" was probably added by mistake later, based on the (eventually) issued
recording.

MEDITATIONS LINER NOTES

Nat Hentoff

Nat Hentoff interviewed Coltrane for these liner notes, sometime between late November 1965 and mid-1966 (*Meditations* was released around September 1966).

I asked John Coltrane to what extent this album was an extension of his incantatory *A Love Supreme* (Impulse AS-77, A-77). Both albums obviously focus on Coltrane's religious concerns. I use the word "religious" not in any sectarian sense but rather in the sense that Coltrane's persistent searching in music is simultaneously a searching for meaning in the world and for his place in the world.

"Once you become aware of this force for unity in life," said Coltrane, "you can't ever forget it. It becomes part of everything you do. In that respect, this is an extension of *A Love Supreme* since my conception of that force keeps changing shape. My goal in meditating on this through music, however, remains the same. And that is to uplift people, as much as I can. To inspire them to realize more and more of their capacities for living meaningful lives. Because there certainly is meaning to life."

Other than this comment, Coltrane prefers not to be specific about the various sections of the album. He expects that each listener will react in different ways to what he hears. And Coltrane adds that it doesn't matter what particular religion—if any—a listener professes because "I believe in all religions."

I noted that in his live appearances, as on this record, Coltrane has been adding to what long was his basic quartet structure. Rashied Ali is here, for example, on drums along with Elvin Jones. "I feel," Coltrane explains, "the need for more time, more rhythm all around me. And with more than one drummer, the rhythm can be more multi-directional. Someday I may add a conga drummer or even a company of drummers." (In a San Francisco engagement in January, 1966, after this record was made, Coltrane had two drummers plus an African percussionist in his complement.)

On this set, there is also another tenor, Pharoah Sanders, as of now a regular member of the Coltrane group. "What I like about him," says Coltrane, "is the strength of his playing, the conviction with which he plays. He has will and spirit, and those there are the qualities I like most in a man." [. . .]

"There is never any end," Coltrane said at the conclusion of our conversation about this album. "There are always new sounds to imagine, new feelings to get at. And always, there is the need to keep purifying these feelings and sounds so that we can really see what we've discovered in its pure state. So that we can see more and more clearly what we are. In that way, we can give to those who listen the essence, the best of what we are. But to do that at each stage, we have to keep on cleaning the mirror."

And that is what *Meditations* is about—cleaning the mirror into the self, going as far through the looking glass as is possible each time. Making music as naked as the self can be brought to be.

Nat Hentoff

INTERVIEWS WITH JOHN COLTRANE

Shoichi Yui, Kiyoshi Koyama, Kazuaki Tsujimoto, et al.

The following transcriptions are from three separate interviews in Tokyo on July 9, 1966. The first was a press conference in the Magnolia Room of the Tokyo Prince Hotel. A number of Japanese journalists asked questions— these journalists included Shoichi Yui (who passed away in 1998), a prominent jazz critic in Japan who was awarded the Order of Culture about Jazz; and Kiyoshi Koyama, who used to be editor in chief of the Japanese jazz magazine *Swing Journal* and who still writes about jazz. The questions were translated for Coltrane by promoter Ennosuke Saito (the press conference was attended by the entire band, but it appears that all the questions were directed at Coltrane). The second was an interview, also in the Magnolia Room, conducted by students from Waseda University. The third was an interview by Kazuaki Tsujimoto in Coltrane's hotel room.

Questions were asked in Japanese and then translated into English for Coltrane, whose responses were then translated into Japanese for the journalists. The questions have been heavily edited for readability and clarity, but Coltrane's responses are presented as accurately as possible, with only light editing to remove hesitations, misspoken words, and the like. (An exception is the question in the first interview to which Coltrane responds, "I would like to be a saint." I've tried to transcribe this as literally as possible, including the interpreter's questions, to capture the nuances of the exchange.)

These tapes were provided by journalist Kaname Kawachi of TBS (Tokyo Broadcasting Station), which broadcast excerpts from these interviews on the radio program "Modern Jazz This Week" in 1966. The tape recorder was turned on and off a number of times, and there are breaks where the tape reel had to be changed; I've indicated these instances with "[*tape gap*]."

First Interview: Magnolia Room, Tokyo Prince Hotel

Ennosuke Saito: What is jazz? What do you think that jazz is?

John Coltrane: Well, let me put it this way. I myself don't recognize the word "jazz." I mean we are sold under this name, but to me, the word doesn't exist. I just feel that I play John Coltrane, he plays Ferrell [Pharoah] Sanders, and all down the line we just try to express what we individually feel. To me it's the music of individual expression.

[Coltrane is asked to introduce the band.]

John Coltrane: Members of the group? Ferrell Sanders on tenor saxophone. And this is Alice McLeod, piano. Rashied Ali, drums. James Garrison is not here, he's the bassist.

Ennosuke Saito: When I asked you about what jazz is for you, you said this is "individual expression." When you play yourself, if there are many other people listening to you that don't understand you, do you want, and do you try to make them understand what you play? Or would you rather not think about it?

John Coltrane: Well, we try, yeah. Mm hmm. 'Course it has to be a two-way—understanding is—it works from both ends. I mean it works from the listener and from the musician who has a desire to present himself. He hopes, too, that others will understand. But if they don't that means that they also have to try too, you see.

Ennosuke Saito: Well, the next question is, John, that when you play to express yourself—in other words, express what you are, what you think and what you want to do—does it include in your playing when you play music, through music you want to express something which lives in you? Is that right?

John Coltrane: I think this is true, I think this is true.

Ennosuke Saito: OK. Then: What is the very first and basic thing that you would want other people to understand from yourself, like maybe, say in a man's life, the many aspects—do you have kind of a political idea or idea in art, or anything like that? What's the very first thing that you want to express to people?

John Coltrane: I would say love, first, and to strive, second. Although they go together in some kind of way.

Alice Coltrane: [*to John*] Explain that love, honey.

John Coltrane: [*to Alice*] Just *love*. Period. So—what do you mean, smilin'?

Alice Coltrane: Do you mean personal, sexual?

John Coltrane: The love that holds the universe together. [*laughs*]

Ennosuke Saito: Why did you add the extra tenor player to your group?

John Coltrane: Well first, I like his work, I like the way he plays. And I feel that I need another horn to express certain ideas.

[*tape gap*]

Ennosuke Saito: It seems, judging from all the news sources in the States, that modern jazz today in the States does not draw a large audience. Do you recognize that modern jazz is drawing a smaller audience these days?

John Coltrane: No, I don't think so. I don't think so.

Ennosuke Saito: Has it been about the same?

John Coltrane: Well, for us it's been about the same, you see? And from what I can hear for some people it goes—it's a thing which is hard to tabulate this way because it goes with the individual there; one man will be in ascendancy, and another man, his career will be going this way at the same time. So, you know, where it might be going down for certain individuals, for this one it's going up because his music is being accepted. And this is always the case in the States;

it's always good for some and it's bad for others. And this is the situation that exists now.

Ennosuke Saito: I see. Well, generally speaking, it's not true that there's less interest in modern jazz in the States.

John Coltrane: I don't think so. I think that the people who are genuinely interested in [*unintelligible word*] music are still this way, you see, and always will be.

Ennosuke Saito: Returning to the previous question about you adding Ferrell, there are many different horns, of course, like trumpet or trombone; was there any particular reason that you needed a tenor sax?

John Coltrane: Well, [*laughs*] I needed—let's say that it's not only the instrument the man plays but it's the man himself, see? And, to me this is very important. Ferrell is the type of young man who I appreciate, and I admire his philosophy and his outlook towards life; I feel that this is the kind of thing that I want in the band so it doesn't matter *what* he'd play, you see? It's the spirit, you know? It's the spirit. Not the instrument.

Ennosuke Saito: If you could—it doesn't have to be limited to modern jazz, it includes classical or, everything—if you could please name three musicians that you like or respect and the reason why.

John Coltrane: Well, let's say, I'll start with, say, Ravi Shankar.

Ennosuke Saito: Ravi Shankar?

John Coltrane: Yeah. And Ornette Coleman. And Carlos Salzedo—he's not living at this time, but he's one of my favorite musicians. He was a harpist. Shankar is a sitarist. . . . Could someone else answer some questions too? Could some of the other members of the group answer questions?

Alice Coltrane: You're doing all right, John.

John and Alice Coltrane being interviewed in the Magnolia Room of the Tokyo Prince Hotel, July 9, 1966. PHOTOGRAPH BY TAKASHI ARIHARA. COURTESY OF *SWING JOURNAL.*

[While John Coltrane's comments about Carlos Salzedo and Ravi Shankar are being translated, he can be heard joking and laughing with Alice about his having to answer all the questions.]

[tape gap]

Ennosuke Saito: The gentleman [one of the journalists] apologizes that he has been repeating asking questions to you, alone, but now, as his final question, he wants to know, ah, what, or—and how, ah, you would like to be in, uh, ten or twenty years later. How you—you would like to be, well, in, uh, what kind of, uh, situation, you would like to, uh, um, establish.

John Coltrane: As a, as a musician, or what, as a person? Or—

Ennosuke Saito: Um, let's say about—as a, as a person.

John Coltrane: In music, or—as a person. . . . I would like to be a saint. [*John laughs, then Alice laughs.*]

Ennosuke Saito: You would like to be a saint, huh?

John Coltrane: [*laughs*] Definitely.

[*While Coltrane's response is being translated, someone (possibly Pharoah Sanders) says something to John, who laughs.*]

[*tape gap*]

Ennosuke Saito: The love that you mentioned at the beginning of this press conference.

John Coltrane: Mm hmm.

Ennosuke Saito: You want to express love through music. Does this word, "love," mean to you the love that is described by the life of Christ, Jesus Christ? Or the love which includes the kind of love between a man and woman, or the love of parents for children?

John Coltrane: Well, I really can't, I can't—I couldn't separate any of it. I think they all are certain degrees of that [*unintelligible*] of the one Christ, or maybe Buddha, or Christian, or of all of them. And all of them, I think it's the same one, that *one*, that all of them describe. It's from which it all comes [*unintelligible*], path, the love you have for your work, it's all of the manifestations of that one, to me.

Ennosuke Saito: Which includes everything.

John Coltrane: Yeah.

[*tape gap*]

Ennosuke Saito: [It's been said that the reason McCoy Tyner and Elvin Jones] resigned from your group was that there was a conflict between your idea on music and theirs. Was that right? Or do you think there were other reasons?

John Coltrane: Well, I don't know. I think you'll have to ask them. I don't know, 'cause I don't know just what [*chuckles*] their reasons are. You'll have to ask them.

[*tape gap*]

Second Interview: Magnolia Room, Tokyo Prince Hotel

Question: I believe you are a Christian, but what kind of God, as it is, in your mind?

John Coltrane: Well, I would say this—I don't know, I don't like to try to define God. Because I think he's beyond any definition that I could give.

Question: And you think you know there is God.

John Coltrane: I feel something.

Question: We would like to know about what you think of the United States and what you think of America.

John Coltrane: Hmm. Well, I'll tell you, at this time I don't have much to say for nationalistic tendencies anyway. Because I believe that it's up to individuals, each man, to know himself in order for it to really be a better world.

Question: We would like to ask, what do you think when you are playing?

John Coltrane: [*sighs*] Oh, boy. Well, there are various considerations. I would say I think of the chords at times, I think of meditations at times, and rhythms at times, and—I don't know what else.

Question: What do you think about Malcolm X?

John Coltrane: I admired him. I admired him.

Question: What do you think about the "new thing" in modern jazz?

John Coltrane: I like it.

Question: [How do] the problems of colored people influence you in your playing?

John Coltrane: I don't know. I don't know.

Question: What do you think about Ornette Coleman?

John Coltrane: Well, he's a great leader.

Question: Is that all?

John Coltrane: That's enough. [*laughs*] That's enough to be, to really be that. He's a great leader.

[*tape gap*]

Question: About the problems of colored people again, would modern jazz be the tool to fight over with the problem?

John Coltrane: I don't know. I couldn't answer that.

[*tape gap*]

Question: What has changed you between—when you were recording for Atlantic Records, your playing was very mechanistic and your improvisation was also so. And in *Ascension* and some other records you're playing very free, freely, that you have changed very much. What has made you change?

John Coltrane: Life is change. You know?

Question: Pardon me?

John Coltrane: Life itself has changed. So I guess just being alive, [*laughs*] you know.

[*tape gap*]

Question: What do you aim in playing different instruments?

John Coltrane: You mean like playing soprano or tenor?

Question: Yes.

John Coltrane: Well, to expand the means of expression.

Third Interview: Coltrane's Hotel Room

Kazuaki Tsujimoto: Do you have a comment about classical music?

John Coltrane: Classical music.

Tsujimoto: Yes.

John Coltrane: Well, I don't know, I may be wrong on this—the term "classical music," in my opinion, means—to me, I think it means the music of a country that is played by the composers and musicians of the country, more or less, as opposed to the music that the people dance or sing by, the popular music. I don't know, what do you think about it—do you agree with that?

Tsujimoto: Well—[*laughs*]

John Coltrane: So in other words, I mean, there are classical musics all over the world, different types of classical music. And I don't know if I'm correct on this, but that's the way I feel about it. And as far as the types of music—if you would ask me what we are playing, and to go beyond what I've said already, I feel it is the music of just the individual contributor. And if you wanted to name it any-thing, you could name it a classical music. See?

Tsujimoto: Have you ever studied classical music?

John Coltrane: Nothin' but the type that I'm trying to play. [*laughs*]

Tsujimoto: Say something about Sonny Rollins' playing.

John Coltrane: Well, he's a wonderful instrumentalist and musician.

Tsujimoto: When did you last see him?

John Coltrane: He was at the Village Vanguard, I've forgotten, just several months ago.

Tsujimoto: You mentioned Ornette Coleman is great. Do you have another com-ment about him?

John Coltrane: Well I said he was a great leader.

Tsujimoto: A leader.

John Coltrane: Yes, and this is—to me, that's a great thing to be.

Tsujimoto: Roland Kirk.

John Coltrane: He's another great instrumentalist.

Tsujimoto: Modern Jazz Quartet.

John Coltrane: That's a very good quartet.

Tsujimoto: Charlie Mingus.

John Coltrane: I admire his work.

Tsujimoto: How about Miles Davis?

John Coltrane: Well, he's [*laughs*]—he was a *teacher*. [*laughing*] Yeah.

Tsujimoto: Did you learn some instrumental technique from Miles Davis?

John Coltrane: Well, there are things that I learned from Miles that—it's hard to put 'em into words, but there are things that a musician needs to know, and then you can *hear* it, although it's hard for me to put it into words. But on hearing it I sometimes can try to bring it out in my playing. That's all I can say. I learned quite a bit there.

Tsujimoto: Some people say they cannot understand your music. And some say, "That is not jazz." Well, you answered very beautifully, but once again I'll ask: What answer do you give to those questions, "I don't understand your music, I don't understand your playing"? Do you have a comment?

John Coltrane: Yes, I have it, and you would like to know the answer to this.

Tsujimoto: Mm.

John Coltrane: Well, I don't feel there's an answer to this. I think that it's just a—it is either a thing that they, the person who doesn't understand, *will* understand in time, or upon repeated listenings; or it's a thing that he never will understand. And, you know, that's the way it is; there are many things in life we don't understand. [*laughs*] And we go on anyway.

Tsujimoto: What do you do at home, or outside, if you have time, so-called leisure time?

John Coltrane: Well, I haven't had much leisure time in the last fifteen years, and when I get any I'm usually so tired I just go somewhere and just lay around, you know, for two weeks—if I can *get* two weeks. And most of the time my mind's still on music.

Tsujimoto: In 1963 Japanese tenor saxophonist Hidehiko Matsumoto was invited to the Newport Jazz Festival. We had a recent interview with him and he told us that whenever you have time you always exercise and exercise and exercise [practice, practice, practice].

John Coltrane: You mean on the horn?

Tsujimoto: Yes.

John Coltrane: Well, it's either there, or sometimes it's here [*probably indicating his head*], you see? Quite a bit is just here [*laughs*], you know, and at the piano.

[The interviewers attempt to ask Coltrane a question that seems to relate to a criticism Coltrane occasionally received—that he "practiced" on stage—but the language barrier is too great and Coltrane doesn't understand what they're asking him. They move on.]

Tsujimoto: Do you have a favorite recorded solo from when you were with Earl Bostic?

John Coltrane: With Earl Bostic? I didn't make any records with him.

Tsujimoto: You didn't make any records?

John Coltrane: No. I played with him, but we didn't re—we recorded, but I didn't have any solos.

Tsujimoto: Do you have some comment about the Vietnam War?

John Coltrane: Well, I dislike war, period. So therefore, as far as I'm concerned, it should stop. It should have *been* stopped. And any other war. Now, as far as to understand the issues behind it, I don't understand them well enough to be able to tell you just how this could be brought about, but I only know that it should stop.

Tsujimoto: A related question about this war: among your people, do they have special opinions about this war?

John Coltrane: Well if so, I don't think a consensus has been made on it. I mean, I don't know of any that's been made.

Tsujimoto: They asked you about this earlier, but if you could more clearly answer about religion. I think that you belong to one of the religions, is that correct?

John Coltrane: As I told the young man, the student—I told him, and I couldn't answer this. —I don't talk much, you know, but you've got me talkin', man! For hours I've been talkin', and I'm not a talker. [*laughs*] But I thought about this question after I had answered it as best I could, and I felt that what I didn't tell him was what I really wanted to. He felt that I was Christian. And I am by, as far as birth— my mother was, and my father was, and so forth, and my early teachings were of the Christian faith. Now, as I look out upon the world—and it's always been a thing with me—to feel that all men know the truth, see? So therefore I've always felt that even though a man was not a Christian, he still had to know the truth some way. Or if he was a Christian, he could know the truth—or he could *not*. [*laughs*] It's according to whether he knew the truth, and the truth itself doesn't have any name on it, to me, see? Each man has to find this for himself, I think.

[*tape gap*]

Tsujimoto: In this moment, what do you have in your mind for the future—in a larger sense, what is your theme about your music?

John Coltrane: Oh, I would—I'll tell you. I believe that men are here to grow themselves into the full—into the *best good* that they can be. At least, this is what *I* want to do. You know? This is my belief, that we are supposed to—*I* am supposed to grow to the *best good* that I can get to. And as I'm going there, becoming this, and what I become, if I *ever* become, this will just come out of the horn. So whatever that's gonna be, that's what it will be. I'm not so much interested in trying to *say* what it's gonna be; I don't know. But I just hope, and I realize that good can only bring good.

Tsujimoto: Self-cultivating.

John Coltrane: Yeah.

Tsujimoto: Would you please recommend to us, in terms of recorded music—what do you suggest?

John Coltrane: My music?

Tsujimoto: Yes.

John Coltrane: The music that I like best, or the music that I have recorded?

Tsujimoto: Yes, the music that you have recorded.

John Coltrane: The music that I've recorded that I like best. [*laughs*]

Tsujimoto: What are they?

John Coltrane: I don't know. [*laughs*] I don't know.

Tsujimoto: You have had lots of recorded music.

John Coltrane: I don't know. I don't know. It's hard to say. I'll tell you this, though, some of the best hasn't been recorded. [*laughs*] Recordings always, you know, recordings always make you—just a little bit—you tighten up, you know?

Tsujimoto: If you have time during your stay here in Japan, do you particularly want to visit or see something in Japan?

John Coltrane: Well, if we have time, I'd like to see some of the temples, and I'd like to hear some Japanese music, you know, some of the classical—what is this instrument, the kouty, or—

Tsujimoto: Koto.

John Coltrane: Koto. I'd like to hear some of this. And I'd like to maybe go to some rural areas to see some of the traditional type of living.

Tsujimoto: You mentioned the koto.

John Coltrane: The koto, yeah.

Tsujimoto: When Roland Kirk was in Japan, he bought a charumera. That's sort of like an oboe.

John Coltrane: Yeah, I want to go to the music store and see what I can find, you know? Those are things I'd like to do.

Tsujimoto: Can you send some comment to Japanese modern jazz fans through this microphone? Say hello?

John Coltrane: Well, [laughs] hello! Thank you, and we're glad to be here and we hope to see you and play for you.

Tsujimoto: Well, thank you very, very much for a great interview with you, Mr. John Coltrane.

John Coltrane: Thank you, thank you.

Tsujimoto: Thank you.

[tape gap]

Tsujimoto: —smoking and drinking, you know?

John Coltrane: Yeah, yeah, yeah, yeah, yeah!

Tsujimoto: Thank you very much Mr. John Coltrane.

John Coltrane: OK.

Tsujimoto: I was so surprised that they said you eat vegetables more than meat.

John Coltrane: I don't quite understand.

Tsujimoto: I asked someone what you eat, and they said that you mainly eat vegetables.

John Coltrane: Yeah, and fruit, you know.

Tsujimoto: They call that a vegeteranianist, or something.

John Coltrane: A vegetarian, yeah, mm hmm.

Tsujimoto: Are you now?

John Coltrane: I am now, yes, mm hmm.

Tsujimoto: How do you keep up your energy, eating just vegetables? Why did you decide to be a vegetarian?

John Coltrane: Well, I feel that—I guess it's more of a spiritual reason than any other reason with me, because I find that it causes me to be a much calmer person. Nerves, you know. I'm much calmer, you see. That's with me, I don't know if it would be the same with everybody, you see? [*laughs*] This I found out, in my own experiments I found this out. And I have less trouble, you know, being in command of my passions and emotions and so forth. And my body has less work to do in grinding this food up, so therefore I have more energy.

Tsujimoto: Well, that's great, but I'm too skinny.

John Coltrane: Well, [*laughs*] you gotta get some milkshakes! [*both laugh*] I want to get like you, see. If I could get like you, I'd—yeah, I got too much of this on here, now.

INTERVIEW WITH JOHN COLTRANE

Frank Kofsky

On Thursday, August 18, 1966, Frank Kofsky took the train to Deer Park in Long Island, New York, a few miles from John Coltrane's Dix Hills home. Coltrane met Kofsky at the train station and drove them to a nearby shopping center. Kofsky then interviewed Coltrane for about an hour as they sat in Coltrane's car.

Originally published in the September 1967 issue of *Jazz & Pop* (pages 23–31) and reprinted in Frank Kofsky's *Black Nationalism and the Revolution in Music* (New York: Pathfinder, 1970, revised edition 1998), this version is a new transcription from the audiotape and thus differs in minor details from previously published versions.

Frank Kofsky: The people I was staying with have a friend—a young lady—and she was downtown at one of Malcolm X's addresses[1]—speeches—and lo and behold, who should plop down in the seat next to her, but John Coltrane. [*both laugh*]

John Coltrane: Yeah.

Kofsky: So, right away, that whetted my curiosity, and I wanted to know how many times you had seen him, and what you thought of him when you saw him, and so forth.

Coltrane: That was the only time.

Kofsky: Were you impressed with him?

Coltrane: Definitely. Definitely.

Kofsky: What exa—

Coltrane: That was—

Kofsky: No, go on.

Coltrane: Well, that was the only time. I had to, I felt I had to see the man, you know. And, I was living downtown, and I was in the hotel, and I saw the posters, and realized that he was gonna be over there, so I just said, well, I'm goin' over there, you know, and see this cat, because I had never seen him, and I was *quite* impressed.

Kofsky: That was one of his last speeches, wasn't it? I mean, it was toward the end of his—

Coltrane: Well, it was toward the end of his career. Towards the end.

Kofsky: Some musicians have said that there's a relationship between some of Malcolm's ideas and the music, especially the new music. Do you think there's anything in that?

Coltrane: Well, I think that music, being an expression of the human heart, or of the human, of the *being* itself, *does* express just what is happening.

Kofsky: So, then, if—oh.

Coltrane: I feel that it, it expresses the whole thing—the whole of human experience at any, at the particular time that it is being expressed.

Kofsky: What do you think about the phrase, the "new black music," as a description of some of the newer styles in jazz?

Coltrane: Well . . . I don't know. Phrases, I don't know. They don't mean much to me, you know, and it's just because usually I don't make the phrases, so—

Kofsky: That's right.

Coltrane: [*laughs*] I don't react too much to 'em. I mean, it makes no difference to me one way or another what it's called.

Kofsky: If you did make the phrases, could you think of one that you—

Coltrane: I don't know what the hell I, I don't think I have a phrase. I don't have, I don't think there's a phrase for it, you see, that I could make.

Kofsky: The people who use *that* phrase argue that jazz is particularly closely related to the black community and it's an expression of what's happening there. That's why I asked you about your reaction to Malcolm.

Coltrane: Well, I think it, I think it's up to the individual, you can call it what you may, for any reason you may. Myself, I have—I recognize the artist, and I recognize an individual. I see his contribution; and, when I know a man's *sound*, well, to me that's him, you know, that's *this man*. And that's what I recognize. And, I don't like—labels, I don't bother with.

Kofsky: But it does seem to be a fact that most of the *changes* in the music—the innovations—have come from black musicians, or—

Coltrane: Yeah, well this is how it is. How it is.

Kofsky: Have you ever noticed—since you've played all over the United States and in all kinds of circumstances—you ever notice that the reaction of an audience varies or changes if it's a black audience or a white audience or a mixed audience? Have you ever seen that the racial composition of the audience seems to determine how the people respond?

Coltrane: Well, sometimes, yes, and sometimes, no.

Kofsky: Any examples?

Coltrane: Well, no. I mean, sometimes it might, it might appear to be one; you might say, well—it's hard to say, man, you know, sometimes people like it or don't like it, no matter what color they are.

Kofsky: You don't have any preferences yourself about what kind of an audience you play for?

Coltrane: Well, to me, it doesn't matter.

Kofsky: What kind of—

Coltrane: I just, I only hope that whoever is out there listening, I hope they're enjoying it; [*laughs*] that's the—you know—if they're not enjoying it, then I'd rather not hear.

Kofsky: If people do enjoy the music, how would you like them to demonstrate this? Do you like an audience that's perfectly still and unresponsive, or do you like an audience that reacts more visibly to the music?

Coltrane: Well . . . I guess I like an audience that does show its, you know, what they feel; to respond.

Kofsky: I remember sometimes when you've played the Jazz Workshop in San Francisco, you really got that kind of an audience that you didn't get when you played Shelly's Manne Hole in Los Angeles, and it seemed to me that that had some effect on the music that you played.

Coltrane: Yeah, because it seems to me that the audience that partic—the audience by—in listening, there is in an act of participation going on there, you know? And when you know that somebody is maybe moved the same way that you are, to such degree, or approaching the degree, it's just like having another member in the group.

Kofsky: Is that what happened at the *Ascension* date? People who were there—did they get that involved, for example?

Coltrane: I don't know. I was so doggone busy; [*laughs*] I mean, I was worried to death. That was my, you know, that was the way I felt. I couldn't really enjoy the date, as if it hadn't been a date. If it hadn't been a date, then I would have really enjoyed it. I'm trying to get, you know, time and everything set, and I was just too busy, myself. But I don't know, I hope they felt something, you know—they felt this. To hear the record, I mean, I enjoyed it; I enjoyed all of the individual contributions on that.

Kofsky: It's a beautiful record.

Coltrane: I enjoyed it.

Kofsky: That's probably the one record that I've had to listen to the most number of times to get everything that's on it.

Coltrane: You know, we got another take out on it now. Did you know that?

Kofsky: That's what Bob Thiele told me. He said he'd mail me the other one.

Coltrane: Yeah.

Kofsky: What do you think, then, about playing concerts? Does that seem to inhibit the interaction between yourself, your group, and the audience?

Coltrane: Well, on concerts, I have—the only thing that bugs me on concerts would, might be a hall with poor acoustics, or acoustics which we can't quite get the unit sound, you see? But as far as the audience, it's about the same. [*unintelligible*]

Kofsky: I wasn't too impressed with the acoustics on Friday night's concert.

Coltrane: No, I wasn't either.

Kofsky: I was sitting right down in front, so I could hear most of what was going on, but even then, it didn't sound—

Coltrane: No. I couldn't feel. I couldn't feel it.

Kofsky: You could tell, the musicians, they can't hear each other and therefore they can't get themselves together.

Coltrane: No, it's like the wind; you fell into the wind.

Kofsky: Yeah. [*laughs*] Another reason I asked you about Malcolm was because, you know, I've interviewed about a dozen and a half musicians by this time, and the consensus seems to be that, especially the younger musicians talk about the kind of political and social issues that Malcolm talked about, when they're with each other. And some of them say that they try to express this in the music. Do you find that in your own groups, or in the musicians you're friendly with, that these issues are important to you and you do talk about them?

Coltrane: Oh, well, they're *definitely* important; and as I said, they are, the issues are *part* of what *is*, you know, at this time. So naturally, as musicians, we express whatever, whatever it is.

Kofsky: Do you make a conscious attempt to express these things, or do you feel that it just—

Coltrane: Well, I tell you, myself, I make a conscious attempt, I think I could say truthfully that in music I make, or I have tried to make, consciously, an attempt to change . . . to change what I've found in music, you see. And, in other words, I've tried to say, "Well, *this*, I feel, could be better, [*laughs*] you see, in my opinion, so I will try to do this to make it better." And this is what I feel that we feel in any situation that we find in our lives—when there's something we feel should be better, we exert an effort to try and make it better. So it's the same socially, musically, politically, in any, in any department of your life.

Kofsky: Most of the musicians I have talked to are very concerned with changing the society and they do see their music as an instrument by which society can be changed.

Coltrane: Well, I think so. I think music is an instrument. It can create the initial, just, the *thought patterns*, that can create the changes, you see, in the thinking of the people.

Kofsky: In particular, some musicians have said that jazz is opposed to poverty, and to suffering, and to oppression; and that therefore, that jazz is opposed to what the United States is doing in Vietnam. Do you have any comments on that subject?

Coltrane: On the Vietnam—and the government?

Kofsky: Well, you can divide it into two parts.

Coltrane: Uh, let's see.

Kofsky: The first part was whether you think jazz is opposed to poverty and suffering and oppression; and the second part is whether you think, if so, jazz is therefore opposed to the United States' involvement in Vietnam.

Coltrane: Well, in my opinion I would say yes, because I believe that in my opinion of jazz—we'll call it, now—which [*laughs*] I'll talk about that later.[2]

Kofsky: OK, well, call it what you want.

Coltrane: [*laughs*] Yeah, call it what you want. To me, it is, it is an expression of—to me, it's music; and this music is an expression of highest, to *me*, higher ideals, you see?

Kofsky: Mm hmm.

Coltrane: So therefore, brotherhood is there; and I believe with brotherhood, there would be no poverty. And also, with brotherhood, there would be no war. So, I mean, to me, I agree with them in this statement. I agree.

Kofsky: That also seems to be what most of the musicians feel. David Izenson, for example, said almost the same thing when I talked with him, Monday. He said,

"Well, we're saying in our music is that we want a classless society, without these frictions, and without the wastes, and without the warfare." . . . Would you care to comment on working conditions for, quote, "jazz" musicians? Do you think that jazz artists are treated as they deserve to be treated; and if not, can you see any reasons why they wouldn't be.

Coltrane: Well, I—I don't know, it's according to the individual. Well, you find many times a man may feel that the situation is all right with him, where another man might say, "Well, that situation is no good for you," you see? So it's a matter of a man knowing himself, just what he wants, you know, and that way, I mean, it's according to his values, you see. If he doesn't mind a certain sort of treatment, then I'm sure he can get, so he can find it somewhere. If he does mind it, then he doesn't have to put up with it. In my opinion, at this stage of the game, where I'm at now, stage, I don't care too much for playing clubs, consistently. Now, there was a time when this felt all right to me, because my music, I felt I had to play a lot to work it out, you see? But now I don't think [*laughs*] that that was absolutely where it was at; but I had to find that out myself.

Kofsky: It's like moving to the country.

Coltrane: Yeah. I had to go through *this* scene, you know, where now I don't feel this is necessary. I think that it is a matter of being able to be at home and *in*, to go into *yourself*, you know, more. In other words, like the years before, I was playing, you know, every night, and as such, I don't feel—I don't—the situation involving the clubs is not an ideal one for me, now.

Kofsky: What is it about clubs that you don't like?

Coltrane: Well, actually, we don't play this, uh, the sets, forty-minute kind of thing anymore, you see, and it's very difficult to always do this kind of thing, now—and now, the music, changing as it is, there are a lot of times when it doesn't make sense, man, to have somebody drop a glass or, you know, or somebody ask for some money right in the middle of Jimmy Garrison's solo. You know what I mean?

Kofsky: I know exactly what you mean.

Coltrane: Something's *happenin'* in there, you see? And, these kind of things are calling for some other kind of presentation, I think.

Kofsky: In other words, these really are artists who are playing, yet they're really not being treated like artists; they're like part of the cash register—just ring up the money.

Coltrane: Yeah, I think the music is rising, in my estimation, it's rising into something else, and so we'll have to find this kind of place, you know, to be played in.

Kofsky: Why do you think conditions have been so bad for producing art by the musicians? What do you think causes these poor conditions that you've spoken of?

Coltrane: Well, I don't know; I don't really know how it came about, you see. Because I do know there was one time when a musician played more dances, you know, and they used to play theaters and all this; and, well, this took away one element, you know, but still it was *hard work* these guys had to do. [*laughs*] Because I remember some of those one-nighters that were pretty, pretty difficult, you know. But it just seems that the music has been directed by businessmen, I would suppose, who know how to arrange the making of a dollar, and so forth. And, and maybe often the artist hasn't really taken the time himself to just figure out just what he's—or if he *does* feel it should be presented [*laughs*] some other way, you know? And I think these are the things which are being thought about more now.

Kofsky: That's what I find, too. Do you think the fact that almost all of the original jazz musicians were black men and have continued to be throughout the generations, do you think this encouraged the businessmen to take advantage of them and to treat their art sort of with this contempt—ringing up of the cash register in the middle of a bass solo?

Coltrane: Well, I don't know, it—

Kofsky: Most of the owners, I've noticed, are white.

Coltrane: Yeah, well, this could be, Frank, this could be. I don't know.

Kofsky: How do you think conditions are going to be improved for the musicians?

Coltrane: Well, there has to be a lot of self-help, I believe. They have to work out, you know, their own problems in this area.

Kofsky: You mean, like, like for example, the Jazz Composers' Guild was trying to do, by organizing?

Coltrane: Yeah, I *do* think that was a good idea. I do, I really do; and I don't think it's dead. I mean, it was just something that couldn't be born at that time, but I still think it's a good idea.

Kofsky: The first time—this is the history of all kinds of organizations in this country—is that they're not always successful the first time. But I think it's inevitable that musicians are going to try and organize and protect themselves against, um—for example, I was at the Five Spot Monday night, and I figure that there are about a hundred tables in there; and two people at a table, comes to about seven dollars and fifty cents a set, at three drinks a set. That means he's making seven hundred and fifty dollars, say, a set, and he has five sets. And I know the musicians for that night aren't getting anywhere *near* five times seven hundred and fifty dollars, or even two times seven hundred and fifty dollars. So actually, it turns out that these businessmen are not only damaging the art, but they're even keeping people away.

Coltrane: Yes, it's puttin' them uptight, lot of people, man. I feel so *bad* sometimes about people coming to the club, like I can't play long enough for them, because, [*laughs*] you know, they're hustling you on. God, they come to hear you play and you get up, you have to play a little bit, and split. These things, you know, you have—something has to be done about it.

Kofsky: If it hadn't been for Elvin taking, you know, the bartender aside, I couldn't have stayed there, because I ran out of money after a set.

Coltrane: Mmm.

Kofsky: Do the musicians who play in these newer styles look to Africa and Asia for some of their musical inspiration?

Coltrane: I think so; I think they look all over.

Kofsky: Do they look some places more than others?

Coltrane: And *inside*. [*laughs*]

Kofsky: Yeah, and inside. I heard you, for example, talking about making a trip to Africa, to gather musical sources. Was that the idea?

Coltrane: Well, I intend to make a trip to Africa to gather, just to gather whatever I can find, particularly the musical sources

Kofsky: Do you think that musicians are more interested in Africa and Asia than in Europe, as far as the music goes? Well, just in general.

Coltrane: Well, the musicians have been exposed to Europe, you see. So it's the other parts that they haven't been exposed to, which I think they're trying to—at least, I speak for myself, I'm trying to, to have a rounded, you see, education.

Kofsky: Is that the significance of those rhythmic instruments that you've incorporated into your group—to give it a sort of Middle Eastern or African flavor?

Coltrane: Well, if so, maybe so, but it's just something I *feel*, you see?

Kofsky: Why do you think that the interest in Africa and Asia is growing at this particular time?

Coltrane: Well, it's just time, for this to come about, that's all. It's just a thing at this time.

Kofsky: Bill Dixon suggested it might have something to do with the fact that many African nations became independent in the 1950s—

Coltrane: Mmm.

Kofsky: —and changed the way the Negroes in this country looked at themselves; it made them more aware of the African heritage and made them more inter-ested in going back and looking for it. Do you think there's anything to that line of thought?

Coltrane: Yeah, yeah, that's part of it.

Kofsky: Another question along the same lines is: It seems that group improvisa-tion is growing in importance—for example, what you did with Pharoah [Sand-ers] when you were both playing simultaneously.

Coltrane: Mm hmm.

Kofsky: And also, of course, *Ascension*. Do you think that this is a new trend now, or not a new trend, but do you think that this is growing in importance now, this playing together?

Coltrane: Well, maybe. I don't know, it seems to be happening; [*laughs*] I don't know how long it's going to stay here, but at this time, it does seem to be.

Kofsky: Why do you think that's taking place now?

Coltrane: I don't know why, I don't know why, it just *is*, that's all.

Kofsky: But it is there—I'm not making something up when I say I think it?

Coltrane: No, I feel it, I understand, but I don't know why.

Kofsky: And another question about the new music: I've noticed that a lot of the new groups are pianoless; or even in your case, where you have a piano, some-times you'll have the piano lay out during a solo, or parts of a solo. Why is this coming about at this particular time? Why the desire to de-emphasize the piano or, not to de-emphasize it, but to give it another kind of position in the group—another kind of role?

Coltrane: Oh, I don't know, because, see, I still use the piano, and I haven't reached the point where I feel I don't need this role. And I might assume that—I don't know, *maybe* it's because the—well, when you're not playing on a given progression, see, well, you don't need, don't really need anybody there to state these things, see. And if it would get in your way to have somebody goin' in another direction and you tryin' to go in this, then it would be better for you not to have a piano, see.

Kofsky: It seems that the direction the horns are going in, too, is to get away from the twelve-tone scale—to play notes that really aren't on the piano.

Coltrane: Mmm.

Kofsky: The high-pitched notes, the shrieks and screams.

Coltrane: Yeah.

Kofsky: I don't know what words you use to describe those words but I think you know what I mean. Sounds that were considered "wrong"—well, still are considered wrong by some people. Now, if you play those notes that really aren't on the piano, and you have the piano there stating notes that are on the piano, do you feel that this gives some kind of a clash that you'd rather avoid in the group?

Coltrane: I suppose that's the way some men feel about that. As I say, I still use the piano, so I haven't reached this point yet [*laughs*] where, you know, the piano is a drag to me, you know, to that degree. Only thing, I, I don't, we don't *follow* what the piano does any more, because we all move in our own directions, see. I like it for a backdrop, you know—of its sound.

Kofsky: You do have the piano, though, lay out a fairly large part of the time.

Coltrane: Well, after a while, I always instruct the piano players that whenever they wish they can just lay out, you know, and let it, let it go on as it is. Because after a while, lots of times, the pianists, well, they get tired [*laughs*], you know, so I say, "Well, you know, if you can't think of anything else to play—just stroll."

Kofsky: When I talked to you a couple of years ago in Los Angeles and I asked you if you ever would consider adding another horn to the group, you said, probably the thing you would do is, if you added anything, you would add drums. [*Coltrane laughs*] Did you have in mind then these kind of things that—

Coltrane: I don't even know, man, but I guess so. And that's just—I feel, I still feel so strongly about drums, I really do.

Kofsky: You said you were listening to African music and you noticed that if you played that with some of your music that it still all sounded right because anything you played over the drums—

Coltrane: Yeah, I feel very strongly about these drums. But I just—I, I experimented in it, but we didn't have too much success. I *believe* it would have worked, but, you know, Elvin and McCoy, they, they couldn't hold, they had—it was time for them to go.

Kofsky: It doesn't necessarily have to be two drums. It could be just drums and another rhythm instrument. Like—that's what I was really referring to, not Elvin.

Coltrane: Yeah, I think so, too. Now, I think it could come in different forms, shapes, you know; I just, just don't know how to do it, though.

Kofsky: After all, though, the things that you were playing up there Friday night, those are rhythm instruments, too. Not all rhythm instruments are drums.

Coltrane: Oh, that's true. That's true.

Kofsky: That's what I meant, when I said if you, that's what you had in mind.

Coltrane: Mm hmm, yeah.

Kofsky: Speaking of Elvin and McCoy, that reminds me of something Sun Ra said, and I'll repeat it. I'll make it clear that I don't put any faith in it, but since he said it, and he told me to tell you, I thought I'd pass it along. He says that you hired Rashied [Ali] as a means of driving Elvin and McCoy out of the band, because you didn't want them in the band in the first place, but that was your way of doing it. Do you want to answer that?

Coltrane: No, I don't. I don't. I was, I was trying to do something. There was—I was trying to do something. Please . . . there was a thing I wanted to do in music, see, and I figured I could do *two* things: I could have a band that played like the way we used to play, and a band that was going in the direction that this, the one I have now is going in—I could combine these two, with these, you know, with these two concepts going. And it could have been done.

Kofsky: Yeah. Sun Ra is quite bitter, and claims that you've stolen all of your ideas from him, and in fact that *everybody* has stolen *all* of their ideas from him.

Coltrane: There may be something, [*laughs*] may be something to it. [*both laugh*] I've heard him and I know—I know that he's doing, he's done, some things that I've wanted to do.

Kofsky: How do you feel about having another horn in the group, now, another saxophone? Do you feel that that in any way competes with you or that it enhances what—

Coltrane: Well, it helps me. It helps me stay alive sometimes, because I find that physically, man, the pace I've been leading has been so hard. So sometimes, I've just been a little, you know—and I've gained so much weight, you know, Frank, that sometimes it's been a little hard physically. [*laughs*] And I feel that I like, I like to have somebody there in case I just don't, can't get that strength. I like to have that strength in that band, you know, from someone. And Pharoah is very strong in spirit and will, see, and these are the things I like to have up there. I like to have that strength, you know.

Kofsky: Well, *strength*, that's the word for the band now, strength and energy.

Coltrane: Energy, yeah. I like to have this energy, too.

Kofsky: Do you feel that spurs you on, the presence especially of a man as powerful as Pharoah?

Coltrane: Any—*yeah*, all the time, there's always got to be somebody with a lot of power, you see, like, because Elvin, in the old band, Elvin had this power.

Kofsky: Mm hmm. Do you think that Ra—

Coltrane: I always have to have *somebody* there with it, you know? [*laughs*] Rashied has it, but it, it hasn't quite unfolded completely, you know, but it's—all he needs to do is play.

Kofsky: That was my impression, too, that he really was feeling his way ahead in the music and didn't have the confidence Elvin had. But then, of course, look how long Elvin was with you before he actually started to—

Coltrane: Yeah, he was there, Elvin was there for a couple of years—although Elvin was ready from the first time I *heard* Elvin, [*laughs*] you know, he was, I could hear the *genius* there. But he had to really *play*—you have to start *playing* steadily, steadily, and every, every night, or however you're gonna play. You have to keep building and then, then it comes out. Like with Miles it took me around two and a half years, I think, for it to start developing, you know, like it was going to—taking the shape that it was going to take.

Kofsky: That's what's so tragic about the situation of the younger musicians now, is they don't have that opportunity to play together.

Coltrane: Yeah, it certainly needs to be done. It should be happening all the time and the men would develop sooner.

Kofsky: Don Cherry has a new record out. And I think it's a beautiful record, on Blue Note, and one of the reasons I think it's so good is because here he has a group that's worked together for a few months.

Coltrane: Yeah.

Kofsky: And so he knows how to get—put—something together for all of the men, that isn't just a "date."

Coltrane: Yeah, I'm hip. Yeah, I'm hip.

Kofsky: I know you are, because you kept the group alive that way.

Coltrane: Yeah, I sure tried to.

Kofsky: Have you listened to many of the other younger saxophonists besides Pharoah?

Coltrane: Yes, Albert Ayler,[3] first. I've listened very closely to him. And he's something else.

Kofsky: Could you see any relationship between what you were doing and what he was doing? In other words, do you think that he had developed out of some of your ideas?

Coltrane: I don't—not necessarily; I think what he's doing is, it seems to be moving music into even higher frequencies, you see.

Kofsky: To me, it appears that some of the things that you did—

Coltrane: It's like, maybe where I left off, may be where he started, [*laughs*] or something, you see.

Kofsky: Well, in a sense, that's what I meant.

Coltrane: Yeah, not to say that he, you know, would copy this or that, but it's just that he, you know, he filled an area that it seemed that I hadn't gotten to. [*unintelligible*]

Kofsky: It seemed that to me, it appeared that your solo on "Chasin' the Trane," that he had developed some of the ideas that you put out there and he had expressed them in his own way, but that this was one of the points from which he had begun. Had you ever thought of it in that light?

Coltrane: No, I hadn't.

Kofsky: Do you ever listen to that record much?

Coltrane: Only when—at the time it came out, I used to listen to it and wonder what happened to me. [*laughs*]

Kofsky: What do you mean?

Coltrane: Well, it was a sort of surprising thing to hear this back, you see, because—I don't know, it came back another way.

Kofsky: How did it come back?

Coltrane: Well, it was a little longer than I thought it was and it, it had quite a bit of a, fairly good amount of intensity in it, you know, which I, I hadn't quite gotten into a record, recording before, you see.

Kofsky: You were pleased with it. I think it's a—

Coltrane: You know, to that—to a degree. I mean, not, not that I could sit there with it and, you know, love it forever.

Kofsky: Well, I know you'd never be pleased with anything you did for longer than a week! [*laughs*]

Coltrane: I just felt that—I realized that I'd have to do that or better, [*laughs*] you see, from then on.

Kofsky: I think it's a remarkable record and I also think you ought to go back and listen to it.

Coltrane: Maybe so.

Kofsky: Because—yeah, because I see a lot of the younger—well, I don't see any saxophonist now who isn't playing something that you have at least sketched out before.

Coltrane: No, I'm, uh . . .

Kofsky: Archie [Shepp], it seems to me is the one who has gone the farthest in the direction of his own style, but if you listen to Archie three or four years ago with Cecil Taylor, he was playing those up and down triad things that, you know, that—really one of your, your trademarks. But maybe you don't want—maybe, you know, you'd rather not think about that, so—

Coltrane: No, you know, because like it's, it's a big reservoir, man, that we all *dip* out of, [*both laugh*] so, you know, a lot of times you'll find that a lot of those things—I'd listened to John Gilmore kinda closely before I made "Chasin' the Trane," too. So some of those things on there are really direct influences of listening to this cat, you see. But then I don't know who he'd been listening to, so—it's growing, you know?

Kofsky: Right, so it really is a reservoir. Yeah.

Coltrane: Yeah.

Kofsky: It's too bad that he's never had a recording that demonstrated what he could do.

Coltrane: Yeah, I like him, man.

Kofsky: Everybody talks about him, and yet—I've listened to, you know, a number of Sun Ra records, which I guess is the only place you can really hear him.

Coltrane: Yeah, well, you probably have to hear him stretch on his own, or something.

Kofsky: Right.

Coltrane: Because I've heard him do some things which are really beautiful.

[*tape gap*]

Impulse released *John Coltrane and Johnny Hartman*
and *Impressions* simultaneously, circa July 1963.

Kofsky: After "Chasin' the Trane" came out and then *Impressions* came out, you
did a sort of change of pace. You remember you did the album with Duke and
the *Ballads* [album], and, the Johnny Hartman album.

Coltrane: Yeah.

Kofsky: Whose idea were those albums? Were they yours, or were they Impulse's?

Coltrane: Well, I tell you, I had some trouble at that time. I did a foolish thing. I, I got dissatisfied with my mouthpiece [*laughs*] and I had some work done on this thing, and instead of making it better, it, it ruined it. And it really, it discouraged me, you know, a little bit, because I couldn't—there were certain aspects of playing—that certain *fast* thing that I was *reaching* for—that I couldn't get, you know, *push*, because I had damaged this thing, so I just had to curtail it. [*laughs*]

Kofsky: Until you got another?

Coltrane: Well, actually, I never found another, but after so much of this layin' around and making these kind of things, I said, "Well what the hell, you know, I might as well go ahead and do the best I can," you see. But at that moment, it was so vivid in my mind—the *difference*, in the, in the—what I was getting on the horn—it was so vivid in *my* mind, that I couldn't do it. Because as soon as I'd do it, I'd hear it; and it just discouraged me, see. But after a year or so passed, well, I'd forgotten. [*laughs*]

Kofsky: That's funny, because, you know, I think I know your music as thoroughly as any nonmusician, yet that wouldn't have been apparent to me, I don't think.

Coltrane: Yeah, well, that's a funny thing, man. That's one of the mysteries. And to me, as soon as I put that horn in my mouth, I could hear it, I could feel it, you know. So I just stopped, I just went into other things.

Kofsky: The reason I asked that was because you recall that was around the time you had Eric [Dolphy] in and out of the band.

Coltrane: Yeah.

Kofsky: And there was a whole wave of really hostile criticism. I'm sure you remember.

Coltrane: Yeah, and this, this, this was—*all of this* was at the same time, so you can see how, how it was. I needed all the strength I could have at that time; and maybe some of these things might have caused me to feel that, well, you know, damn, I, I can't get what I want out of this mouthpiece, so I'll work on it.

Kofsky: You think this might have undermined your self-confidence to a degree?

Coltrane: It could have, it certainly could have. Could have.

Kofsky: Why do you think there's been all this hostility to the new music, especially in your case?

Coltrane: *Oh, man*, I, I never could figure it out, you know? And I wouldn't, couldn't even venture to answer it now. Because as I told them then, I just felt that they didn't understand. [*chuckles*]

Kofsky: Do you think that they were making—

Coltrane: So I feel that they didn't understand, that's all.

Kofsky: Do you think they were making as conscientious and as thorough an attempt to understand as they could have?

Coltrane: At times I didn't feel they were, because I did offer to them, I think in this article in *Down Beat*, I asked, I asked if any of you men were interested in, you know, trying to understand, let's get together and let's talk about it, you know? I felt if they were really genuinely interested or thought there was something here, that they—instead of just condemning it, what you don't know about it, if you want to discuss it, let's talk about it. But no one ever, you know, came forth, so I don't think they were really—they didn't want to know what [*laughs*] *I* had to say about it.

Kofsky: I think it frightened them.

Coltrane: Well, it *might* have.

Kofsky: Bill [Dixon] said—you know we talked about this at great length—and he said, "Well, these guys, it's taken them years to pick out 'I Got Rhythm' on the piano, and now the new music comes along and undermines their entire career, which is built around understanding things based on—"

Coltrane: Yeah, yeah, it could be. I dug it like that too. I said, "Well, it could be a real drag to a cat's career, if he figures this is something that he won't be able to cope with and he won't be able to write about," you see, and if he can't write about it, he can't make a living at this; and then I realized that, so, I quieted down. I didn't, I wouldn't allow myself to become *too* hostile [*laughs*] back, you know, in return. Although there was a time I, I kind of froze up on the people at *Down Beat*. I froze because, I don't know, I felt that there was something there that wasn't—I didn't, I felt that they were letting their weakness direct their actions, which I didn't feel they should have, you see.

Kofsky: Of course, that makes me want to kill all those people, because—

Coltrane: Well, man, you know.

Kofsky: Because I get so much pleasure out of your music.

Coltrane: Yeah, well, the test, the test was for me. [*laughs*] That's what it was for, you know. They could do what they wanted to do. The thing was for me to remain firm in what I was doing. But it, that was a funny time—a period in my life, because I went through quite a few changes, you know, like the home life—*everything*, man, I just went through so many—*everything* I was doing [*slaps hands*] did this.

Kofsky: The perfect wrong time to hit you.

Coltrane: Everything, everything I was doing [*slaps hands*] hit like that.

Kofsky: Yeah.

Coltrane: But it was a hell of a test for me, and coming out of it, it's just like I always heard, man: when you go through these crises and you come through them or come out of them, you're definitely stronger, you know, in a great sense.

Kofsky: Yeah, if you, if you can surmount them.

Coltrane: Yeah.

Kofsky: Did the reaction of Impulse to these adverse criticisms have anything to do with those records that we talked about?

Coltrane: The *Ballads* and the—

Kofsky: Yes, the *Ballads* and the—

Coltrane: Well, I don't know. I think Impulse was interested in having what they might call a balanced sort of thing, a diverse sort of a catalogue, you know, and I don't find nothing wrong with this myself, you see. I like, I like—in fact, most of the songs I even write now, or have been written, the ones that I really consider songs, are ballads. So there's something there, that I mean, I really love these, love these things.

Kofsky: They're beautiful. No question about that.

Coltrane: And these ballads that came out were *definitely* ones which I felt at this time. And I, I chose them; and they seemed to be something that were laying around in my mind—from my, [*laughs*] you know, youth, or somewhere—that I just had to do. And they came at this time, when the confidence in what I was doing on the horn had flagged, it seemed to be just the time to clean that out. And Johnny Hartman—a man that I'd had stuck up in my mind somewhere—I just felt something about him, you know, I don't know what it was. And I liked his *sound*, I thought there was something there I had to hear, you know, so I looked him up and did that other one, see. And although I—really, I don't regret doing those things at all.

Kofsky: You shouldn't.

Coltrane: No, no, I don't regret it.

Kofsky: Because Johnny Hartman went with, in my opinion, went with the quartet perfectly. Those are the only six songs I knew the words to!

Coltrane: Yeah, me too. [*both laugh*]

Kofsky: Eight. Is it six or eight? Six, yeah, six. Right.

Coltrane: Yeah, I don't regret doing those.

Kofsky: No, no.

Coltrane: The only thing, I do regret not having, you know, kept that same attitude, which was, you know: I'm gonna do, no matter what. That was the attitude in the beginning, but as I say, there was a whole lot of reasons why [*laughs*] these things did happen.

Kofsky: There's ups and downs and that was one of the downs.

Coltrane: Yeah. That was one of the downs.

Kofsky: Do you think that learning how to play the soprano had anything to do with the change in your style from what it had been, say—

Coltrane: Definitely, definitely. Yeah, it certainly did.

Kofsky: How so? Could you spell it out?

Coltrane: Well, the soprano, by being this small instrument, I found that playing the lowest note on it was like playing the, one of the middle notes in the tenor. So therefore, after I got so I could—my embouchure would allow me to make the upper notes, I found that I would, I would play *all over* this instrument, you see. And on tenor, I hadn't always played all over it, because I was playing certain ideas which would just run in certain ranges, octaves, see. But by playing on the soprano and becoming accustomed to playing from that low B-flat on up, it soon got so when I went to tenor, I found myself doing the same thing, you see. And this caused the change or the willingness to change and just try to play the, you know, as much of the instrument as possible.

Kofsky: Did it give you a new rhythmic conception too?

Coltrane: I *think* so, I think so. A new, a new shape came out of this thing, and patterns—you know, the way the patterns would fall.

Kofsky: It seemed to me that after you started playing soprano, and particularly after *My Favorite Things*, then you started feeling that same kind of a pulse on the tenor that, that hadn't been there in your work before.

Coltrane: I think it's quite possible, quite possible. In fact, the soprano started—the soprano's one of the reasons I started [*laughs*] getting dissatisfied with that tenor mouthpiece, see, because the sound of that soprano was actually so much closer to me in my *ear*, or there's something about the presence of that sound, you know, that, that to me—I didn't want to admit it—but to me it would seem like was better than the tenor—or I liked it more, see? And I didn't want to admit this damn thing, because I said, "Well, the tenor's my horn, this is my favorite." But this soprano, or maybe it's just the fact that it's a higher instrument, it just, it started pulling my conception, you see, [*laughs*] it really was headed, going into this instrument.

Kofsky: How do you feel about the two horns now?

Coltrane: Well, the tenor is the power horn, definitely; but soprano, there's still something there in just the, just the voice of it—that I can't—it's really beautiful, something that I really like, you know.

Kofsky: Do you regard the soprano as an extension of the tenor, or—

Coltrane: Well, at first I did, but, I don't know, now it's, it's another voice, it's just another voice.

Kofsky: Did you ever use the two horns on the same piece, as you did on "Spiritual"?

Coltrane: I think that's the only time I've done that. Sometimes in clubs, if I feel good, I might do something like this—start on one and end on another, you know—but I think that's the only one on record that was like that.

Kofsky: What prompted Pharoah to take up the alto? Was that to get away from the two-tenors sound?

Coltrane: I don't know, I don't know.

Kofsky: Did you talk it over with him?

Coltrane: No, this is something he wanted to do, and about the same time, I decided I wanted to get one, so we both got 'em.

Kofsky: I haven't heard you play the alto, yet. Do you play it much in—

Coltrane: I played it in Japan. I played it in Frisco a little bit, but I've had a little trouble with the intonation of it. It's a Japanese make that they new thing they're trying out, so they gave us these horns to try, and mine has to be adjusted at certain points where they're not quite in tune, so I don't play it, but I like it.

Kofsky: I saw a picture of you with a *flute*. Are you playing that too now?

Coltrane: I'm learning. I'm learning it.

Kofsky: You're always learning, aren't you?

Coltrane: I hope so. Always trying to learn.

Kofsky: I looked at the *Down Beat* Critics' Poll two years in a row, and both years, this year and last year. Both years, I noticed this: that European critics are much more in favor of the new music than the American. Almost, say, 50 percent or 60 percent of them would vote for new musicians, whereas, only, say, about a quarter of the American—

Coltrane: Isn't that something?

Kofsky: Is this what you found in Europe and—

Coltrane: Yeah.

Kofsky: Well, let me just say, is this what you've found outside the United States, that your music is more favorably received by the critics, the power structure, shall we say, than, than in the U.S.?

Coltrane: Well, I'll tell you, in the new music, I believe—and when I say the new music, I mean most of the younger musicians who are starting out—I know that they definitely have found a quicker reception in Europe than they have here. And, when I started, it was a little different, because I started through Miles Davis, who was an accepted musician, you see, and they got used to me here in the States. Now when they first heard me with Miles here, they did not like it. [*laughs*]

Kofsky: I remember. I remember [*unintelligible*].

Coltrane: So, anything, it's just one of those things, anything that they haven't heard yet and that's a little different, at first, they're gonna reject it, at first, man. But the tide, it will roll around, the time when they will like it. Now, the States, by being here with Miles and running around the country with him, they heard more of me here and, consequently, they began to accept it before they did in Europe, because they hadn't heard me in Europe. But we find, when we went to Europe the first time, well, it was a shock to them there, you know. Like, they booed me and everything in Paris, because, well, they just weren't ready to listen. But now I find, the last time I was in Europe, it seems that, the new music—they've, they have really, [*laughs*] you know, they opened up, man. They can hear it there better than they do here.

Kofsky: I think that part of this is because what's happening in the new music is analogous to what's happened in painting, say, and sculpture and literature; and the people who appreciate jazz in Europe are much more aware of this than—

Coltrane: I see.

Kofsky: What do you—

Coltrane: Well, I don't know.

Kofsky: See, in Europe, jazz is regarded as a serious art, whereas here, it's regarded as, well, I don't know—

Coltrane: Whatever it is.

Kofsky: As part of the nightclub business.

Coltrane: Yeah.

Kofsky: Otherwise, you couldn't have a magazine like *Down Beat*. I know Albert [Ayler] is going back to Europe, and I know that there are many of the younger musicians who want to get away from the States because of that thing—they, they just don't feel that there's any hope for them here. Do you remember Third Stream Music, what was called Third Stream Music?

Coltrane: Mm hmm.

Kofsky: Did you ever want, feel much of an inner urge to play that kind of music?

Coltrane: No.

Kofsky: Why do you think it didn't catch on with the musicians? Was there anything about it that suggests why it was never very popular with them?

Coltrane: Well . . . I don't know. Well, like it was an attempt, it was an attempt to, to create something, I think, with more of a label, you see, than through true evolution.

Kofsky: You mean, it didn't evolve naturally out of the desires of the musicians?

Coltrane: I don't, I don't think so. Well, it—maybe it did; I don't—I can't say that. It was an attempt to do something which is—evolution *is* about trying, too, you know? [*laughs*] But there's something in evolution that, man—it just happens when it's ready, although you have to try, also, and this just seemed it wasn't really where it was coming from, you know. It was a, it was a—what was it? An attempt to blend, to wed two musics, right? That's what it really was?

Kofsky: Well, that's what it was supposed to be.

Coltrane: Yeah.

Kofsky: You said that—talking about saxophone players—that there was a common pool that everybody dipped into. Maybe here, there wasn't enough of that pool, I mean, for people to dip into.

Coltrane: Well, I just think it wasn't time. It hadn't—it was an attempt to do something at a time when it just wasn't time for this to happen, and therefore it wasn't lasting. But there may have been some things that came out of this that have been beneficial in promoting the, the final change, which is coming. So nothing is really wasted, although it might, you know, it might appear to have failed or not succeeded, you know, the way that men felt they would have desired it to.

Kofsky: Even the mistakes can be instructive if you know how to utilize them.

Coltrane: Definitely. [*chuckles*]

Kofsky: Do you make any attempt, or do you feel that you should make any attempt, to educate your audience in ways that aren't musical? It's obvious that you want your audience to understand what you're doing musically, but do you feel that you want them to understand other things, too, and that you have some kind of responsibility for—

Coltrane: Sure, I, I feel this, and this is one of the things I am concerned about now. I just don't know how to go about this. I, I wanted to—I want to find out just how I should do it, you know. I think that it's going to have to be, uh, very subtle; I mean, it's—you can't, you can't ram philosophies down anybody's throat—and the music is enough! [*laughs*] You know, and that's philosophy. But I think the best thing I can do at this time is to try to get *myself* in shape, you know, and *know myself*. If I can do *that*, then I'll just play, you see, [*laughs*] and leave it at that. And I, I believe that will do it, if I really can get to myself, and, and really, and then be just as I feel that I should be, and play it, you see. And I think they'll get it, because music goes a long way—and it really is—it, it can influence.

Kofsky: That's how I got interested in all those things I was talking about earlier—I mean, in Malcolm X, and so forth. I might not have come to it, or come to it as fast, if it hadn't been for the music. Because that was my first introduction to something beyond my own horizons, and that made me think about the world I was living in.

Coltrane: Yeah! That's, that's what I'm sure of, man, I'm *sure*, I'm *really sure* of this thing. And as I say, there, there are things which, as far as spirituality are concerned, which are very important to me at this time, and I've got to grow through certain, you know, phases of this to other understandings and more, you know, consciousness and awareness of just what it is that I'm supposed to, you know, understand about it; and I'm sure all this will be part of the music, which is, to me, you know, I feel I want to be a force for good.

Kofsky: And the music, too?

Coltrane: Everywhere. [*laughs*] You know, I want to be a force for *real good*. In other words, I know that there are bad forces. You know, I know that there are forces out here that bring suffering to others and misery to the world, but I want to be the opposite force. I want to be the force which is truly for good.

Kofsky: I don't have any more of my prepared questions to ask you—or my improvised questions to ask you. [*both laugh*] 'Cause we had a lot of questions here that were related just to you. All those questions about music I don't ask of the other musicians; but I've always had a very special interest in your work, so I took this opportunity. I don't know when I'll ever get the chance to sit you down with a tape recorder again, [*both laugh*] so I took this chance. Do you have anything else that you'd like to get on here?

Coltrane: I think you, man, well you just about covered it, I believe, just about covered it.

Kofsky: Do you mind, or do you have any objection if I publish this interview someplace?

Coltrane: Well, the only thing I would like is that you might send me, before you do?

Kofsky: The transcript? OK.

Coltrane: Yeah. Send the transcript.

Kofsky: The reason I say that is because you are now a person of such significance and such influence that things coming from the mouths of other people, which could be, just be disregarded, could not so easily be disregarded when they come from you.

Coltrane: That's true. That's true.

Kofsky: And I know since, from what you said that you're sincere in wanting to be a force for good, and I think this is one way of getting it in front of a lot of people is by printing this sort of thing. So I'll type, I'll have a transcript typed up and send it to you and you can have it.

Coltrane: Yeah, well that's the only thing I ask.

Kofsky: I'll indicate where the shopping carts were rattling. [*laughs*]

Coltrane: Yeah. [*chuckles*] Yeah.

Kofsky: OK, you can take me back and dump me at the train station, if you want.

Coltrane: All right. What time is it, now?

Kofsky: It's about twelve after one.

Coltrane: [*starts car*] What time is the train?

Kofsky: About one-thirty. So we timed it. I'll just leave the thing [the tape recorder] running till we get there.

Coltrane: Yeah.

Kofsky: Something else may come up.

Coltrane: It was going pretty good.

Kofsky: I hope you didn't think those questions were too silly.

Coltrane: No, man. This, uh—much better than I could ever do. I don't think it's an easy job to really come up with questions, either. I don't think it's an easy job. I mean you have to be thinking about something, yourself.

Kofsky: Yeah, well, that's the thing. You know, if you can't play this music—

Coltrane: There's Ascension Lutheran.[4] [*laughs*]

Kofsky: Yeah. Oh yeah, how about that! They named it after the record, huh? [*both laugh*]

Coltrane: A beautiful church.

Kofsky: It looks nice from the outside.

Coltrane: Yeah, man.

Kofsky: Yeah, if you can't play it, then if you're going to write about it, you have, I think, an obligation to do it as conscientiously as possible.

Coltrane: I believe it, man. [*unintelligible*]

Kofsky: And always when it's a question of your opinion versus the musician's opinion, to give the benefit of the doubt to the musician, because he knows the music far better than you'll ever know it. In other words, you have to be humble, but—

Coltrane: I understand, yeah, I believe this.

Kofsky: A lot of guys aren't humble; they get arrogant because they think they have some kind of power.

Coltrane: Yeah, well, that's one of the causes of this arrogance—the idea of power. But then you lose your true power, which is to be part of all, you see, and the only way you can be part of all is to understand it.

Kofsky: To understand it, yeah.

Coltrane: And you have to—that means you have to, when there's something you don't understand, you have to go humbly to it. You know, you don't go to school and, say, sit down and say, "I know what you're getting ready to teach me," you know, you sit there and you learn. You open your mind. You absorb. But you got to be quiet, you have to be still to do that.

Kofsky: That's what so annoyed me about all of that stuff that they were saying about you in sixty-one, and so forth.

Coltrane: Oh, that was, well, that was hell. That was very—I couldn't *believe* it, you know, it just seemed so *preposterous*. It was so *ridiculous*, man, it just—I just—that's what bugged me. It just was so absolutely ridiculous, because they made it appear that we didn't even know the first thing about music—the *first* thing, [*laughs*] you know. And there we were really trying to, you know, push things on.

Kofsky: Because they never stand still.

Coltrane: No, they never do.

Kofsky: Well, I know that later generations will look—

Coltrane: And Eric, man, as sweet as this cat was and the musician that he was—it hurt me, you know . . .

Kofsky: To see him . . .

Coltrane: . . . seeing him get hurt in this thing, you see?

Kofsky: Do you think that this possibly contributed to the fact that he died so young?

Coltrane: I don't think so, I don't know. But Eric was a strong cat. I don't know. Nobody knows *what* caused Eric, or what he passed from, so there's a mystery about it, you know?

Kofsky: I didn't mean that it was directly, but I mean—

Coltrane: Indirectly?

Kofsky: Yeah.

Coltrane: I don't know. The whole scene, man. He—well, he couldn't work [*unintelligible*].

Kofsky: That's what I meant, really. Emotional—

Coltrane: I don't know just how—he always seemed to be a very cheerful young man, so I don't *think* that would push him, you know.

Kofsky: That way.

Coltrane: I don't think so, because he, he had an outlook on life which was very, very good—optimistic. And he had this sort of thing, friendliness, you know—to everyone, a real friend. He was the type of man who could be—he was as much a friend to a guy he'd just met today as he was to one he'd known for ten years, you know? So, this, this kind of person, like that, I don't think it would really hurt him to the point where he would do something to hurt himself, consciously *or* unconsciously.

Kofsky: Mm hmm. Mm hmm. That friendliness was one of the things that has impressed me about the musicians here. I really didn't expect to be greeted with open arms, because I am an outsider, after all. And yet I have been amazed constantly at how eager the musicians were to cooperate once they got the idea that I was sincere and that this wasn't a joke or a con or something of that nature.

Coltrane: Yeah, well, man, I think that's all, that's all we need is sincerity, you know? And empathy. What is that, what is that word?

Kofsky: That's the word—"empathy." It means identification with other people. Becoming—

Coltrane: Becoming what we really are.

Kofsky: Yes, and being considerate of other people and not trying to damage them with—treating them, in other words, with the same care that we would want to be treated ourselves.

Coltrane: Truly. Yeah.

Kofsky: There *is* a restaurant in this town. [*both laugh*]

Coltrane: Maybe a hotel somewhere. A motel, rather. Not a hotel.

Kofsky: Not a hotel.

Coltrane: No. No hotel.

Kofsky: Do you live far, outside of wherever we are, now?

Coltrane: Well, I guess I'm about four, five miles down the road. [*chuckles*]

Kofsky: You really sound like Farmer John. [*both laugh*] Reminds me of my boyhood, I grew up in a place like this.

Coltrane: Yeah, man, when I come up here and now I have to do all, get everything I want to get, you know.

Kofsky: That's right, because you—

Coltrane: I got to go to the store, and do all that, because I don't want to come back up here. Yeah, well I've, I've gone through this. I don't know, I think I want to get closer to town, because, I don't know, maybe there's something I can do in music, you know—maybe I can get a place, a little room or something to play in. Hopefully, maybe I can do that.

Kofsky: Everybody else has those lofts down in Cooper.

Coltrane: Yeah.

Kofsky: But I mean, that's not really suitable for you, anymore. It's OK—it's one thing when you're in your twenties, but—

Coltrane: Yeah. Yeah, I don't want a loft, but I don't know, maybe there's something I can get to play in, just some place to, to be able to work, you know, or give somebody some work in.

Kofsky: Where do you play at home? I heard you practicing over the phone, at least I thought that was what I heard.

Coltrane: Yeah, well, anywhere. I've just got a—there's a room over the garage that I'm getting fixed now to—I think it's going to be my practice room. You know, sometimes you build a room and it ends up you still go in the toilet, so I don't know. [*both laugh*] I hope I like it, but—I was, I was in the living room then, or just anywhere. I keep a horn on the piano. And I have a horn in my bedroom—

a flute's usually back there, because when I go there I'm tired so I lay down to practice.

Kofsky: About how many hours a day do you play, would you say?

Coltrane: Not too much at this time. I find that it's only when something is, is trying to come through, you know, that I, that I really practice. And then it's, it's—I don't even know how many hours, you know—it's just all day, on and off.

Kofsky: Until it comes.

Coltrane: Yeah. But at this time, it's, uh—there's nothing that's coming out, now. It's just, I'm kind of taking in.

Kofsky: I was very surprised to hear you practicing at all, because I just couldn't conceive of what you could find to practice! But I know it isn't like that.

Coltrane: No, you know, I *need* to practice, man. It's just that I want something to practice, and I'm trying to stick around now and find out what it is that I want to—area, you know, that I want to get into.

Notes

1. Coltrane researcher David Tegnell has determined that this was most likely the speech Malcolm X gave on April 8, 1964, at the Palm Gardens Ballroom on 52nd Street in Manhattan.
2. In this interview, Coltrane didn't return to the subject of his opinion of the term "jazz," but he'd made his feelings clear in the Tokyo interview a few weeks earlier (see page 266).
3. Coltrane pronounces it "*Ail*-er."
4. Coltrane is referring to Ascension Lutheran Church, which is located at 33 Bay Shore Road in Deer Park, New York, and is across the street from the parking lot where the interview was held (see www.ascensionlutheran.org).

LIVE AT THE VILLAGE VANGUARD AGAIN! LINER NOTES

Nat Hentoff

Nat Hentoff interviewed Coltrane for these liner notes, probably sometime in the summer or early fall of 1966 (the album was released around November 1966).

Along with his extraordinary musicianship, the especially impressive quality of John Coltrane is his insistence on continuing to explore himself and his music each time he plays. This is a point Albert Ayler has made—that Coltrane could have stopped quite comfortably on one of his previous plateaus, but he refuses to stop. And as Coltrane goes on, he acts as a powerful stimulus to others not to stop.

Musician-critic Don Heckman, in reviewing a Coltrane performance for *Down Beat*, distills the nature of that part of Coltrane's power to seize and hold his listeners: "What makes his work so special is the fact that even though Coltrane can probably do anything he wants as an improviser, he constantly sets goals for himself while he plays that require an outpouring of the most demanding personal energies. Few players of Coltrane's generation continue to place such demands on themselves, and the great magic is that he more often than not finds the resources within himself to meet these demands. The resulting personal esthetic odyssey makes almost every exposure to his work a memorable experience."

As is the case in this recording made at New York's Village Vanguard on May 28, 1966. Both songs have long been part of the Coltrane repertory, but again Coltrane has found in them the base for new dimensions of expressiveness.

Of "Naima," he points out: "In its structure, it's a simple melody over pedal tones. The outside goes from an E-flat pedal to A-flat. The bridge is over a B-flat pedal tone and then back to outside pedal tones. Also I guess you could say that piece uses suspension of chords."

Coltrane's initial statement of the melody focuses once more on the essential lyricism that characterizes all his music. It is a lyricism that can be exceptionally sensitive to nuances of mood and color but that is always based on strength—a strength and openness of feeling that allows for that lyricism to pass through a wide range of transformations.

Pharoah Sanders follows on tenor. His solo, also lyrical in its own forceful terms, underlines Coltrane's assertion that "Pharoah is constantly trying to get more and more deeply into the human foundations of music." That concern is clear, for example, in the spectrum of speech-like sounds he creates and also, I feel, in the complexity of his rhythmic designs over an enormously powerful implicit pulse. "He's dealing in the human experience," Coltrane adds. And as the human experience is multidimensional and seemingly fragmented but actually rooted in the kaleidoscope of the self, so Sanders's solo here is acutely, turbulently, compellingly personal.

After Sanders, Coltrane returns to close the circle of this particular plunge into music-as-being. It is "Naima" as it has not been heard before, and will never be heard again in this way. For each Coltrane performance is a whole unto itself that cannot be duplicated.

"My Favorite Things" begins with further proof of how singularly creative a bassist Jimmy Garrison has become. "Jimmy," Coltrane emphasizes, "has been a great influence within the group. Certain things have occurred in the ways in which our music has gone that definitely reflect his approach to bass playing. The way, for example, he solos without rhythm accompaniment. That influenced us. And the mood that his solos set. Knowing what he is capable of helped a lot of the music to take shape. He was always in mind. As for his solo work as such, it's difficult for me to put into words what makes it so outstanding. Of course, there's a remarkable sense of structure. But it's more than that. There's an intuitive sense at work too—he just knows what to hit and when to hit it."

I asked Coltrane about the song itself. Hadn't he tired of "My Favorite Things" after all the times he'd played it. "No," he answered, "because once you go into the solos it's wide open for any kind of creation you can get going." This is improvising. That way no song need ever go stale.

After Garrison's astonishingly resourceful solo, the rhythm section and Coltrane on soprano saxophone begin to illustrate Don Heckman's point that "all the carefully evolved steps in Coltrane's musical development . . . have now been assimilated in what is, for me, the most brilliant total improvisational style in jazz."

A key reason for the presence of Rashied Ali in the group is his contribution toward that totality of improvisation. "The way he plays," Coltrane explains, "allows the soloist maximum freedom. I can really choose just about any direction at just about any time in the confidence that it will be compatible with what he's doing. You see, he's laying down multi-directional rhythms all the time. To me, he's definitely one of the great drummers."

Pharoah Sanders follows with an intensity, a fierceness of commitment that makes him sound at first like a man possessed. But I find, after listening to him again and again, that the evolving impact of his playing on me is not that of a man possessed by external forces. What we're hearing—if we allow ourselves to hear—is a man trying to strip himself to the marrow of being. Coltrane puts it this way: "Pharoah is a man of large spiritual reservoir. He's always trying to reach out to truth. He's trying to allow his spiritual self to be his guide. He's dealing, among other things, in energy, in integrity, in essences. I so much like the strength of his playing. Furthermore, he is one of the innovators, and it's been my pleasure and privilege that he's been willing to help me, that he is part of the group."

A ferociously spiraling dialogue between Sanders and Coltrane sets Sanders into further searching and then the two intersect again at full emotional speed.

Throughout, from the start of the album, there is the persistently apposite piano of Alice Coltrane, John's wife. Her value to the group, Coltrane says, is that "she continually senses the right color, the right textures, of the sound of the chords. And in addition, she's fleet. She has real facility."

Coltrane on soprano saxophone concludes the piece with yet another startling, sometimes shattering demonstration of sustained improvisation. At the conclusion, Sanders has switched to flute. (Incidentally, Coltrane, otherwise heard on soprano all the way through "My Favorite Things," also doubles on bass clarinet in the dialogues.)

What's ahead for Coltrane? "More writing," he says. "I'm trying to work out a kind of writing that will allow for more plasticity, more viability, more room for improvisation in the statement of the melody itself before we go into solos. And I'd like that established point of departure to be freer rhythmically. Also I've got drum fever. I'd like to continue exploring the use of more than one drummer, as we did here with Emanuel Rahim. And I'd like more horns."

Is there never a stopping point for him? "No," he answered emphatically. "You just keep going all the way, as deep as you can. You keep trying to get right down to the crux." The crux of music. The crux of life. For Coltrane there is no separation between the two.

NAT HENTOFF

"JOHN COLTRANE: MY IMPRESSIONS AND RECOLLECTIONS"

Babatunde Olatunji

Coltrane and Nigerian-born percussionist Babatunde Olatunji were friends and, eventually, collaborators; as detailed here, Coltrane helped Olatunji open the Olatunji Center of African Culture in 1967. Part of Coltrane's performance there on April 23, 1967, was recorded and eventually released as *The Olatunji Concert: The Last Live Recording*.

This rare, previously unpublished manuscript is located at the Institute of Jazz Studies (IJS) at Rutgers University in New Jersey.

If there is any kind of experience one encounters in the business, John Coltrane had a taste of it all. John Coltrane—a soft-spoken, quiet, unassuming soul of a brother—saw and experienced how recording companies can and will use an artist, pick his brains, and make a sucker out of him. He coped with managers and booking agents; many who as parasites, kept the artist on the go—living in suitcases, changing hotel rooms day after day, city after city—with no regard for his or her health, and yet the artist would have nothing to show for it money-wise. He dealt with shrewd operators in the music business who decided which tune is going to be in the "Top Ten" around the country by giving payola to program directors and, most of the time, to ignorant disc-jockeys whose knowledge of the music they spin tantamounts to nothing.

When John Coltrane finally made it into the "Big-Time"; when "they" finally decided that he had "arrived", many critics of the music he loved and played couldn't understand his form of expression and the extent of his creativity. They did not know that Coltrane was a genius from childhood. He—like many young Black musicians who were denied the opportunity for growth and creativity (from conception to birth) during the unchallenged years of segregation, injustice, and complete disregard for human dignity and decency in the music business—survived the gradual process of a peaceful but damaging indoctrination.

Some people still believe that his decision not to perform in public halls, theatres, and Jazz rooms was an escape mechanism to avoid criticism of his music by self-appointed Jazz authorities, and jealous ego-maniacs. But I can truthfully say that John Coltrane made his decision because:

1. He knew that he had reached the highest level in applying his knowledge of the music taught in school and therefore had to explore other sources if he was to reach another pinnacle of achievement in creativity and provocative expression (i.e. of our trials and tribulations, failure and success; the joy and sadness—the universal truth of a universe in perpetual motion of an unending horizon).

2. He was tired of being "Taken" by concert promoters who usually capitalized on the growing fame and public acceptance of a talented struggling artist who, after being in obscurity, suddenly came to the limelight—built, managed and protected by those who can and will determine who makes it to the "Top". Being a person not known for a violent display of emotions, he refused to sell his soul for a mess of pottage.

Umoja—Unity

These two reasons more than anything else brought us closer than ever before. In the early 1960s 'Trane would always come to see and hear me and the musical group which included giants like Yusef Lateef, Chris White, Rudy Collins, etc., at Birdland and the Village Gate (now known as the Bottom & Top of the Gate). After shows, he would come quietly to say how much he enjoyed the session and especially the polyrhythmic rendition in various compositions. The conversation always ended by him saying, "We need to do an album together. I need to learn something about the culture, the language, the music of my ancestors." 'Trane tried to get Impulse to sign me up in 1964, but the deal was blocked.

In 1965, when he came to see my show at the Afrikan Pavilion of the New York World's Fair, I told him that my dream to open an Afrikan Cultural Center in Harlem will materialize after the Fair. He was glad to hear that, and promised to do anything he could to help and be a part of the Institution. As a genuine and generous brother, he wired two hundred and fifty dollars as contribution towards the renovation of the loft which was last occupied by an optical company leaving behind corroded pipes and gadgets bolted from the ground up—and against the walls. Because of the terms of our lease which reads and dictates taking the premises as it is, it took quite some time to clean up the messy mess from which the landlord shrewdly excused himself. 'Trane would always call and comment on the sign "Coming Soon—Olatunji Center of Afrikan Culture" and how he was looking forward to the official opening. The sign remained for a year and a half due to legal problems which could have been avoided if I had not been associated with inexperienced young Jekuredi lawyers. (Jekuredi is an Afrikan slang for mediocre).

On July 19, 1966, the Board of Standard and Appeals voted unanimously granting permission to establish the Center provided I meet the Board of Ed's specifications required for such establishments. This meant more money. 'Trane got the news and sent me another two hundred and fifty dollars by Western Union. A few days later he called and requested a meeting to discuss an idea he had been contemplating on for quite some time. My response was an immediate yes, "let's meet". Two days later John Coltrane came and was pleased at the progress being made. When I told him about the electrician who demanded and received a thousand dollars advance towards installation of lights and never came back to fulfill his contractual obligations, Coltrane's reaction was a gentle shrug of his shoulders with a serious, stern look on his face while muttering these words, "You can't even trust your own these days."

After a few minutes of silence he opened up the conversation by asking me if I would be willing to join him and brother Yusef Lateef to form an organization or a trio without any specific grandiloquent titles or high sounding catchy names, but a union that would bind three of us together to accomplish certain goals. I asked him what he had in mind.

John Coltrane said, "Tunji, I am being tired of being taken and exploited by managers, club owners and concert promoters. I worked too hard to get where I am today and still don't get adequately compensated for my talent. I hate to see promoters manipulating one artist after another. When you get a bad review, that means your concert price is going down. They don't really care about you, your music, what you are trying to accomplish artistically, nor do they give a damn if you are up today and down tomorrow because they know they will soon discover another victim!"

I asked him, "What do you think we should do, because I am tired of the whole thing myself."

Kujichagulia—Self-determination

Trane answered and said, "Look Tunji, we need to sponsor our own concerts, promote them and perform in them. This way we will not only learn how to take a risk but will not have to accept the dictates of anybody about how long you should play, what to play and what you get."

What else can any right thinking Black musicians say to that—but, "Amen! Amen! Amen!"

When you realize the fate of giants like Charlie Parker, Dinah Washington and many others, it is quite understandable why men like Coltrane decided against a continuous exploitation of talent, as well as a complete disregard and disrespect for his intelligence.

Ujima—Collective Work & Responsibility

Without any delay, Coltrane, Yusef Lateef and I met at the Center a few days later. At the meeting we arrived at the following decisions:

1. To regard each other as equal partners in all categories.
2. Not to allow any booking agent or promoter to present one group without the other two members of the Triumvirate.
3. To explore the possibility of teaching the music of our people in conservatories, colleges and universities where only European musical experience dominates and is being perpetuated.
4. To book halls and theatres in major U.S. cities for our presentations for [the] 1967–68 concert season.
5. That the premier concert be presented in New York City.

I was given the task of investigating the availability of halls like Carnegie Hall, Lincoln Center and others for our Premiere Concert in New York City. With speed and enthusiasm, I contacted Carnegie Hall officials, but all available week-end dates in 1967 were already taken. Lincoln Center offered and convinced me to accept Sunday evening, January 14, 1968.

Ujamaa—Cooperative Economics

After communicating with my two brothers, a check for $1000.00 to which each of us contributed $333.35 was sent to Mrs. Louise Homer with the contract on June 19, 1967.

The date was agreed upon to give us adequate time for planning and rehearsal with our respective groups as well as several joint rehearsals.

Nia—Purpose

Before this agreement was finalized 'Trane, who had refused many engagements and refused to make any public appearances that year, agreed to open the Center's Sunday Afternoon Happening, the sole purpose of which was to bring great Black musical groups back to Harlem thus changing its tarnished image as well as improve and restore its cultural tradition and pride.

Kuumba—Creativity

On April 23, 1967 the Olatunji Center of Afrikan Culture, Inc. presented John Coltrane and His Quintet in "The Roots of Africa" for two continuous performances; 4PM–6PM and 6PM–8PM. The concert which was well publicized and advertised in newspapers and on radio brought hundreds of people both Black and white from all areas of the city. The huge attendance for both shows proved that 'Trane was still popular and respected by those in the business. It demonstrated to all present that, despite all rumors, he was in the best of spirit and shape; still the master of his instrument, still determined not to allow the display of collective immorality, injustices, prejudices and dishonesty by many in the business destroy his and the universal commitment of some towards good and the desirability of truth.

This philosophy of life, Coltrane put into practice in his dealings with those who walked and worked with him.

Ujamaa—Alternate Master

After the successful concert which featured his loyal and talented wife on piano, Coltrane asked for the receipts of all spent ($425) on the promotion and gave it back to the Center for the following week's coming attraction. He also divided the balance of what was left ($500.00) after paying each musician the union scale for each concert as was agreed upon with the Center.

Ujima—Alternate Master

He was convinced that we can build and help our institutions survive through genuine support and dedication, the lack of which led many into the deep sea of financial chaos and extinction.

The concert was recorded by a very close friend of the family whose name I cannot recall. I wasn't too concerned at that time about the recording. I was too excited, maybe, because I was honored like many who saw what is now regarded as his last public appearance.

Imani—Faith

I left New York early in July 1967 for a two week engagement in Minneapolis, Minnesota with the January 14, 1968, engagement at the Lincoln Philharmonic Hall in what was supposed to be billed "An Evening with John Coltrane, Yusef Lateef, and Olatunji—In the Roots of Afrika," a closely guarded secret—only to hear on the radio about the sudden, untimely death of my brother, a friend, a colleague, a wholesome spirit, a giant of a soulful soul.

Since his death in July 1967, the music of John Coltrane has been the topic of scholars in the field, in lecture halls. It is so ironical and paradoxical that the man whose creative expressions (not improvisations) were too heavy, complicated, and incomprehensible to Jazz critics and enthusiasts now has his name immortalized in the minds of millions, his music now taught in colleges and universities and his spirit free like those of our ancestors whose noble deeds and way of life will forever remain a source of inspiration in our relentless struggle for survival.

There have been and there will be many more articles, stories and poems written about John Coltrane the man, the super-musician since he joined the great majority in July 1967.

To those of us who knew him well and confided in him, it was an honor and a privilege. To those who had the opportunity and could not relate, what a pity.

KULU SÉ MAMA LINER NOTES

Nat Hentoff

Nat Hentoff interviewed Coltrane for these liner notes, probably in mid- or late 1966. Though it consisted of material recorded in 1965, *Kulu Sé Mama* wasn't released until early 1967. It was the last Coltrane album released before his death on July 17, 1967 (the album *Expression* was released shortly thereafter).

Juno Lewis is a drummer, a drum maker, a singer, a composer. Born in New Orleans in 1931, he is now based in Los Angeles. It was there John Coltrane met him through mutual friends, and the result was the first side of this album, which was recorded in Los Angeles.

Lewis is a proud man, proud of his tradition, as the accompanying poem makes clear. The composition "Kulu Sé Mama" (or "Juno Sé Mama") is described by Lewis as a ritual dedicated to his mother. Lewis's poem [. . .] supplies the programmatic content of the piece as well as its emotional base and its emotive intentions.

I would only add that the performance is an absorbing, almost trance-like fusion of tenderness and strength, memory and pride. And fitting its ritual nature, the singing and much of the playing by the horns have the cadences of a chant. For all its length, the work has an organic totality; and at the end, there is a fulfilling sense of achievement—of a long nurtured and developed story finally being told. This, by the way, is Juno Lewis's first appearance on records. His singing is in an Afro-Creole dialect he cites as Entobes. His drums include the Juolulu, water drums, the Dome Dahka, and there are also bells and a conch shell.

As the poem makes clear, Lewis's primary present goal is the establishment of an Afro-American Art Center, "a home for the homeless, future sons of drums." He wants it to be international in scope, and proceeds from this album will go towards actualizing that dream.

The two John Coltrane compositions which make up the second side are further musical essays on Coltrane's insistent belief in the perfectibility of man. "Vigil," Coltrane points out, "implies watchfulness. Anyone trying to attain perfection is faced with various obstacles in life which tend to sidetrack him. Here, therefore, I mean watchfulness against elements that might be destructive—from within or without."

Coltrane adds: "I don't try to set standards of perfection for anyone else. I do feel everyone does try to reach his better self, his full potential, and what that consists of depends on each individual. Whatever that goal is, moving toward it does require vigilance." And as the performance shows, that vigilance is not without its tensions. Listening to Coltrane work through his own challenge may well stimulate self-confrontation in the rest of us. Each listener, of course, will himself be challenged in a different way. For many, the basic beginning will be that described by Don DeMicheal in a *Down Beat* review of Coltrane: "This music . . . opens up a part of myself that normally is tightly closed, and seldom-recognized feelings, emotion, thoughts well up from the opened door and sear my consciousness." "Welcome," Coltrane explains, "is that feeling you have when you finally do reach an awareness, an understanding which you have earned through struggle. It is a feeling of peace. A welcome feeling of peace." And accordingly, the performance is serene. Temporarily serene, for in Coltrane's view of man in the world, there are always further stages to work your way toward. The striving is ceaseless. It is not striving in competition with others, but rather a striving within the self to discover how much more aware one can become.

NAT HENTOFF

"'TRANE'S GONE"

Herb O'Brien

This brief reminiscence, published in an obscure underground newspaper shortly after Coltrane's death, paints a concise portrait of Coltrane as an extremely generous man—generous with his time (taking tickets at the door to give the ticket taker a break), generous with his money (taking a pay cut so the club's employees could get paid), and generous with his music (performing a two-hour matinee for four people).

My Favorite Things

Sometimes he'd lay out of a set and walk to the rear of the house [nightclub] to listen to his rhythm section. There'd always be standees there leaning against the back wall. He'd find a spot, light a smoke and just listen quietly. You couldn't help noticing him in the crowd there. He was the one who wasn't snapping his fingers or humming or saying "yeah" out of time.

If Elvin or McCoy or Reggie did something he particularly liked a small smile would cross his usually impassive face; but it was his eyes I remember. He had happy eyes.

One night I was taking tickets and the room was jammed and I hadn't been to the john for hours. He glanced over at me then walked over and said, "My guys want to be alone with themselves a while, you go on, I'll get the tickets." And he did.

The joint never had enough money, and in jazz rooms the rule was you had to pay the musicians first (in that jazz room anyway). One payday night he walked into the manager's office and heard me being asked whom I thought wouldn't mind getting paid. He interrupted us, it was the only time I ever heard him interrupt anyone, and said, "Give me half of mine for my guys and pay your own help with the rest . . . I'm cool for a while." And he was. He spoke very little on the

From *The Seed: Voice of Chicago Underground*, August 11–25, 1967, volume 1, number 6, page 7 stand or off. He didn't call his sets but would just walk out on stage and stand there 'til the talkers quieted down and then he and his men would play. The contract said something about forty minutes up and twenty off. Often he'd get into something and play an hour and a half, yet nineteen minutes later he'd be walking out to stand quietly waiting for the talkers to finish their sets so he could start another of his.

We had matinees on Sundays. They were never very well attended, that is if you think in terms of total numbers present. One Sunday just four people showed up. One of his men started to say something about giving back the money and splitting. He [Coltrane] got up, walked out on the stage, stood there a second then spoke quietly into the mike to the four people scattered out in the room. "What are you doing way out there, get up here." As the four moved up to take seats at the foot of the stage he turned to his men and said, "Dig Yourselves." And they did, for two hours.

Beyond an occasional funny cigarette he never did anything the Fuzz would frown on, yet he never looked down on those who did, he'd just say, "I don't need to get any higher than I am."

John Coltrane, dead at forty. Dig yourselves.

QUOTABLE COLTRANE

Opener

"Could I have the beer opener?"

—John Coltrane at Van Gelder Studio, May 11, 1956,
immediately after recording "Woody'n You"

Thelonious Monk

"I always had to be alert with Monk, because if you didn't keep aware all the time of what was going on, you'd suddenly feel as if you'd stepped into an empty elevator shaft."

—John Coltrane, quoted by Nat Hentoff in the liner notes to
Giant Steps (Atlantic 1311)

A Small Sound

"I can't play [the alto saxophone anymore]. I don't like my sound on that at all. I get a small sound on it, you know?"

—John Coltrane to Ralph J. Gleason, May 2, 1961

This Winding Road

"But now I prefer the rhythm [section] to be free. [*laughs*] I had to get it beat into my skull, but [*laughs*] I accept this principle now. At first I wasn't sure, because I was delving through sequences and I felt that I should have the rhythm [section] play the sequences right along with me, and we all go down this, you know, this winding road. But after several tries and failures and failures at this it seems better to have them free to go as they, you know—as free as possible. And then you superimpose whatever sequences you want to over what they're doing."

—John Coltrane to Michiel de Ruyter, November 19, 1961
(audio available at http://mdr.jazzarchief.nl/interviews/coltrane)

Coltrane and the Million-Dollar Groove

"Coltrane is exceptionally conscientious in his attitude toward audiences. He genuinely desires to give the most he can of himself, and he becomes irritated when he feels he has not been able to play at his maximum capacity. After a set one night which certainly satisfied this listener, Coltrane, perspiring heavily in his dressing room, kept muttering, 'I couldn't get a groove out there. I'd pay a million dollars to get a groove.'"

—Nat Hentoff, "John Coltrane: Challenges Without End,"
International Musician, March 1962, pages 12–13

Fun with Duke

"Coltrane, who is considered by his peers to be in the very front rank of experimenters, recorded recently with Duke Ellington. 'Was it fun?' I asked. 'Fun! I was scared to death!' Coltrane replied."

—Ralph J. Gleason, "Coltrane, the Venturesome,"
San Francisco Chronicle, March 29, 1963, page 39

Storm Clouds in "Alabama"

"Bob Thiele asked Trane if the title ['Alabama'] 'had any significance to today's problems.' I suppose he meant literally. Coltrane answered, 'It represents, musically, something that I saw down there translated into music from inside me.' Which is to say, Listen. And what we're given is a slow delicate introspective sadness, almost hopelessness, except for Elvin, rising in the background like something out of nature . . . a fattening thunder, storm clouds or jungle war clouds."

—LeRoi Jones (Amiri Baraka), from the liner notes to
Coltrane Live at Birdland (Impulse! A[S]-50)

Writing for the Band

"The thing that I'm gonna concentrate on is trying to write for the band. That I'm gonna do first, and If It becomes necessary through the music to have another horn, then I'll do it. And if not, I'll just stay with a quartet. But I think it's important that first I get the music. [. . .] I would only accept a financial loss if I was gonna reap something musically, see? And as it is now, the music doesn't demand another horn because it's all worked out between just the rhythm section and one horn. But as I say, if, in a year or two, if the things that we're gonna start writing for the band, if they reach the point where they sound like they call for another horn or if we need another horn to really express these ideas, then I'll have to get one. Even if it means making less."

—John Coltrane to Michiel de Ruyter, October 26, 1963 (audio available at http://mdr.jazzarchief.nl/interviews/coltrane)

A Thousand Rhythms

"I'll tell you the truth—John [Coltrane] wanted somebody to play [drums] next to Elvin [Jones], and I turned him down. I had played with John three times in 1964, and the closest Elvin came to losing his job was me taking it [   ] John came over quietly and said, 'Sunny, how you doing? Would you like to play?' But Elvin was playing so great that night, it froze me in my tracks. After [Elvin Jones] jumped and ran Albert [Ayler] said 'You still wanna do this?' I said, 'Yeah . . .' And we played, man. McCoy sounded different, Jimmy was singing with me . . . it worked. Elvin came back and was sitting there with a drink and he was enjoying himself! I came off the stand and we had a drink together and we became buddies. He calls me Big Man ever since. [. . .] Later I told John 'Elvin never let nobody play with you but me, and I'm never gonna lose the friendship I have with him . . . You're gonna make him hate me.' John sat there quietly and said, 'Sunny, I hear a thousand rhythms . . .'"

—Sunny Murray, interview by Dan Warburton, Paris, November 3, 2000 (www.paristransatlantic.com/magazine/interviews/murray.html, accessed September 23, 2009)

Tribute to Eric Dolphy

"Whatever I'd say would be an understatement. I can only say my life was made much better by knowing him. He was one of the greatest people I've ever known, as a man, a friend, and a musician."

—John Coltrane, quoted in "A Tribute to Eric Dolphy,"
Down Beat, August 27, 1964, page 10

Truth in Music

"I wouldn't want to give up the use of chords, if what I want to do can be accomplished by using those devices. I'm not sure whether the chord system will survive, but I do know it will be used very differently. I don't want to take anything away from music; I want to add to it. I prefer not to answer the controversy about 'anti-jazz.' If someone wants to call it that, let him; I'll continue to look for truth in music as I see it, and I'll draw on all the sources I can, all the areas of music, all the things there are in the world around us to inspire me. It takes many people to effect a complete change in any system."

—John Coltrane, quoted in *Esquire*, September 1965, page 125

Purely Experimental

"Saxophonist John Coltrane caused a sensation when he played Los Angeles' It Club last month. Added to his regular rhythm section of pianist McCoy Tyner, bassist Jimmy Garrison, and drummer Elvin Jones were bassist Donald Garrett and drummer Frank Butler. Tenor saxophonist Harold [*sic*; Ferrell 'Pharoah'] Sanders also was on some sets of the 10-day gig. According to some observers, the sound level when Jones and Butler got warmed up, was, to say the least, intense. When asked if the expansion of his group was permanent, Coltrane, who has used two bassists and extra horn men on several occasions, said that it wasn't. 'This is purely experimental,' he told *Down Beat*. 'I just wanted to see how it would work out. I may try it again later.'"

—"News and Views: Potpourri," *Down Beat*, December 2, 1965, page 12

As If for the First Time

"Sometimes I wish I could walk up to my music as if for the first time, as if I had never heard it before. Being so inescapably a part of it, I'll never know what the listener gets, what the listener feels, and that's too bad."

—John Coltrane, quoted by Nat Hentoff in the liner notes to *Om* (Impulse! A[S]-9140)

Strange Career

"I've had a strange career. I haven't yet quite found out how I want to play music. Most of what's happened these last few years has been questions. Some day we'll find the answers."

—John Coltrane, quoted in Leonard Feather's "Jazz Undergoes Transition, Finds Beat Getting Bigger," *Milwaukee Journal*, March 5, 1966, Green Sheet, pages 1–2

My Being

"My goal is to live the truly religious life and express it in my music. If you live it, when you play there's no problem because the music is just part of the whole thing. To be a musician is really something. It goes very, very deep. My music is the spiritual expression of what I am—my faith, my knowledge, my being."

—John Coltrane, quoted in Paul D. Zimmerman's "The New Jazz" (with Ruth Ross), *Newsweek*, December 12, 1966, pages 101–104, 106, 108

The Real Risk

"The real risk is in not changing. I have to feel that I'm after something. If I make money, fine. But I'd rather be striving. It's the striving, man, it's that I want."

—John Coltrane, quoted in Paul D. Zimmerman's "Death of a Jazz Man" (with Ruth Ross), *Newsweek*, July 31, 1967, pages 78–79

No Notes

"I would like to put out an album with absolutely no notes. Just the titles of the songs and the personnel. By this point I don't know what else can be said in words about what I'm doing. Let the music speak for itself."

—John Coltrane, quoted by Nat Hentoff in the liner notes to
Expression (Impulse! AS 9120)

Always Strive

"To perceive again and this time it must be said, for all who read to know that no matter what, it is all with God. He is gracious and merciful. His way is in Love, through which we all are. Wherever and whoever you are, always strive to follow and walk in the right Path and ask for aid and assistance . . . herein lies the ultimate and eternal happiness which is ours through His grace. Ohnedaruth, John Coltrane."

—John Coltrane, liner notes to *Infinity* (Impulse! AS-9225)

CODA: TRANE'S THREE WISHES

1. "To have an inexhaustible freshness in my music. I'm stale right now."
2. "Immunity from sickness or ill health."
3. "Three times the sexual power I have now. And something else too: more natural love for people. You can add that on to the other."

> —John Coltrane to "Nica" (the Baroness Pannonica de Koenigswarter), quoted in *Three Wishes: An Intimate Look at Jazz Greats*, compiled and photographed by Pannonica de Koenigswarter (New York: Abrams Image, 2008), page 61

APPENDIX A

Interview with Franklin Brower

C. O. Simpkins

C. O. Simpkins interviewed Franklin Brower, Coltrane's boyhood friend, at Brower's apartment in New York City in the fall of 1972, as part of his research for *Coltrane: A Biography*. At the time of the interview, Brower was 47 years old and had enjoyed a long career as a reporter for newspapers such as the *Philadelphia Afro-American*. Here he provides a firsthand account of Coltrane's days in High Point. The full interview, with extensive annotations by Coltrane researcher David Tegnell, will be published in Simpkins and Tegnell's forthcoming book, *Coltrane's High Point*. Tegnell wrote the introduction for this interview and transcribed it; both the interview introduction and the interview itself follow here.

Franklin Dewitt Brower and John Coltrane grew up as childhood friends in High Point, North Carolina. Although Franklin was a year older than John, the two boys befriended one another at an early age and passed through elementary and high school as classmates. Throughout his youth, Franklin Brower lived just down the street from John Coltrane, at 218 Underhill Avenue; 1930 census takers found him residing at this address with his parents, Thomas (age 41) and Janie (34), and five siblings, Lee (17), George (16), Willie (13), Janie (11), and Carl (2). This already crowded household also included five relatives—two of Janie's sisters, her brother-in-law, and two nieces, as well as two roomers. Such living circumstances were typical of many Underhill families, for whom home ownership was possible only by combining income from several residents. The Brower home was valued at $2,500, roughly equal to that of Reverend W. W. Blair, that is, the house at 118 Underhill, where Coltrane lived. Thomas A. Brower made his living as a barber. Both of Franklin's aunts and one of the roomers worked as hand ironers at a laundry (probably High Point Steam Laundry); his uncle was employed as a laborer at a golf course (probably Emerywood Country Club), and the second roomer as a cook at a college (probably High Point College).

Franklin Brower and John Coltrane took divergent paths through school. At Leonard Street (Elementary) School, both John Coltrane and Franklin Brower excelled as students. But once in high school, Brower flourished as a student, while Coltrane languished. Franklin graduated first among boys in his William Penn High School class, third, overall. Moreover, he served as editor of the student newspaper in both his junior and senior years, as vice-president of the student council during his senior year, and as treasurer of the senior class. John, on the other hand, focused almost exclusively on learning his musical instruments, largely in solitude. Consequently, at the end of each of his last two years at William Penn, Franklin Brower's classmates voted him most studious boy. In their senior year, these same classmates deemed John Coltrane most musical boy.

Brower and Coltrane remained close through much of much of their youth, but as differences emerged, their friendship gradually cooled. Upon graduating from high school, in June 1943, Brower and Coltrane left High Point together for Philadelphia, but once there, neither seemed especially interested in continuing their relationship. Over the ensuing years, they saw each other only intermittently.

Brower's recollections are best understood in historical context. In the wake of Negro disfranchisement throughout the South (imposed during the decade 1890–1900), many members of the African American aspiring class sought to regain the vote and achieve full citizenship by living responsibly and respectably, pursuing education, and dedicating themselves to the uplift of the Negro race. In High Point, a number of Underhill residents subscribed to such notions, and tried to instill in their children their values of self-discipline, thrift, and hard work through the churches and schools. Moreover, these families furthered this agenda by advertising their children's accomplishments in the Colored News column of the Segregationist newspaper, the *High Point Enterprise*. Consequently, the students of Leonard Street School, Fairview Elementary School, and William Penn High School grew up under glass, as it were, acutely aware of their role as race exemplars. Yet, William Penn students represented only a fraction of High Point's African American community: less than half of the town's Negro children attended school past seventh grade, and fewer than a quarter graduated from high school. The *High Point Enterprise* routinely highlighted this disparity by trumpeting news of "Negro" crimes, while burying the Colored News column in its back pages. We may surmise that John Coltrane early recognized the futility of adhering to the path prescribed for William Penn students, and deliberately departed from it, knowing that even his best scholastic efforts could gain him only a menial job after graduation. Franklin Brower, on the other hand, never wavered in his commitment to respectability and racial uplift. Brower's insistence, thirty years after his high school graduation, that Coltrane, as a 15- or 16-year-old boy, had betrayed his group's code speaks to the hold such ideas had both on him and on the community in which he and Coltrane grew up.

C. O. Simpkins: When did you first come in contact with John?

Franklin Brower: Well, actually, Coltrane and I grew up together in North Carolina in High Point. See, he was born in Hamlet, North Carolina. That's, actually, that's what's listed in all the books, but he was still a preschool kid when he came to High Point. From what I gather, his grandfather was a Reverend Blair, and did some preachin' around High Point.

Simpkins: Yeah, I went down there. Down to Hamlet. And that's where he was born, Hamlet. That's right.

Brower: I imagine you didn't find out too much about John in Hamlet. Did you get to High Point?

Simpkins: I went to High Point, too.

Brower: Because, well, actually, see this house. Did you see his house in High Point? His home there?

Simpkins: One-[eighteen] . . . Underhill Street.

Brower: On Underhill Street. I lived at 218 Underhill Street, which is further down . . .

Simpkins: It's down the hill?

Brower: You go down the hill, then you go down further. [. . .] I don't remember Reverend Blair at all, it's the grandfather. But I remember the grandmother, Mrs. Blair. [The] first I can remember Coltrane is, like, in the first grade or second grade, or somewhere along that line. Well, I'd be goin' home from school, I'd stop by his house, 'cause we went to Leonard Street School, which meant that, on my way home, I had to pass his house, and I can just remember a little, playin' around in his yard, there. And, somehow or another, we just became friends. And that situation existed throughout our school years.

Simpkins: Do you remember anything about that time? Any things you did together . . . in first and second grade?

Brower: Well, no, not that early. See, in the school system down there, and I imagine all over, they have, I guess, it's what they call a track system. They give these [State] tests at the end of the year [. . .] your class rankin' was A or B. And the children, A-, A-class, were the children who stood highest on these tests, and Coltrane and I just were naturally in the same class. We were always in the A-class. And matter of fact, Coltrane . . . as I first recall him as a student [. . .] was one of the top students. Somehow, I don't remember our first three or four years. Only thing I remember [of] our first four years, like in fourth grade, I remember that some girl came to town, her name was Annie LeGrand.

Simpkins: Annie LeGrand?

Brower: Yeah, Annie LeGrand. She was from out of town, she wasn't a native High Pointer. She came there like to stay with a relative, and Coltrane and I took an interest in her, and thought she was nice. But that's the fourth grade, we was in Mrs. Whitted's class, but as far as the schoolin' itself, studyin' and stuff like that, I remember in the fifth grade, at the first rankin' of students accordin' to the tests that I can remember [. . .] I stood number one, and, then, I don't know where Coltrane stood, but in the sixth grade, I was, like, number two, and some girl named Lula Stanton was number one, but in the seventh grade, I fell to number three, and as I remember, I think Coltrane was one of the two people that stood higher than me. But even though he was a good student, say, in those years, somehow or another after he went to high school, he lost interest, in bein' a stand-out student, he didn't make the honor lists, anything like that. I don't know what happened to John. But we were still tight in those years, I mean, he was a student who passed his work, but he didn't stand out [as he had in elementary school]. So, like I said, I just remember that fourth grade situation, and I never will forget this girl, Annie LeGrand. I mean she just came to town, even if this became somethin' of a—well, no, I can't put her down, after she started goin' with a very handsome fella, a guy named Harvey Beck. And they were engaged in a certain activity, which we thought was a little wild for people their age, but then later on there was also a girl named Eloise Monroe that had the same situation where she came in from out of town, and Coltrane and I had strong feelings about her, but we were very young then, and I remember these little things, at a time when Coltrane and I weren't that much interested in, say, making girls, just the idea that—or even goin' with girls, you know? Matter of fact, we didn't even start thinking about datin' girls until we was junior in high school. But these early years, like in, say, up until around when we was about twelve years old, before we went to high school, we had the usual interests, I mean we would play ball, stickball, and he was athletic, you know? But he didn't have any interest in music [or] show any interest in music at all, say, until he was about in his junior year, maybe his sophomore year in high school. But in those elementary school years, he was just [a] typical kid. I think one thing you have to sort of picture, since you've been to High Point, and to sort of give you an idea of the type of growin' up that John was involved in, [he] had certain, maybe several, influences on him, was the fact that he did grow up on Underhill. It may seem kinda silly to think there was, anybody who really knows High Point, to think there was any kind of snobbery, or that a street address could mean anything, but the fact was that Underhill was really one of the more desirable, if not the most desirable, streets for a Negro family to live on. One thing, it was paved completely, at a time when, I would say, easily, three-quarters of the people, the Negro people in this city, still stayed on dirt roads. And not only that, it had more two-story houses than the average street. Coltrane's house was a fine house, sittin' on the top of that hill, there, and on one side Dr. Gannett built a nice house, and on the other it was Parhams, and across the street the Ingrams, and the other two-family houses like the Drakes', Williamses', Kenos', the Browers', and further down the hill there was another family called the Carl D. Ingrams, which was different from that other family. Matter of fact, I saw Dillard Ingram, who owned that house, not so long ago, he's still gettin' around [*unintelligible*] into big fights. He's sort of a poolroom operator, bondsman, always had his hands in somethin' nice to turn money.

So [. . .] the Coltrane home was usually referred to as Reverend Blair's house. [Coltrane] grew up on a street, that if you said you lived there, you didn't necessarily lord it over anybody, you know what I mean? It wasn't that everybody on there were professional people; the average person on there just had a routine job in a lotta instances, you know, but the families that had been somehow or another lucky enough to buy a house on that particular street would, sort of, carried a certain quality to be able to say [. . .] that you were from Underhill, that you lived on Underhill. [. . .]

I mean, those things can have an influence on your life in a Southern city, as well as in a Northern slum. In other words, it means, in a way, who your neighbors are, who your friends might turn out to be. And I imagine, in our case, if we both didn't stay on the same street, we would probably never gotten as tight as we did, even though there was other people, other boys, other youths, that was growin' up at the same time. Matter of fact, we grew up with a lotta schoolteacher kids, you know, it seemed like our class and most schoolteachers' sons, and one guy, Bernard Baker, who became a broadcaster at a radio station in Winston Salem, there, I forget the name of it, but right after the war, when I used to go back to North Carolina, I used to hear Bernard broadcast from this station. [One of the] first Negro, all Negro, stations in, in that area, you know? And there was Julius Michael, and Charles Whitted, his father was the Principal of Leonard Street School, and that type of situation.

Simpkins: Was there any clique, was there any formation of cliques in the community?

Brower: Well, actually, there was certain sons, certain boys, from certain families—you know, I often used to think about the fact that I, as a, a top student, didn't make the school patrol, but John did. He made it, with the schoolteachers' kids, and a few other boys. It wasn't so much, I mean, I don't know what held me back—in a sense, I've, I've always had my difficulties, even though I've been acknowledged, say, to be a leading student, and all of that—some way, I've always tended to rub people slightly wrong. But John, he was, he's the kind of person that people liked, teachers liked, and he just seemed to have had good training, which is not to say that I had bad training, but there was nothin', nothin' that tended to offend people, you know—he didn't do anything of that nature, see? And I was somewhat jealous because I didn't make the patrol, because it entailed a trip to Washington, during the Spring season, and I remember Coltrane and them makin' that trip, and I'd never even been on a train, and I used to want . . .

Simpkins: When was that trip?

Brower: It must have been around, say, when he was in the fifth grade or so.

Simpkins: And what qualifications did you [have] to meet?

Brower: They just picked you for bein' a school patrol . . .

Simpkins: Patrol boys?

Brower: Yeah, Patrol Boys they called it. [. . .] The job only entailed standin' patrol at street corners, and there was a rail, a railroad crossing, you may have noticed that railroad that went through the city, it's in a sunken area. Well, when we were first goin' to school, it wasn't, it was on [an] even level with the street. Now, actually you've been there since—I haven't been home since sixty-four, and they've done a lot of redevelopment. [. . .] At that time, it was even with Washington Street, and when you came across, you had to make sure that the trains weren't comin', so, one of the patrol boys was to make sure the kids got across these crossings safely. It wasn't all that terribly dangerous, because the train probably only came through town about three or four times a day, you know. But, maybe a little more, see actually High Point, itself [was] supposed to be the highest point between Washington and Atlanta on the Southern Railroad, so that's how it more or less got its name, see. So, like I say, he made the patrol boys, and he deserved it, in the sense of bein' an outstandin' student, and a very mannerly kid, and, like I said, it sort of, bein' from Underhill, kept him . . .

Simpkins: But you were also from Underhill, too.

Brower: Yeah, it helped him because—but I mean the Brower family was much more numerous, than, say, Coltrane, Coltrane was like an only, he was definitely an only kid. Mary Lyerly was his cousin, she grew up with him, and was almost like a sister to him, but basically, he was just an only child, and, wasn't anything. [. . .] I mean somehow or another the Brower family being as big as it was—I had about six brothers—I mean, I wouldn't say that any action on anybody else's part should have affected my situation in school, but somehow or another, when you come from a big family, you got a whole lotta people workin' for ya or against ya, in a way, but Coltrane, bein' a single boy, was almost, like, on his own, see. Whatever he did was for himself and nobody else had to affect his life, so, like I said, he stood well, with the teachers. In those days, like I say, he was a very good student; that's in elementary school years . . .

Simpkins: Was there any cliquishness with regard to people not on Underhill Street?

Brower: There was no such thing as social snobbery, you know? But the idea was . . .

Simpkins: Still, it was a good place to be.

Brower: If you say you're from Underhill, it sorta indicated that your family had gotten a nice place to live. It wasn't like, see, I remember, for example, Burns Hill [. . .] wasn't anything wrong with those people, but it was sorta way out in the woods, like, you had to walk through, over, nothin' but dirt roads to get there. And then there was other streets, even like the one that runs parallel to Underhill, Eccles Street.

Simpkins: Were the white streets paved?

Brower: Well, not exclusively, but much more.

Simpkins: What about sidewalks? Did they have sidewalks?

Brower: Well, sidewalks, no. [. . .] In our area, the sidewalk situation was left up to the individual person. The city didn't have anything to do with it.

Simpkins: What about for the whites?

Brower: I don't know about that. They may have done it, see, because there was, of course, a situation where the whites probably did a lot of things for themselves that we probably weren't even aware of. But I do know, like, say, Miss Parham, who stayed next to the Coltranes, she had her sidewalk paved, but the Coltranes didn't. It was merely the fact that they never got around to doin' it; it wasn't that—most times it was probably they couldn't afford it. A lotta people, just, they didn't do it; they never got around to doin' it, you see [. . .] only about ten percent had paved sidewalks. [. . .] Seemed like, you didn't have a sidewalk, you didn't worry about it. So, I don't think that that had much value as far as people's thought was concerned. But I'm sayin' that, actually, you didn't go out and say, well, look, I'm from Underhill, you from Moon Street, and try to be a big shot about it. I'm just sayin' that somehow or another that was an important street, in the sense of a residential street.

Simpkins: Do you remember any other incidents, any other situations, or any other things that you all did together?

Brower: Well, whenever, as I think back, it's just more or less what we were interested in. [. . .] I can't quite place the period, but we was in our pre–high school period, and we liked to read Doc Savage stories. That's a pulp magazine. [. . .] And it probably sold for ten cents a copy, and Doc Savage, he was like the head of a gang of guys that were sort of scientific Americans, and their job was to go out and fight evil. No matter where it was. And, of course, they were always up against unusually diabolical forces, and sometimes they would really get jammed up. And he had a couple cohorts there, one of 'em was named Ham and another one was named Monk. Anyhow, we got a great kick outta readin' those stories, because, the more unusual their opposition was, the more we liked it. I remember one time, we even tried to duplicate it by composin' a story ourselves. I think John did the drawin'. I think he took some paper, and just folded it over into a book, booklet, like. And I tried to write the story, and Coltrane tried to do the drawing part. And we also liked the Shadow stories.

Simpkins: Shadow stories?

Brower: Yeah, that was another pulp magazine, called the Shadow. Chief character was a guy named Lamonte Cranston, they had him on the radio in the forties, you know, they used to say, "The Shadow knows . . ."

Simpkins: Oh, yeah.

Brower: ". . . what evil lurks in the hearts of man," somethin' like that. That was a pulp magazine, too. So that was our chief, nonschool reading during one period.

Simpkins: Did you try to duplicate that also?

Brower: No, no, we didn't try to do—we didn't go so much for the Shadow, even though we read him, and we knew all about him . . .

Simpkins: We he a black man, or was he . . .

Brower: No, he was some sort of, a professional man, but he had a way, when he got involved in solvin' mysteries, he assumed sort of a shadowy aspect, so that's how he got his name.

Simpkins: A shadowy aspect.

Brower: But Doc Savage, like I said, Doc himself, was a man of brilliant mind; he surrounded himself with brilliant guys, but no matter how brilliant he was, there was always a time when they were in hot water, and they had to figure ways of gettin' out, and Coltrane and I were intrigued by these stories. As a matter of fact, we were the only kids I knew that read 'em. I know there was another fella there named Willis Hinton, who used to like to read the Wild West stories, but Coltrane and I never did get interested in those, even though I remember Willis and I used to be messin' around with those Western books, I forget just what my interest was with Coltrane . . .

Simpkins: Do you know how old you were, at that time? Was it late in pre . . .

Brower: Yeah, it would have to be anywhere up to around twelve or thirteen, maybe twelve, I would say, because he was probably about twelve or thirteen.

Simpkins: Was it after his father died?

Brower: Yeah, uh huh. And [. . .] we also read comics. I think the comic strip we liked the best, most liked was, we had an interest in Mandrake, Dick Tracy. Ones like Moon Mullins, and that type, didn't particularly interest us. We was always interested in somethin' involvin' mystery, and solvin' of crime, you know? And, uh, somehow or another, we had the same interest when it came to the movies. I don't recall that John was as much a movie bug as I was, perhaps then again, he was. But I know I used to have to go to the movies every Saturday [for the] cowboy pictures, but I know he musta been goin' because he was interested in certain serials, like he was interested in Flash Gordon. [. . .] And I remember there was a Dick Tracy serial one time that both he and I got very excited about. One reason, had a guy named Ralph Byrd as the, he was playin' Dick Tracy, and there was a colored fella in town that looked so much like Ralph Byrd. But anyhow, we followed that series, and there were several others. [. . .] I guess it was more or less because of the way the pictures would end every week, you know. You gotta come back next week to see what's happenin'. Actually, the stories, themselves— I see these Flash Gordon pictures on television now, and the stories themselves are very sickenin', I mean in the sense of bein' anything really exciting, but to our young minds, boy we were really concerned about what's going to happen next week, and we'd be discussing the whole week, what's gonna happen to this guy when he, like jumped off the mountain on his horse and last time we seen him the horse was goin' one way and he was goin' another, you know? And you go there the next week, the guy didn't even jump off the mountain.

Simpkins: Yeah, yeah. Did you go to church together?

Brower: No. That's the one part of our social life that we didn't share. I went to St. Marks.

Simpkins: He went to St. Stephen.

Brower: That's right [. . .] and that threw him in connection with certain people. You know, I was aware of that situation, like, there was certain families that [. . .] they had heard of me, the *Browers*, they hadn't heard of *me*, you know, but then, the Coltranes would be somebody *to* them, quite simply because their families knew each other from church, and particularly since his [grand]father had been a minister, and a lotta these older people that I'm talkin' about, they knew Reverend Blair—not his father, but his grandfather. [So] they sorta gave John the big treatment. I mean, I wasn't jealous or anything, but I do remember those type of situation. I get the same thing happenin' in my case, because of my father bein' a big man in our church, whenever I could meet people, and they be start talkin' to me, like, and John would be ignored to a certain extent, and that's because they even didn't hardly know his family. But we didn't go to church together, just like I said, we just, in our schooling . . .

Simpkins: Was he on any teams in elementary school?

Brower: No, we didn't have no teams in elementary school.

Simpkins: You didn't have a softball team, or . . .

Brower: No.

Simpkins: Did you have a thing where you played softball?

Brower: Yeah, well, we used to play softball and he used to play with us. We, you could always count on him for any type of team sport. I remember we used to, even tried to organize a baseball team, we even played the white boys.

Simpkins: Did you beat 'em?

Brower: I don't recall what the score was. I know, I remember I used to try to do all the pitchin', but I don't even remember what position John played. He was the type that could catch and he could do anything athletic. He wasn't no real misfit on the athletic field. He was kinda, he wasn't a big fella, but he wasn't smallish, either. He was, I guess in high school he must of weighed about a hundred and fifty pounds, or so, like that. I mean, he took a certain amount of pride in tryin' to be good, without ever gettin' any ideas that he had the makings of any kind of a star. Just that when he out there, he was hustlin' and tryin' to do good as he could. [. . .]

Simpkins: What was his personality like in elementary school.

Brower: Well, in elementary school, like I said, he was just a good mannerly kid. Never . . .

Simpkins: Towards you, though.

Brower: Well, towards everybody. In other words, there was nothin', the teachers couldn't find any fault with him. [. . .] He was always dressed neatly. Well, his parents never seemed to have suffered too much from the Depression. By that, I mean, bein' an only child, livin' in a house—I don't know what the situation was as far as the mortgage, anything like that—but, bein' from a big family, myself, I knew, things were pretty tight, in our home, but I never got the impression that John ever wanted for food, or anything like that, see. And I spent an awful lotta time in Coltrane's house; [. . .] seemed like, I was in his house all the time, rather than he was in ours. And I think one of the reasons was that in our house, like I said, we had more people—and he come down, he come down to the house, but like, whenever he come down to the house, was like, we're goin' to the park. Or he come down and, we go right on to the park. And I can remember, like, winter days, after school, I end up at his house. And we be playin' games, did a lot of things, like, I don't remember, little games like at Christmas time—another indication that his family was able to care, because he was gettin' a lot of little things for Christmas, and whereas—another thing we used [to] like to do when we was very young was skate, and . . .

Simpkins: Rollerskate?

Brower: Right. We used to get [*unintelligible*] a pair of skates called Union Skates— I never will forget the name, and those were the best skates. They just clamp on your shoe. [. . .] And then, we used to skate, and we was very good at skating, and we could do those hills on Underhill. We used to get to the top of 'em and we'd jump up and spin backwards, you know?

Simpkins: Backwards down the hill?

Brower: And go all the way down the hill, like that. Seemed like—I mean those hills don't seem like nothin' to me now, but in those days, to do that, seemed like it was. I can remember a lotta people used to like to skate. I mean, it don't seem like it's a big thing, now, but in those days even the high school kids used to get skates, and I can remember seein' a lot of older people, I mean older girls and boys, [. . .] and it seemed like a big thing to be skatin' all over town. It's like people ride with a bicycle, now? Yeah, we would skate everywhere. Wherever there were sidewalks, we'd hit it. And like I said, Underhill was a big street for it, because it was paved all the way, and had all these nice hills. So we did do a lot of skating, and that was in our elementary school years. We never had any bikes, so we never did do any bike riding. But we did an awful lot of walkin', particularly on Sundays. On Sundays, after church, we'd get together, before we'd go to the movie at night, and we'd walk through the woods, 'cause there were a lot of wooded areas, at that time, out beyond High Point College. It was a lotta—we'd just be walkin' and talkin'. And we'd walk up through white neighborhoods up Greensboro Road, Montlieu Avenue, I think they call it, all the way up to Main Street, and then we'd hit Main Street, we would walk into the center of town, and we, we didn't think much about white people, in the sense that—there was no oppression, no sense of oppression, you know? I mean, we, we just didn't have anything to do with white people on a social level, but we would go up town, we would mingle with 'em in the department stores. They had the dual fountain system, where colored drink here, the white drink there, but basically, our relationship, as far as dealing with the whites was as though, was no animosity. Because you—in order to go uptown, and you would go up to a certain street, and then it became white, and some of the biggest houses of the whites were located between that point and uptown.

Simpkins: What street was that?

Brower: It would be Washington Street. We walked up Washington Street. Then you get up to [Commerce Avenue]. [. . .] That was the dividin' line, and then you just walk, and then you get up town, there was no such thing as worryin' about etiquette, racial etiquette, or anything like that. But when you went to the movies, you went right on upstairs and didn't think nothin' about it. You wanted a drink of water in the department stores, OK. You wanted to get waited on, you just stood there; you didn't have to defer to the whites or anything, you just—whatever the girl asked you what you want, you told her.

Simpkins: But they would serve the whites first?

Brower: No, uh, uh. No, I mean, I can't recall it, I don't really recall any real snubs, as far as, to indicate that John and myself had any racial scars, like I said—but *just us*, you know—I mean I do know of certain instances where, like, I mean one time there was a, like a big steam laundry there, where there was over a hundred Negro women working there. [. . .] And I had an aunt that worked there and every Saturday she used to take me to the movies. [. . .] Well, I remember one time I went in this restaurant, right next to this place—now, that's where a lot of the women ate at lunchtime. But most of 'em didn't eat in there. You know they go in and get you, a hamburger or somethin' and [you] take it out. So, I just happened one time, I remember, I just decided to sit down in there for some reason, but I sat up, like, up front; I done been in this place so *many* times, you know? I was just a kid, so didn't actually go in there and, say, order me a platter. Whenever I went in there, was for, like, somethin' I could eat out. But this particular time, I don't know why, I decided to sit down. The woman told me, said, "No, you can't sit here, you have to sit back there." I never will forget that incident.

Simpkins: What music did you hear around that time?

Brower: Well, first songs that I think John and I got any excited about were, they built this park out in our end of town, and by that time, Ella Fitzgerald came out with "A-Tisket, and A-Tasket," and Jimmie Lunceford had "Margie." And they used to play these songs on the jukebox out at the park.

Simpkins: Was it a carnival kind of thing, was it an amusement park?

Brower: Yeah, it was an amusement park. In other words, it had a swimmin' pool, and . . .

Simpkins: We could go there? Or was it segregated?

Brower: No, this was strictly for the colored people.

Simpkins: And what about the movies, could you, did you have to sit in a certain section of the movies?

Brower: Oh. Yeah. Umm, hmm. Yeah.

Simpkins: Upstairs or downstairs . . .

Brower: Well, we sat upstairs, and had about four theaters there. Two of 'em had galleries, for the Negroes.

Simpkins: The other two, you couldn't go up there.

Brower: The other two. Then, eventually, they built a fifth one, which was really, became a sort of palatial one. They didn't even build a section for the Negroes there. What they would usually have to do, say a big picture, with Errol Flynn, Clark Gable, some big star like that, they would show it at the Centre—that was their new theater, the Centre Theater—they would show it there—maybe a whole week sometime (dependin' on how big the picture was)—and then on Sunday, they would hold it over for the Paramount. And the Paramount you had to walk way up to the gal—I mean, this was really way up, you know? And then we would go see those pictures on Sunday, and this would usually be our Sunday night amusement, to go to the Paramount.

Simpkins: What other music was heard around that time? Just around the time that he was in—you were in elementary school.

Brower: Well, let's see, now, we finished our elementary school in thirty-nine, but we didn't have that much interest—I know we used to wake up in the morning, right before we go to school, and on the local station there, they had a program— about the only way we absorbed any music, and . . .

Simpkins: Would it be jazz?

Brower: Well, it would be a mixture.

Simpkins: Gospel? Would it be gospel?

Brower: No, no gospel. It would be strictly popular music, and I would say that in our elementary school years, except for those two songs that I mentioned, I don't, I can't recall anything that we even got excited about. But then later, after we got to high school, we were beginning to develop an interest in, say, Glenn Miller, Harry James, I know we used to like to listen to "You Made Me Love You," and "Flight of the Bumblebee," by Harry James, and all of the Glenn Miller stuff, "Chattanooga Choo Choo," and stuff like that. Then I remember there was one piece by Artie Shaw—I just can't think of it—and Charlie Barnet, Tommy Dorsey, all, just the big name bands, you know. I think very little Duke Ellington–type music was played on those stations.

Simpkins: Was Count Basie played much?

Brower: No Count Basie was, hardly. Louis Armstrong; I remember they used, one song they used to play of his that Coltrane and I liked was, "Old man Mose kicked the bucket." I don't [recall] whether or not that was the title of it, but that was the big line, and Louis, that was one of the first songs we heard by Louis Armstrong. [. . .]

Simpkins: They didn't play that much of him or Jimmie Lunceford.

Brower: No, no. They played a lot of Jimmie Lunceford, I mean, Chick Webb they played, but I can't recall the titles, you know? I guess to a certain extent they played Ellington. [. . .] Cab Calloway, I remember, "Hi-de-hi-de-ho," ["The Hi-De-Ho Miracle Man"] and I was well aware of that. I'm pretty sure John listened to that type of stuff, too. But [there] was very little race music, per se. But I will say that, when we started goin' to dances, say, not big dances, but group dances, among our group, you know, the kids. We never went to a dance where you had to pay money to dance to, say, a big orchestra. Well, we had our little dances, I think the big songs that we liked to dance to were, like, "After Hours," Avery

Parrish, and then we particularly liked Billy Eckstine's "Jelly, Jelly." Those kinda songs, you get a girl and kinda, you know, hug her tight, and dance pretty good to, you know? But the big bands, Lunceford and those guys, when they would come down and make personal appearances, [*unintelligible*] they'd come to High Point, would be Greensboro. I remember Reese Dupree used to book 'em, down that area, and the older people, not even high school kids, but people that's already out of school in their twenties and thirties, they would go over to Greensboro, and pay the buck-fifty or buck seventy-five, whatever it was, you know, sometimes I would hear 'em talkin' about those things, I used to wonder what it was like to see these guys in person, not so much to dance, but just to see 'em, you know.

Simpkins: We were going to talk about high school, now. What happened in high school?

Brower: Well, like I say, we finished Leonard Street, thirty-nine, and then started off in high school—tryin' to remember the first years there—pretty much routine. Coltrane and I, we'd gotten older, now, and we still loved to talk—that was our big thing between us, bein' able to just talk, and [we] wasn't always together. We was with other guys, like the drugstore—we used to hang outside the drugstore up on Washington Street—and pretty soon, other people would drift up, and we'd just, you'd just be talkin' . . .

Simpkins: What'd you talk about?

Brower: Well, it's hard to say, hard to recall, I mean, be a lotta stuff about girls, not so much that we, at that early . . .

Simpkins: Same thing I used to talk about.

Brower: That's right, I mean anything can happen, you know, talkin' 'bout the teachers and [. . .] We never discussed what we were gonna do in life, too much, we talk about cars—that's another thing Coltrane and I had a big hangup on, discussing the make of cars, how they looked. We weren't concerned about mechanical, mechanical aspects of cars—I still don't know how to drive (I guess Coltrane went to, got to messin' around with a car—in those days, he didn't have any interest in a car)—but we liked to look at the magazines, and study the models, and try to draw streamlined cars—that's another thing we used to do, try to see who could draw the most *streamlined* cars . . .

Simpkins: This was in high school.

Brower: Yeah, well, this held over from my elementary days. I would say this is, probably, [. . .] our late elementary days, tryin' this, 'cause seemed like as we got in high school, [we] kinda drifted away from the same interests. Seemed like I began to get interested in, say, sports figures. But John never had any interest in sports figures. I used to tell you every name of every baseball player that was in the major leagues, and used to follow the football season, and, basketball—anything pertainin' to sports, I was up on. But John didn't have that interest.

Simpkins: What was he interested in?

Brower: Well, he didn't seem to develop many interests, during this period, before he became interested in music, and, I mean I can't pin him down as bein' interested in anything that he and I shared, you know? Like I said, another fellow, this fella named [James] Kinzer. Have you run across Kinzer?

Simpkins: Yeah.

Brower: Have you talked to him?

Simpkins: Not yet.

Brower: Yeah, well, he and I and Coltrane came up from North Carolina, together. But, "Poche," [*Po*-shay] as I call him; that's what, that's his nickname—Kinzer.

Simpkins: Poche? How do you spell that?

Brower: Probably something like, P-O, P-O-U-C-H-E.

Simpkins: Why did you call him that?

Brower: Well, there was a guy in town named Poche. For some reason, he was a, he had a restaurant, and that's all I can remember [*unintelligible*] start callin' him Poche.

Simpkins: What'd you call John?

Brower: Nothin'. I mean, he never had a nickname. Yeah, just Coltrane or John. I always called him John. I mean, nobody ever called him by his last name, except, probably discussin', I might say Coltrane, rather than John, while talkin'. But he never had a nickname like this name "Trane" that they gave him, that's somethin' strictly from his musical years up here. But he never had a nickname, like, my nickname was "Snooky," and even a lotta people never called . . .

Simpkins: Did he call you that?

Brower: No, he never called me that. That was just like, the family called me that, and the neighbors called me that—I mean, my high school friends, didn't nobody ever called me that. But Coltrane never had a name like that. But like I said Poche was very interested in athletics, and John would participate—I'm tryin' to remember whether or not John ever went out for the football team. But I do know that he just didn't have any interest in sittin' around, talkin' about All-American football players, what they gon' do at Duke this year, what kinda team Carolina's gonna have. We wasn't interested so much in the Negro colleges' teams, as we were in those white teams [. . .] like Duke, and Carolina, and Wake Forest. But John, I can't recall ever, him ever getting too much interested in that. Matter of fact, John never even talked about goin' to college, which was a big thing on Poche and my mind, and, I don't know why, because at that time we was finishing school, and it became quite a serious matter, tryin' to pick what college to go to. Now, I will say that, like I said, John as a student, he sort of drifted back, stayed in the pack, and he seemed to have been satisfied with bad marks, but [. . .] [*tape gap*] I don't know whether the death of his grandmother had much influence on him in that way or not.

Simpkins: When did she die?

Brower: 'Cause like I said, she was a sort of hidden influence. I know she was in the house, and John had a lot of respect for her, and all of that, and I always seemed to have thought that, somehow or another, somethin' happened, that [he] didn't feel impelled to be a standout anymore. [. . .] As a high elementary school student, I guess they sorta pushed on him, not pushed, but, I mean, impressed on him, to do his studying, and make sure, with clarity, toe the mark and everything. He didn't get outta hand, in high school, at all, even though he did begin to sli—[. . .] begin to run around with girls, as mu—he didn't run around with 'em, I mean, get 'em on his mind more. First girl that I can remember Coltrane bein' particularly interested in was a girl named Doreatha Nelson. [. . .]

Simpkins: This is in his junior year, when he began interested in . . .

Brower: Yes, uh huh, he sort of dropped it on me one night, he was sayin', "You know, I know somebody that like you." And so I say, "Who," so he was tellin' me, "Doreatha," you know? But I knew he liked her, because he'd already *told* me he *liked* her, but in a different sorta way. But for some reason, he wanted to play a *game* with me about the girl, you know? But I guess I had indicated to him that *I* liked her, too, so [I] didn't indicate that I was gonna make any play for her. So he began to say, "Well, look, I'm gonna tell her you like her," so I was beggin' him not to. I don't know whether he was serious about it or not, he didn't tell. Eventually, they did have a little fling, but . . .

Simpkins: Little fling . . .

Brower: Yeah, when I say that, I mean, they did go together, but, when I say they went together, it was sorta like—it didn't become a, a real, well, I wouldn't say a hot romance—but there wasn't no such a things in those days—I mean, you become involved with a girl in high school, and you take her home, and, you might go to a movie with her. But mostly, it would be a case of walkin' a girl home. And then if you got bold enough, you drop by her house, on a Sunday afternoon, or somethin' like that, and if her mother liked you well enough, you could stay around and talk to her awhile. So he did get involved with her to a certain extent, but it didn't hold out to the extent that they really said, well, we're for each other, we're not gon' mess around with nobody else. Actually, *she* didn't mess around with anybody else, but in other words, she was still available to, whoever, whoever wanted her, because Coltrane, somehow or another, didn't really push it. But that was the really, first girl that, *only* girl in high school I can remember, of the bunch there that Coltrane really had a real feelin' for, that I can recall. But he did branch out. There was another girl named Ruth Hiatt. Now she was older than John—well, couple years—and she was always kinda out of our circle. So I always sorta looked upon that as, as a sort of, a step in a different direction, as far as lookin' for girls, settin' up a romance with girls, because, it meant that he wasn't just operatin' with somebody that he was familiar with, and so forth. And he used to go down—she lived on a house down on Day Street, which is an offshoot of Underhill—and he—right across the street from what was known as Dan Gray Spring. I, we used to be hanging around Dan Gray Spring, first thing I know, John would be over on her porch. And he'd be over there talkin', and so, we used to be kiddin', "Now, what you findin' so much to talk to about to the girl." As though a guy couldn't talk to a girl [but] about five minutes, and that'd be it. And he'd get over there and get involved in quite a long conversation with Ruth. And Ruth was a pretty nice person, I mean, nice lookin', in a way, and so forth, so—like I said, to me, that was indication that John wasn't just playin' around anymore, I mean, the idea that he would go out and get himself involved with some girl that was altogether out of our circle. See, Doreatha, she was in our class and stuff, and so it wasn't exactly the same type of thing. But, somewhere along the line they began to have little Friday night parties. That's after Miss [Mrs.] Coltrane left High Point. And John became pretty, pretty free, and, there was a guy named Martin, I remember, Robert Davis, Harry Hall; they all used to get together for Friday night parties, and, I don't know would, could happen in those cases, and my imagination, which would be tellin' me certain things must have happened. But I do know they did a lot of drinking, so I think that's John's first introduction to . . .

Simpkins: That was like in late high school?

Brower: That was the last year of high school. His mother wasn't there anymore.

Simpkins: When did she leave?

Brower: Well, she must have left for . . . either while we were juniors or seniors, 'cause . . . probably while we were seniors, she came up this way [North]. I don't know. I always wondered whether it was Newark, or . . . Newark seemed pretty far from Philadelphia, but she didn't have no objection to John comin' to Philadelphia to live. And I'd just say, well—I used to think about it later—I said, "Gee, was it Newark that she was in?" 'Cause when you came to Philadelphia, she, he didn't live with her, 'cause she was, like, workin' on the, livin' on the lot. Domestic work, I think she was doin'. So, she was livin' with the family that she was workin' for. So John came up, he didn't have any real place to stay, but luckily, I had an aunt that knew of a place in her building. So, he and Poche, they were able to get that place.

Simpkins: That was in forty-three?

Brower: Yeah, that was in forty-three. You might make note of [the] fact that one fella that went to high school at the time we did, and was sort of looked up [to] by everybody, including Coltrane, a fella named Carl Chavis. Now, he was a—Carl had everything goin' for him, he was . . . I don't know whether you're familiar with the Chavises of North Carolina, but seems like there's a bunch of people—any time they got the name Chavis—there's a physical attractiveness about 'em, certain complexion, you know?

Simpkins: Light skinned?

Brower: Yeah, light skinned. Not white lookin'. They, their skin is reddish, and their hair isn't white hair, but it's sort of curly-like, and the girls' hair isn't long and fluffy, brown, it's just heavy, dark, hair. So there was Annie Chavis, and I think Carl had an older brother, and there was a sister that was older than Annie, who was about a year behind us in school, but not only was he a handsome chap, very—beautiful smile—he was a big guy—and he weighed a hundred and eighty—and he was one of the first lifeguards out at the park, after they opened it up, and then in high school, he was a football hero, and a basketball star. And he was smart enough to get through class. And then, after he finished William Penn, he went to Morgan. That was at the time when Eddie Hurt was turnin' out almost unbeatable teams, down at Morgan, and if you was goin' to Morgan, that meant you was goin' to, like, Notre Dame, you know? So he spent, he had one or two years at Morgan, playin' for 'em, Chavis did.

Simpkins: Did he know John very well?

Brower: Yeah, umm hmm.

Simpkins: I should check him out, then.

Brower: Well, it, the only thing, he's dead, now. [. . .] He went to Morgan, and he had a couple good years as a football player, then he went into the service, then he got killed while in the service, so they named the—people at Morgan thought well enough of him—they named their gymnasium after him, Carl Chavis Gymnasium. Like I said, it wasn't that he had any direct influence on John's life or anything, it's just that I know that John, and everybody else, thought a lot of Carl, and anybody who knew him, would remember him, and always remember what a great guy he was.

Simpkins: What other close friends did he have, besides James Kinzer?

Brower: Well, let's see, now, I would say, there was this guy Martin that he seemed to have got pretty close to. [. . .] We called him "Red Martin." [. . .] I can't think of Martin's first name. He was some relationship to Mr. Henley, who had the hotel there, and he came, like, late, [. . .] when we was juniors or sophomores in school. Might even have came when we was a freshman, but, he was the kind, like I said, that John picked up during the late years. [. . .]

Simpkins: When his mother left, who was he staying with?

Brower: Well, that left Mrs. Lyerly, there—that's his aunt, Mary Lyerly's mother. And Mrs. Lyerly wasn't too strict, in a way. I mean, she—very nice woman. I thought about, when Mrs. Lyerly died—she came up to Philadelphia later with 'em, and she and John and Mary and all them all stayed together.

Simpkins: When did that happen?

Brower: When did they come to Philly?

Simpkins: When did his mother leave; we can begin there.

Brower: Let's say his mother left, say, this'd be, maybe, sometime in forty-two.

Simpkins: And why did she leave?

Brower: Well, she, I guess she had a chance to come up and get a, what she considered a pretty good job up North someplace. So, she left, and that left, in the house, that left Mrs. Lyerly, John, and Mary. Now, Mary's career had been somethin' like John's—she was like a sister to John—and she had been a good student at one time, but then in high school, she sorta went back in the pack. But like I said, basically, after John's mother left, he began to sorta want to let out, and have a little more fun, there wasn't anything to kinda hold him back. I'm not sayin' he got wild, it's just probably typical of the kids. Somehow or another, I didn't go along with it. That's why I probably speak in somewhat negative terms about little things he did. But he was just a normal guy, in a way. The only thing I will say, that I do know that they started drinkin', which I didn't like. And I remember one time, this Doreatha and I, we came friends—later—and she was in Philadelphia there, for a while, and I was workin' for the *Afro-American*, as a reporter, and she came down, she got a job there, as a secretary. So, one time, I was at her house, and we was talkin', and so I mentioned somethin' about the fact that John and I began to drift apart because he became a thrill-seeker. So, I never will forget, she repeated the word "thrill-seeker" so *contemptuously.* [. . .]

Simpkins: What do you mean, in response to you, or agreeing with what you said?

Brower: Well, she was repeating the word, but she was saying it as though I had uttered something that was absolutely silly, the way I said it, maybe I shouldn't [have said] thrill-seeker, just because he was beginnin' to go out with girls and stuff like that. But like I said, in a way, he was just bein' normal. The only thing I do recall that, they were always talkin' about this, gettin', not drunk, drinkin' whiskey. And so I say, well, what these guys gon' be doin', all that drinkin' whiskey and have these girls with 'em, and, so I figure they were up to some real shenanigans, but, just what happened, I never even found out, because I never pressed nobody. I do know they had these parties, and they'd be talkin' about how much they drank, and that type of thing. [. . .] He and I begin to kinda [. . .] get sarcastic with each other, I begin to make snide remarks about what was goin' on. I never tried to tell him he wasn't doin' right, or anything like that, it's just like, well, "Whatever you're doin', Chief," "I don't go for it, I ain't worried about it, I don't want no parts of it," nor do I look down on him in any way. [. . .] I was kinda jealous, because I guess the guys were havin' fun, and I just didn't go along. Now, I do remember there was a case, there, where [an] insurance agent's wife became kinda liberal with her body, and, guys would start talkin' 'bout this woman, and there was a, a particular, it was, this guy that supposed to have been, you know, makin', doin so much with her, havin', havin' relations with her and everything, was a guy that you wouldn't expect, you know? And then, the word was getting' around that other guys could, could make it [too]. So, I, I think Coltrane, you know, was involved in that bunch, and it might have been his first introduction to sex. I'm not too well up on that, but I do know that this woman, he was talkin' like he had done somethin'; she was known to really be givin' it up to all these young school kids. She wasn't that much older than they, but she was definitely, like, in her twenties, and these boys were all sixteen and seventeen.

So, basically, I would say that he started gettin' interested in music. First interest I knew, he started buyin' *Down Beat* magazine, around his junior year, and I didn't have any interest in *Down Beat*, and I used to, sorta, act like he was buyin' a Mickey Mouse book or somethin', like, "What you buyin' that magazine for," but he begin to be interested, he begin to study the ads, particularly, I noticed, like he was interested in the ads on certain instruments, and things like that. Now, I don't know, did, when you were in High Point, did you hear about a guy named Haygood or Haywood [Charlie Haygood]?

Simpkins: Mm hmm, but I never did get to see him, though.

Brower: Is he still livin' or did they, did they say he's livin'?

Simpkins: Somebody gave me a long list of people that I should see, and I think the name was written down on that. That's right, he had a band! And they said that he was gone, I think that's what happened. But they didn't say anything about him bein' dead.

Brower: Well, he was in his forties, then, so that would easily make him pretty old, now, see. But he had a restaurant, and . . .

Simpkins: Where?

Brower: Up on Washington Street, there, and it was a big clean place, but he did the cookin', and [. . .] he had a saxophone, and he used to, when things weren't busy, he'd be sittin' back in the kitchen, or sometimes be out, in among the tables with his saxophone. So, he was one of the people that I knew John was seein', in reference to his interest in music, but they didn't have a school band, at that time. The only musical activity that they engaged in was with an a cappella group that Professor Burford organized.

Simpkins: Was there a community band?

Brower: Well, there might have been some sort of a band. There was a man named [Warren] Steele. Did you ever . . .

Simpkins: Yeah, I heard about him.

Brower: Yeah, well, he had some sort of band that was different from jazz music, I think. He wasn't so interested in that type of music, and I think John got in contact with him. See, these were things where he became involved with people, he was sorta doin' it, and I wasn't, I wasn't aware. We [would] still get together, we'd be talkin', you know? We could stand out on the corner there, Drake, at the Henley Hotel, at the corner there—hotel, they might have torn it down, I think they tore it down. It was at the head of Underhill, right where Underhill ran into Washington Street.

Simpkins: I know where that is.

Brower: Uh huh. [. . .] Actually, it was a lady by the name of Drake that had a confectionery, and we would stand there and talk and talk and talk, until almost twelve o'clock, which was very late, then. Like I said, I can't tell ya, you can't recall the conversations. And we used to go in the pool halls. And that was one of the few recreations available, to us, after we got into high school. We used to like to shoot pool, but he never gambled; he never got any vices from pool. And, I'm tryin' to think, let's see, outside of that, just outside of singin', I don't know of any other interests.

Simpkins: Was he involved in Student Council and things like that?

Brower: No. [. . .]

Simpkins: What was it like, personally, in high school, then.

Brower: Well, in high school, it was still very congenial. Didn't have no enemies. I can't think of any instance—I'm trying to think if Coltrane ever got involved in a fight with anybody; and I can't think of one.

Simpkins: Why was that? Did he ever get into any arguments?

Brower: No. He wasn't even the kinda guy that really got into big debates about anything. In other words, if you're sittin' around, you're talking, I wouldn't say that he didn't try to make a point. But I'm tryin' to say that Coltrane and I were generally, for ourselves, we generally saw so much eye to eye, that he and I never even had any real difference of opinion. [. . .] We used to, we used to kid each other about what's a better car, which car looks better and all that type of stuff. But to say, discussin' some philosophical, little aspect of life, or what was worthwhile [. . .] seemed like we never had any discussions of that type, at all. [. . .]

And I'm tryin' to think of all the other guys that we knew, that passed through our lives in high school, and that knew John, like I know him, but, I can't recall anybody that he ever had any difficulty [with].

There was one other thing I was thinkin' about. And that was the fact that in later years, when John began to play with the professional bands, I think that I was the first person to make note of him in public print. It happened that I was workin' for the *Afro-American* in Philadelphia at the time, and John came out of the service, and had been playin' around Philadelphia, but I hadn't been followin' him [closely]. You could hear about him, and when I talked to Kinzer, he'd be tellin' me John is doin' this and John is doin' that, and then sometime I stopped over the house—this is when he was stayin' up on North Twelfth Street—and this guy . . .

Simpkins: This is when he was living with his mother and his aunt Bettie . . .

Brower: Yeah, well, his mother seemed to have been still livin' someplace else, most of the time. But Mrs. Lyerly was at this place, this apartment, and then Mary was there. Then, Mrs. Lyerly died sometime during that period. I just can't remember when she died, but when I mentioned her before, I was gon' say that one thing I intended to do was write Mary a letter and just tell her that all the time I knew Mrs. Lyerly, I'd found her to be a very nice woman, and I was sorta indicatin' that after John's mother left High Point that Mrs. Lyerly didn't make a point of bein' tight on him—strict—which was just as well. I'm not sayin' that she had that responsibility, but I'm sayin' that these little things that John did, just beginnin' to drink and so forth was done while he was supposedly under the care of Mrs. Lyerly, I would say. But I'm pretty sure that when his mother left, Mrs. Lyerly must have had the understandin' that John . . .

Simpkins: How could I get that notice that you put in the *Amsterdam News*?

Brower: Well, it wasn't the *Amsterdam News*, it was the *Afro-American*, right? [. . .] And I don't recall the year, but it would be sometime around forty-nine, I'd imagine. See, I left the *Afro* in late fifty. [. . .] But what happened was, I knew that he was with Gillespie, or—most likely it was Gillespie . . .

Simpkins: Right. Forty-nine.

Brower: Uh huh, but they were supposed to appear at the—no, they were making an appearance at the Earle Theater, in Philly, you know with the big band—stage show place, left of Market, and . . .

Simpkins: That's near his house.

Brower: And I knew that he was gon' be there, so I wanted to write a little story[1] about this kid, came up from North Carolina, bought himself a sax, went into the Navy, came out, and now he was beginnin' to play with name bands. But, I didn't have the details I wanted, about who [he'd] been giggin' around with in Philadelphia [. . .] I was a pretty conscientious person, as a reporter, and I did want to have a little more details to make it a complete little story. But, seemed like, I was very busy, and I never did get up to John's house—and even if I'd got there, might not have caught him. [. . .] So I ended up havin' to make it like I did, but just in outline, I omitted the fact that he came outta North Carolina.

Note

1. The article is "Dizzy's Saxist Realizes Dream: Coltrane Finally Ends Up at Earle," *Philadelphia Afro-American*, November 5, 1949, page 8 (reproduced in Lewis Porter, *John Coltrane: His Life and Music*, page 77). In the article, Brower does in fact mention that Coltrane was from North Carolina.

APPENDIX B

Interview with Isadore Granoff

Steve Provizer

Coltrane studied music at the Granoff Studios in Philadelphia from the mid-1940s until the early 1950s (though not continuously, as he was often on the road with various bands). Steve Provizer interviewed Isadore Granoff, head of Granoff Studios, on October 20, 1969.

Isadore Granoff: What do we start with? I'm just trying to find out the time Coltrane was a student here and I have to dig up cards and I don't know where to look for them.

Steve Provizer: Do you have any personal impressions of him? How do you remember him?

Granoff: Coltrane came in here somewheres around, as my memory serves me, around '41 or '42 as a student.[1] He had studied with Matthew Rastelli, one of the leading clarinetists and saxophonists in the city. He studied quite a number of years with him, and we always found that after he was through with his regular lessons he would start to improvise, and we felt that there were very, very few students who could do improvisation as this young man did. In many instances, Mr. Rastelli would call me up and say, "Come on up, I want you to listen to what John does, that I can't do! It's impossible for me to do! It's just something new." In other words, from the very moment that he learned his instrument, he wanted to revolutionize it, which he did. It was most interesting to hear him, because at first we didn't understand. He was doing things and we didn't understand what they meant. He willed his mind to capacity to do something different with the instrument.

From *Kord Magazine*, date unknown.

Provizer: Did your studios offer classical training?

Granoff: First he had classical training, that's right. Then he had some popular work that the teacher himself was able to give him, since his teacher was quite a performer, the best known man in town. Anyway, we gave him a classical background. That was the greatest help to John Coltrane, and many others, who dreamed to enter the jazz field; that they knew their instruments by classical means and were able naturally, from there on, to do what they wanted. He was a very conscientious boy, even with his classical work. I mean, he took it to heart.

Provizer: Did Coltrane study composition?

Granoff: Composition, that's right. And, of course, that gave him the chance to do arranging for his band. He could put down on paper what he was doing. That's why afterwards we had guys following John Coltrane. Everyone thought it was a new thing. Everyone was dreaming that this was going to be one of the greatest things in music, when they heard him. On many occasions he arranged concerts here at the school where he displayed his art. Many, at first, couldn't understand it. But they took a great interest, students as well as teachers, to find out what Coltrane meant by jazz. I would say Coltrane was the first to lead in this field.

Provizer: You mean in and around Philadelphia?

Granoff: I think anywheres in the country, because I considered him, and so did others, as the best in the world. He was rated in a number of magazines as the greatest in the world. He had a good background here. There were some very able boys he used to get together and rehearse with. He had a jazz quartet. Percy Heath played with him then on bass. Georgie ["Butch"] Ballard was the drummer. John would get together with these young men and rehearse many hours a day. He would try all the compositions that he wrote. At that time, we knew "popular," but we didn't know the meaning of "Jazz."

Provizer: What kind of proficiency did Coltrane have when he came to Granoff studios?

Granoff: Actually, when he came he was a beginner. He studied here for many years, at least about eight or nine years. When he came I don't think he knew what the sax was like.

Provizer: I spoke with some friends from his home town, and he apparently switched instruments in high school, though he started playing about the age of thirteen.

Granoff: He probably did play, but he didn't know how to read music when he came to Granoff.

Provizer: He must have been 22 or 23 when he came?

Granoff: No, I think he was younger than that, a little younger than that. He studied very diligently. Really one of the finest workers I have known. He used to work seven, eight hours a day at his instrument, and in composition he worked about two hours a day, and he was always working or rehearsing his band, wanting them to play his compositions. Actually, half the time of Coltrane's rehearsing with the band was taken up with his own works.

Provizer: Did you have opportunities to speak with Coltrane in private?

Granoff: Yes, we spoke many times.

Provizer: Any thoughts . . .

Granoff: Well, he was a respectful individual, and most grateful to us for his training. He expressed it in many ways. He sent me a collection of his work that he composed as well as played. He was, as I said before, very diligent. When he had to be here, he arrived an hour early, waiting on the steps for the school to open up. Then he would run into his studio, and you wouldn't see John until his band would get together after school hours.

Provizer: He was obsessed with his music, then?

Granoff: Yes. He said after a few years' study he was going to do something else with the instrument.

Provizer: Most people say he was very quiet.

Granoff: He was a very quiet individual and sort of shy. And he was well-bred, I would say. He wouldn't go out of his way to show his talent. He was a humble fellow with the other students. Having the other students for an audience would inspire him.

Provizer: Did Coltrane have another job when he attended Granoff studios?

Granoff: Later on he started to play with groups at night, but nothing else I know of. Well, that's about all I can tell you now.

Provizer: Thank you very much.

Note
1. Coltrane moved to Philadelphia in June 1943. His mother bought him a used alto sax in September 1943, and he could have started at Granoff as early as then, although it may have been a year or two later.

CREDITS

"A Statement of Musical Purpose," printed by permission of Antonia Andrews, executrix of the Estate of Juanita Coltrane.

"The *Afro* Goes to a Be-Bop Concert," by Rufus Wells, *Baltimore Afro-American* (late city edition), January 12, 1952, pages 1–2. Used with permission from the Afro-American Newspapers Archives and Research Center.

Interview with John Coltrane, by August Blume, Baltimore, June 15, 1958. This is the first publication of the full interview. Excerpts have previously been published in *Jazz Review* (January 1959, page 25); *John Coltrane: His Life and Music*, by Lewis Porter (University of Michigan Press, 1998); and *The John Coltrane Companion*, edited by Carl Woideck (Schirmer Books, 1998). The audio is available at http://slought.org/content/11161/.

"Correspondence with Fans," printed by permission of Antonia Andrews, executrix of the Estate of Juanita Coltrane.

"Correspondence with Journalist Bob Snead," printed by permission of Antonia Andrews, executrix of the Estate of Juanita Coltrane.

"Letter to Dickson Debrah Kisai," printed by permission of Antonia Andrews, executrix of the Estate of Juanita Coltrane.

"'Trane on the Track,"*Down Beat*, October 16, 1958, pages 16–17. Courtesy of the *Down Beat* Archives.

"Honest John: The Blindfold Test," *Down Beat,* February 19, 1959, page 39. Courtesy of the *Down Beat* Archives.

Giant Steps liner notes, reprinted by permission of Nat Hentoff.

Interview with John Coltrane, by Carl-Erik Lindgren, Stockholm, March 22, 1960. The audio is included on the Dragon Records issue of the Stockholm concert.

"The John Coltrane Story," as told to Björn Fremer, *Jazz News*, May 10, 1961, page 3. Reprinted by permission of Björn Fremer. Originally published as the liner notes to the Swedish LP issue of *Chambers' Music* (Sonet SLP28), 1960.

"Coltrane on Coltrane," by John Coltrane in collaboration with Don DeMicheal, *Down Beat,* September 29, 1960, pages 26–27. Courtesy of the *Down Beat* Archives.

"Coltrane—Man and Music," by Gene Lees, *Jazz News,* September 27, 1961, pages 5–6. Reprinted by permission of Gene Lees.

Interview with John Coltrane, by Ralph J. Gleason, San Francisco, May 2, 1961. From The Ralph J. Gleason Interview Collection and Jazz Casual Productions, Inc. Copyright © Jean R. Gleason. Reproduced by permission.

"Countdown at Abart's: New King of Jazz Taking Flight Here," by Tony Gieske, *Washington Post,* June 17, 1961, page A13. Reprinted by permission of Tony Gieske. All rights reserved.

"Accent on Jazz: The King Wears a Cockeyed Crown," by Tony Gieske, *Washington Post,* June 25, 1961, page G4. Reprinted by permission of Tony Gieske. All rights reserved.

Africa/Brass liner notes, reprinted by permission of the Verve Music Group, a Division of UMG Recordings, Inc.

"Live" at the Village Vanguard liner notes, reprinted by permission of Nat Hentoff.

"Conversation with Coltrane," by Valerie Wilmer, *Jazz Journal*, January 1962, pages 1–2. Reprinted by permission of Valerie Wilmer.

"Jazzman of the Year: John Coltrane," *Down Beat's Music 1962—The 7th Annual Yearbook*, pages 66–69. Courtesy of the *Down Beat* Archives.

"John Coltrane and Eric Dolphy Answer the Jazz Critics," by Don DeMicheal, *Down Beat*, April 12, 1962, pages 20–23. Courtesy of the *Down Beat* Archives.

"Letter to Don DeMicheal," printed by permission of Antonia Andrews, executrix of the Estate of Juanita Coltrane, and Dr. C. O. Simpkins.

"On the Town: Coltrane's Back Better than Ever," by Tony Gieske, *Washington Post*, August 31, 1962, page B11. Reprinted by permission of Tony Gieske. All rights reserved.

Duke Ellington & John Coltrane liner notes, reprinted by permission of the Verve Music Group, a Division of UMG Recordings, Inc.

Interview with John Coltrane, by Jean Clouzet and Michel Delorme, Paris, November 17, 1962 ("Entretien avec John Coltrane," *Les Cahiers du Jazz*, number 8, 1963, pages 1–14). Reprinted by permission of Michel Delorme.

"After Dark: His Solos Run 45 Minutes Long," by Ken Barnard, *Detroit Free Press*, April 12, 1963, page B-5. Reprinted by permission of the *Detroit Free Press*.

"The Trane Rolls In to Create a Miniature UN," by Bob Hunter, *Chicago Daily Defender*, May 16, 1963, page 16. Used with the permission of the *Chicago Defender*.

Interview with John Coltrane, by Michel Delorme and Jean Clouzet, Paris, November 1, 1963 ("Coltrane 1963: Vers la Composition," by Michel Delorme, *Jazz Hot*, December 1963, pages 10–11). Reprinted by permission of Michel Delorme.

"The Jazz Bit: A Chat with John Coltrane," by Louise Davis Stone, *Chicago Defender*, August 1, 1964, page 10. Used with the permission of the *Chicago Defender*.

"Coltrane Shaping Musical Revolt," by Leonard Feather, *Melody Maker*, December 19, 1964, page 6. Reprinted by kind permission of Lorraine Feather.

A Love Supreme liner notes, reprinted by permission of the Verve Music Group, a Division of UMG Recordings, Inc.

"John Coltrane," by Joe Goldberg, from *Jazz Masters of the Fifties* (Macmillan, 1965). Copyright © 1965, by The MacMillan Company, Copyright © 1993 by Joe Goldberg. Reprinted by permission of the Estate of Joe Goldberg and Henry Morrison, Inc., its agents.

"Coltrane, Star of Antibes: 'I Can't Go Farther'," by Michel Delorme and Claude Lenissois ("Coltrane Vedette d'Antibes: Je ne peux pas aller plus loin," *Jazz Hot*, September 1965, pages 5–6). Reprinted by permission of Michel Delorme.

Interview with John Coltrane, by Michiel de Ruyter, Antibes, Juan-Les-Pins, France, July 27, 1965. The audio is available at http://mdr.jazzarchief.nl/interviews/coltrane/.

Meditations liner notes, reprinted by permission of Nat Hentoff.

INDEX